STARWALKING

STARWALKING

SHAMANIC PRACTICES FOR TRAVELING INTO THE NIGHT SKY

PAGE BRYANT

BEAR & COMPANY
PUBLISHING
SANTA FE, NEW MEXICO

LIBRARY OF CONGRESS CATALOGING-IN-PUBLICATION DATA

Bryant, Page.
    Starwalking : shamanic practices for traveling into the night sky / Page
Bryant.
       p. cm.
    Includes bibliographical references.
    ISBN 1-879181-36-3
    1. Stars—Religious life. 2. Stars—Mythology. 3. Astrology.
4. Shamanism. 5. Astral projection. 6. Spiritual life. I. Title.
BL438.B79   1997
291.2'12—dc21

                                       97-13044
                                          CIP

Bear & Company, Inc.
Santa Fe, NM 87504-2860

Interior text design: Melinda Belter

Cover design: © 1997 by Lightbourne Images

Cover Illustration: Scott Guynup

Editing: Sonya Moore

Printed in the United States of America by BookCrafters

9 8 7 6 5 4 3 2 1

This book is dedicated to the Star Gods, who brought
the Light of Wisdom to Earth.

TABLE OF CONTENTS

LIST OF ILLUSTRATIONS   ix

PREFACE   xi

ACKNOWLEDGMENTS   xxv

EDITOR'S NOTE   xxvi

PART ONE: JOURNEYING INTO THE
GREAT STAR NATION

Chapter 1   Grandfather Sun–Grandmother Moon   5
Chapter 2   Constellations and the Fixed Stars   19
Chapter 3   Star Power for Personal Growth   33
Chapter 4   Comets and Meteors: Messengers of the Gods   47
Chapter 5   The Ancient Art of Starwalking   65
Chapter 6   Pathway to the Gods   91

PART TWO: WHEN THE SKY GODS
CAME DOWN TO EARTH

Chapter 7   Mighty Sirius! Monarch of the Suns   103
Chapter 8   The Stars and the Stones   123
Chapter 9   Skidi Pawnee: Star Cult of the Great Plains   143
Chapter 10   Starwatchers of the Desert Southwest   159
Chapter 11   Visions of the Cosmos Lakota Style   177
Chapter 12   Star Peoples of Mexico   191
Chapter 13   Dogon Star Knowledge   209
Chapter 14   Stairways to the Stars   215
Chapter 15   Star Myths: Our Celestial Legacy   241

CONCLUSION   261

APPENDICES

Appendix 1   Meeting Star Woman   271
Appendix 2   Stargazing Navajo Style   274
Appendix 3   Deep-Sky Objects   276

Appendix 4   Astronomy Glossary   280

Appendix 5   Annual Meteor Showers   282

Appendix 6   Astronomy of the Great Pyramid   283

Appendix 7   Stonehenge and the Ancient Art of Geomancy   284

Appendix 8   Commentary On Lakota Ceremonials
                and Parallel Universes   286

Appendix 9   Reference Section: Constellations   289
                and Fixed Stars

SELECTED BIBLIOGRAPHY   309

NOTES   315

ABOUT THE AUTHOR   323

LIST OF ILLUSTRATIONS

Sun Shrine	16
Lunar Shrine	17
Star Shrine	18,42
Autumn Star Map	28
Winter Star Map	29
Spring Star Map	30
Summer Star Map	31
Circumpolar Star Map	32
Star Mask	37
Star Symbol	37
Drawing-Down Ceremony	40
Star Shield	68
Star Bundles	70
Judaculla Rock	133
Petroglyphs	134, 135
Pawnee Star Symbol	144
Poverty Point Site	223
Bird Motif	225
Hill Works (Ross County, Ohio)	229
North American Nebula	278

PREFACE

The stardome blazes brightly above the ceremonial ground like a great bowl of gems: diamonds, rubies, sapphires, topaz, each illuminating the silhouettes gathered around the leaping balefire. The crisp night air is filled with expectation. The Sky Gods await. The most sacred of ceremonies is about to begin. The Night Star dancers are poised to embark upon a ritual journey that will carry them, as it did the father-priests before them, across the starlit Sky Bridge that stretches from Earth to heaven. The spacecraft they will navigate on their pilgrimage are their minds which, when coaxed by ritual into a mysterious trance, will carry them to their destination. Once there, they will have access, mentally, to the Sacred, the sacred knowledge and power inherent within the Great Star Nation.

The bodies of the Starwalkers are painted yellow and dotted with blue symbols of the Sun, Moon, and stars. The lone chief wears a headdress of eagle feathers that fall down his back in a single trail like a comet streaking across the sky. He is an ordinary man who is this night to be transformed into a Star Chief by merging with the sky dwellers, a transformation that has occurred many times before. The Sky Bridge is a familiar route to him. While it is to Earth that he and his people look for their physical needs, it is to the sky that they must now turn. On this night, the Star Chief stands tall upon the body of his Mother Earth. He and his people will soon enter the realms of their Father Sky. They will fly a merging flight into the domain of the Great Male. They will, once again, move in the spiral reemergence dance that will lift them from the bonds of Earth back into the celestial home of the Ancestors.

Slowly, the dancers begin to rotate around the Star Chief who stands in the center of the human circle, his arms stretched skyward. A low, mesmerizing chant echoes ancient voices into the night. All through the evening's passage, the dancing and singing continue. Bodies sway to the rhythm of the singing. The fire casts eerie shadows on the graceful forms who surrender to the flight of the mind. Drums pound; rattles shake in firm hands. Earth's reality is left behind. The dance goes on; energy is spent.

Finally, dawn brings the daylight of renewal, and with it an opportunity to carry on with life, renewed and reborn. The path the Ancestors walked to the North Star has been trodden once more. And once more the Great Star has given of its power, its stability and strength. The Starwalkers have again brought the stellar power down to Earth for use by the people in their quest for self-discovery and a better life. Yes, at dawn the journey is over, for now. The people will return to living their earthly lives, once more complete, in harmony with Nature. But they will be ever-mindful of the Star Nation above them that gives order to their world. It will forever be the place from whence the Ancestral Spirits came and where they, the living, will someday go.

When I was a little girl people would ask me what I wanted to be when I grew up. Children often get asked that, don't they? My answer usually reflected the mood I was in at the time and where I was along the winding, changing path of childhood. If I was in the mode of wanting to help others, I would say I wanted to be a nurse. In grammar school I loved my second grade teacher, so I wanted to be a teacher. But one day I read a book about the stars, and from then on I wanted to be an astronomer. Today? Well, you know how it goes: Who among us has not said, "If I had my life to live over I would . . . " I am not unhappy about what I have chosen as my life's work. Nor am I unfulfilled. My experiences and what I have learned from them have led me down many roads, each with its own perils and rewards. All those roads have been my teachers. But the longing to study the stars has never left me, and for that I am grateful. I just tucked the longing on the back burner, I suppose, in that special never-forgotten place inside where childhood dreams go.

In the autumn of 1977 that slumbering "astronomer archetype" awakened inside me with the vengeance of an unrequited love. I could no longer deny the urge. I wanted to study the stars. I wanted to go to school and learn about the universe. It was more than a desire; it was an urgent, passionate need. Why it came alive precisely at that time I don't really know. I suppose it was simply the right time. There was a lot going on in my life then. I had recently relocated to Ft. Lauderdale from Tampa, had just entered into a new marriage, was traveling in my teaching work, doing a lot of psychic counseling, and if that wasn't enough, I had my own talk show on WFTL radio six nights a week! Being the perpetual student that I am, most of my free time was spent immersed in books on metaphysics, Theosophy, comparative religions, astrology, Wicca . . . you name it. Now I wanted to take on astronomy! All my studies up to then had been solely on my own. But not this time. I knew I needed a teacher.

One evening I went to the radio station early to cut some commercials for my show and ran into Mike Harvey, my boss and the program director at the time. Somehow our conversation turned to astronomy, and I told him that I had always wanted to study the subject, figuring that he would think that a bit strange for a psychic whose interests were obviously on things nonscientific. But Mike's eyes lit up; astronomy was his passion, and he had been an avid amateur astronomer since he was nine or ten years old! What a coincidence, I thought. (That was before I knew anything about *synchronicity*.)

I immediately jumped at the chance and asked if Mike would consider being my teacher. He seemed really surprised by my request, and although he declined (*his* plate was full too), he thought he knew someone who would. That someone was Barry Perlman, a man with lots of free time on his hands and a degree in astronomy from Boston University. Best of all, he agreed to teach me.

I grabbed up every book I could find on astronomy and read them hungrily. I asked Barry zillions of questions, which he patiently answered. I soon learned that one cannot study astronomy without studying physics too. Have you ever tried to teach yourself physics? Well, with my determination to learn and Saint Barry's help, I pressed on, working with him for two years.

Then we moved to Sedona, Arizona, in 1979, where in 1981 I founded its first amateur astronomy club, Sedona Planetary and Cosmic Education Society (S.P.A.C.E.S.). I found that there was a wealth of retired astronomers, physicists, and astrophysicists living in the area, and invited many of them to speak at the meetings. In 1984 I enrolled in my first (and only) formal astronomy class at Northern Arizona University in Flagstaff, which I attended for one semester. The books in my personal library continued to increase and so did my knowledge.

I am a person with an innate need to share with others what I know. It's just the nature of the beast, I guess. That need led me to being the teacher and writer that I am today. The more I learned about the stars, however, the more I puzzled over how and in what context I could share my knowledge and enthusiasm. One day I picked up *In Search of Ancient Astronomies* by Dr. E.C. Krupp, a book about the astronomy of numerous ancient cultures worldwide. That book gave me direction, changing everything for me. I had long had an interest in ancient peoples, particularly the Egyptians, the Maya, the prehistoric Britons, and the Celts, from the perspective of their religions and spiritual practices. It seemed natural for me to teach about what they knew about the heavens, the *source* of their spirituality and religion.

The rest, as they say, is history. For the past eleven years I have given lectures and workshops on astronomy and archaeoastronomy, the archaeology and astronomy of our ancestors. The experiences I have gained from being a student of the universe and a teacher of what I have learned thus far have led me to write this book.

Who among us has not looked up at the stars and wondered what is really up there? Who has not been captivated by the beauty of the night? Who has not been dazzled by the brilliance of the Morning Star and the Evening Star, or the Full Moon, or the huge red Sun ball sinking into the horizon, giving way to the twilight? We all have, of course. I remember the first time I saw a meteor streak across the night leaving a trail of orange and green light in its wake. I remember when I first saw the Milky Way arcing like a smoky diamond bridge so bright that it seemed to be only a few feet above the floor of the great Sonoran Desert. I remember seeing my first solar eclipse and my first halo around the Moon. However, of all the "firsts" astronomy has given me, the first time I looked through a telescope is the most memorable.

Astronomy books are filled with spectacular photographs, beautiful pictures of star clusters, galaxies, nebulae. How many times I have sat and thumbed through *Astronomy* magazine and related books, admiring page after page of jewel-like globular clusters: red and green and blue nebulae; sparkling new starlights reaching out from behind clouds and mist so thick that they threaten to snuff out the star flames. I knew what beauty the night held. I had seen it in the pictures. So when I had my first opportunity to peer through a telescope I was very excited! Finally I would get to see some of those deep-sky objects I had been looking at in books. And what fantastic sights they would be! Right? Well, not quite. The images I had been viewing were of course time-lapse photographs. Knowing nothing about photography, however, I didn't realize that. What I saw wasn't exactly what I expected.

Looking back I realize that it was actually better than I expected: I was looking not at a picture, but the reality. I will never forget seeing the Great Nebula in Orion for the first time that night. The twinkling jewels of its stars were suspended in what looked like a turquoise-colored cobweb, soft and wisplike, and at the same time piercing and dramatic. I now understood why some astronomers listen to classical music while peering through their telescopes into space.

I have seen the Great Orion Nebula many times since that night almost twenty years ago. Each time its beauty excites me, but never quite like it did that first time. That time my eyes were innocent; that time I went to the sky filled with expectations. I actually learned something about myself that night. Often I approach a new experience . . . or a new friend . . . or a book . . . with overinflated expectations, only to have that person, experience, place, or thing fall short of what I expected it would be. I don't do that anymore . . . well, not as much anyway. I have learned to let myself experience what is rather than what I *want* or *need* it to be. Now I go to the sky on its terms, not mine.

The night sky is fascinating. We have all looked into the face of the Full Moon . . . watched the Big Dipper circle around the skydome . . . seen Orion dominate the cold winter skies. We have all wondered what really lies out there amid all those alien worlds so far, far away. Maybe it is impossible to just *look* at the stars. Something about them naturally makes us wonder what lies beyond what we can see.

But while the night sky captures our imagination, and is a virtual feast for our eyes, the study of astronomy remains for most of us an impossible pursuit. All that math, all that physics! What I have learned about the physical universe has given me a sense of space . . . and time . . . and distance . . . of the matter of stars and planets . . . of the birth and eventual death of Creation. It has made the universe *real* to me.

But the "science" of it all is not enough for me. It is not enough to know what a star is composed of or how it was born. It is not enough to know a galaxy is composed of millions of stars. I want to *know* them, *really know* them. Knowing my neighbors, their names and addresses, and describing the houses they live in, doesn't tell me anything about *who* they are. I want to come to know my celestial relations from the perspective of our holistic interconnectedness. I long to *understand* them and their true spiritual nature. That awareness comes only with *knowing the source of things*. To even attempt this I must go beyond what astronomy, the science, can teach me. I want to know the Sky Gods.

In an article about the philosophical school founded by Plato (c. 428-347 B.C.), Kenneth Stein points us in the right direction: "The Neoplatonists worked out a fully developed esoteric philosophy. When they referred to the stars, we may think their intent was to explain them as modern science does, and we see immediately that their knowledge of physics and astronomy was mistaken. But the Neoplatonists were concerned with a holistic conception of things, a system of interconnected and interacting wholes and its meaning for human beings. It is from this perspective that we must understand their view of the earth and stars. To grasp it is to understand much, not least of all ourselves, in terms of a different order of reality."[1] That's it!

We can have it both ways. We can and must know the universe both scientifically and esoterically. We live in a technologically advanced world where astronomical data and discoveries come in faster than they can be deciphered and understood. Today we know more about the physical universe than humans have ever known. But before we, like the Neoplatonists, can venture into the metaphysics of the cosmos we must realize that there is something magical about the act of studying the stars, and that study helps us overcome the futility we feel with their remoteness.

Starwalking is about the universe and the celestial bodies that exist within it. It is about the night and the sky that have been pondered by sages and philosophers down through the ages; about the mysterious worlds that lie above us, the worlds that poets and artists have sought to describe and define. Most importantly, this is a book about a great and immense body of stellar wisdom so ancient that it is difficult, if not impossible, to trace its origin. This wisdom was a *secret doctrine* that was known only to the initiates of the celestial mysteries, including the priests of Sumer, Babylon, Egypt, and the Atlanteans before them. It was also known to the ancient Greeks, the Maya, and Aztec. It was passed down through the Mystery Schools of various cultures worldwide, maybe the last to have inherited the entire tradition intact.

The wisdom concerns the workings of the universe. It contains a sacred geometry defining the vast Whole; rituals, star maps, and myths that both explained and disguised the true nature and workings of the universe; knowledge of the planets and their revolutions in space. It contains the secrets of sacred architecture that symbolized the cosmos and gave humans the knowledge to build immense smooth-sided and stepped pyramids, mounds, ziggurats, temples, stone circles, and towering obelisks. It contains the secrets of the origin and destiny of the human soul, and a model for the visible and invisible dimension of time/space.

Our ancient ancestors made use of the "power" inherent within individual stars, the esoteric knowledge of the constellations, the secrets of celestial computations and of cosmic order. The cultures who possessed that vast body of wisdom in its entirety were able to answer vital questions about the nature of the universe and make giant leaps in evolution. They taught that all life is sacred and that all is alive, every star, every planet, every tree and stone . . . everything. That knowledge gave them a technology that still puzzles us today.

Where did it come from? And when? Was it Atlantean esoteric tradition? If so, how did they get it? Did Hermes himself come to Earth and decode the celestial secrets before returning to the stars? Was it brought here by amphibian creatures? Did the angels gift it to humankind, or did it come with ancient astronauts from distant star systems? The fact is we don't know. Too much time has passed. And the Tradition, once intact, has long since been fragmented.

As geological and climatic planetary changes occurred, human beings migrated. New cultures sprang up, old ones died out. As the migrations continued the original body of stellar knowledge became fragmented so that it rarely survived as a whole. Today, the cultures that can still lay legitimate claim to any part of the ancient celestial wisdom are severely diminished.

That fact has affected both the knowledge and our lives today. Our modern society has lost touch with the need to view the universe as sacred. We have thrown over the sacred for concrete matter, energy, and information. We no longer think we live in a universe of spiritual beings. As we see it, our cosmos has no sacred destiny. We seem to have little or no clue as to what role we, both individually and collectively, have to play in the overall cosmic drama. We don't know our place in the scheme of things.

Science has become the rule by which we measure practically everything, the hook upon which we hang every "truth." Knowledge gained intuitively has little value in our culture and is too often relegated to the trashbin of superstition. We use imagination to produce fantasies that are the stuff of illusion and delusion . . . the unreal.

Somewhere along the way we suffered a "split" between science and metaphysics. With that separation came a worldview that has violated our spiritual nature and our need to understand ourselves and the world we live in. Now we have two cosmologies. One is purely "scientific," and leaves no room for anything but the "science" of our existence. The other is based on a view of the universe that is constructed from a sum of knowledge gleaned from both the conscious and subconscious levels of our minds. Both affect what we believe, shape and define our values, and influence our behavior. One evolved from the intellect, the other from intuition.

The split between science and metaphysics is not the only one that has affected human society. Another occurred between orthodox religion and "paganism." The former relies upon doctrine and dogma that denies access to God by the common folk and reduces all other lifeforms to mute, unconscious existence. Paganism, on the other hand, brought the stars down to Earth and endowed them with life and personality. Earth's children were reared to know and respect all life as sacred. Both separations have resulted in unanswered questions, unfulfilled needs and, sadly, the apathy we see around us today.

I think the time has come when human beings are ready to and capable of rectifying the psychological and spiritual predicament of being closed off from the universe. We can begin a journey to embrace a scientific knowledge of the cosmos, and use that information to inform and acquaint ourselves with the cosmos again. At the same time we can couple the science with a cosmology that has its roots in the distant past, and that bestows the gift of life and power to all that exists.

We must begin somewhere. Astronomy and physics can teach us about the physical nature of the universe, and that knowledge is vital to the success of our journey. We can also learn what our ancestors knew about the stars, and what their view of the cosmos entailed, through the work of archaeologists, astronomers, and pagan sages. We can retrace their steps into the heavens, muse about their elaborate rituals and fearlessly speculate about the purpose of their sacred myths and formulas. In turn we can apply our intellect and intuition to eventually come to understand the Ancients, their knowledge and the age-old monuments, pyramids, medicine wheels, temples, and stone circles, mute testimony to the reality of that great body of stellar knowledge they inherited.

All this involves putting together the pieces of an ancient puzzle. When complete, the image that unfolds will reveal a theology and a cosmology that have been fragmented and often lost to time. We already have many of the major pieces. They include sacred geometry, mathematics, numerology, geomancy, and meteorology. Now it is time to go about the business of gathering the rest.

Some of the pieces we are looking for exist in the cosmologies of tribal cultures all over the world. Some can be found within the sacred rites of the Native Americans, the Celts, and other Earth-based and star-based religions and star-based societies, both ancient and modern. There are pieces in mythology. Pieces are concealed within the petroglyphs and pictographs etched and painted by ancient hands; others are hidden in the ruins of temples and megalithic sites worldwide. They are found on the walls of dark caves, maybe written on bark scrolls or etched on stone tablets. There are pieces in astrology, the Kaballah, Wicca, and in other Nature-based religions, and in the secret traditions of various magical schools such as the Rosicrucians and the Order of the Golden Dawn.

To find the pieces we have to go to the people and places where the stellar tradition was once known. The Persian Magi in the Holy Land knew it. The priests at Heliopolis in ancient Egypt knew it. The Dogon star priests in Africa know it, as do the modern-day Hopi and Navajo. And there are others . . . many others. Their knowledge did more than explain the workings of the universe to their personal satisfaction. It also gave them a "code" of ethics by which to live and by which they could "enter" the universe. In his introduction to Barbara Hand Clow's *Pleiadian Agenda*, cosmologist and physicist Brian Swimme wrote: "To enter the universe simply means learning the ways of the wider world and how a person is to relate to all this. The first humans felt this to be a deep and pressing challenge. Possibly for as long as 300,000 years, and certainly for at least 40,000 years, humans gathered in the night and pondered the ways of the universe in order to find their way through the Great World. No matter what continents humans lived on, no matter what culture, no matter what era, they gathered in the night—around the fire on the African plains, in the caves of the Eurasian forests, under the brilliant night sky of the Australian land mass, in the long houses of North America—and there they told the sacred stories of the universe, and of what it takes to live a noble human life."[2]

This book represents twenty-eight years of personal study in numerous areas of the wisdom teachings contained within Theosophy, the Kaballah, theology, the spiritual traditions of the Tibetan Buddhists, Christianity, Huna, Spiritualism, and Hinduism. It represents fifteen years of study and experiences with Native American and Celtic religions and spiritual practice. It also reflects eighteen years of interest and study in astronomy and physics. Finally, it delineates a long-time interest in and research into the astronomy of the ancient peoples, megalithic sites, and geomancy. With these "tools" I have sought to make a beginning at recovering the original body of stellar knowledge that came to Earth so very long ago.

The time has come for us to reach out to the stars intellectually, intuitively, and ceremonially. Evidence that it is time is becoming more clear. For example, *The Orion Mystery*, released in 1994 became a bestseller. And what is it about? Evidence shows that the pyramids of Egypt were "nothing less than a replica of Heaven on Earth. With great astronomical precision they were created to serve as the Pharaoh's gateway to the stars."[3] Astrology, an integral part of that ancient body of stellar wisdom not only survives, it thrives because it helps us to acknowledge and understand the planetary and cosmic forces at play in our lives. Movies and television programs about space travel and exploration continue to both entertain and inspire us into thinking beyond Earth to alien worlds and beyond time into a future yet to be lived. The science of archaeoastronomy gains in popularity. Ancient sites like the pyramids, Stonehenge, Avebury, Newgrange, Big Horn Medicine Wheel, the Sun and Moon temples in Mexico, and Machu Picchu . . . all of which have astronomical significance . . . continue to be popular destinations for spiritual seekers. Every lecture and workshop I have offered on the stars over the past decade has been filled. More and more people are turning to "channelers" who offer information from extraterrestrial sources from the Pleiades, Orion, Sirius, and other star systems.

While I neither advocate wholesale acceptance of all these messengers and their messages, nor offer validation for or against their celestial sources, the fact remains that their pronouncements are a bit more than widely received. Writer Jay Kinney gives some true insight into the popularity of the messages from ETs and the channelers that bring them: "Nature abhors a vacuum, and if the spiritual barrenness of modern life has called these messengers forth, we need to acknowledge that at least they are grappling with issues of ethics, spiritual growth, and compassion which rarely make it to the surface in popular culture." (Stein, p.33)

Maybe the most convincing evidence that we are ready to reach for the stars is found in the controversial phenomena of UFOs. Since the 1940s, people from all walks of life all over the world have reported strange aerial sightings. Whether the phenomena are evidence of aliens visiting our planet or not, they continue to fascinate and confound us. The phenomena are real, and so is their effect on society. One of the last books written by psychiatrist Carl Jung is titled *Flying Saucers: A Modern Myth of Things Seen in the Skies*. In it he concludes that UFOs are "a modern myth that has an undeniable psychic aspect."[4] But it is Jung's penetrating insight into human nature that interests me most. In a discussion of the perilous times we are living in (the book was written in the 1950s) he says "[the world] situation is calculated as never before to arouse expectations of a redeeming supernatural event. If these expectations have not dared to show themselves in the open, it is simply because no one is deeply rooted enough in the tradition of earlier centuries to consider an intervention from heaven as a matter of course."(Jung, p.21) Jung is saying that humanity expects a "savior" to come and save us from the mess we've gotten ourselves into. If Jung thought the 1950s were dangerous times, one can only imagine what he would think of the world today! We are in trouble and, as Jung said, "we have no metaphysical certainties" . . . and "rationalistic enlightenment predominates." (Jung, p.22)

So have we created a technological image that is in turn being projected and seen as UFOs? Aliens from outer space, archetypal projections, Sky Gods coming to Earth? I don't know. But the UFO phenomena continue to occur, and they are sky-related phenomena. Perhaps this indicates a collective archetypal awakening that comes as a result of our looking for a way out of our global difficulties. If so, we are looking *skyward* for the answers. Interesting how humans would create a global phenomenon that symbolizes a "coming" or "return" of the gods from the sky. Could it be that there are images stored in our individual and collective unconscious of the events such as those reported in the myths of the ancient Babylonians and the more contemporary Dogon of Africa, where the Sky Gods came to Earth and walked among men? It is a thought worth pondering. We seem to have a deep inner longing to go to the stars.

What does it all mean? I think the answer is clear and simple. We are star born. We are responding to an innate human desire to find out where we came from, and then to go home. Through reason and intuition, meditation, ceremony, visualization, creative imagery, and imagination *we can remember our origin.* There are no "maps," per se. There is only the past with long-forgotten memories. And some of those memories are ancient, the kind locked in the collective unconscious. In *The Beginner's Guide To Jungian Psychology,* Robin Robertson defines Jung's concept of the collective unconscious as consisting of "images and behavioral patterns not acquired by an individual in his or her lifetime, yet accessible to all individuals in all times; 'unconscious' because it can be reached through conscious awareness."[5]

Jung's concept of the collective unconscious may in fact hold an all-important key. It implies that humans have memories of ancient times and the people who lived them. It says that we have memories of the stars. It also says that those memories awaken to express themselves in our dreams, in the events of our lives and times, and in our spirituality (and perhaps in every other aspect of our lives), and give us something to sink our teeth into as we seek to understand the role the Sky Gods have played, and continue to play, in our individual psyches and in the collective human psyche. We inherit being human. And the images or archetypes we all inherit are all the same. It is these images that I believe are now awakening within us, individually first, but ultimately within the entire human race. We can and we *will* remember what we know . . . and have always known . . . about the stars. Those memories will call us home.

ACKNOWLEDGMENTS

This book has been in the process of becoming a reality for a long time. The road was not always smooth. Every bump in the road taught me a lesson, the most important of which was patience. I knew from the onset that the time was right for this information to come to the forefront. Although I was not always entirely confident that I could do the subject justice, I never doubted that I had to write it. . . No book comes together without the efforts of a number of people. This one is no exception. There are many people to thank.

First, I would like to thank my husband, Scott, whose unwavering support for me and whose love for the stars saw me through the difficult times. I must thank the people who have encouraged me in various ways through the years since the book's conception: Wabun Wind, Sun Bear, Ron and Helaine McLain, Don O'Neal, Mark Stevens, Fred Spinks, and Jaine Smith. Thanks also go to the archaeoastronomers, particularly Dr. E.C. Krupp, Von del Chamberlain, and Anthony Aveni, whose pioneering work and knowledge of the sky have opened a door to the ancestral peoples whose connection to the Sky Gods continue to intrigue and inspire us for generations to come. My thanks to Barbara Hand Clow, whose enthusiasm for this book gave me the confidence and push I needed at the time I needed it the most, and for her wise editorial help and suggestions that made the work come together. A special thanks goes to Alisha Henri, who so generously gave of her time in putting the manuscript into the computer during the final hectic hours of this project. I thank Mike Harvey, whose love for the stars has long excited and inspired me. Thank you, Mike, for the telescope whose eye showed me the heavens for the first time. And much love and appreciation goes to Barry Perlman, my first astronomy professor. It was Barry's willingness to teach me and his patience that opened up a part of my soul that has led me to a connection with the night sky I might not have experienced otherwise. And, finally, I must extend heartfelt gratitude and appreciation to my editor at Bear & Company, Sonya Moore. Sonya has taught me what working with an editor is truly about. Her skills, insights, and support for this work have gotten me through many down times and inspired me to write my best book.

EDITOR'S NOTE

Please note the reference information in parentheses in the text. After a source is mentioned for the first time in each chapter (and referenced with an appropriate endnote number), succeeding references to that source are placed in parentheses in the text. This process is done by chapter, and is not a continuation from the beginning to the end of the book, so that references will be pertinent to each chapter.

STARWALKING

SHAMANIC PRACTICES FOR TRAVELING INTO THE NIGHT SKY

PART ONE

JOURNEYING INTO THE GREAT STAR NATION

CHAPTER ONE

GRANDFATHER SUN
GRANDMOTHER MOON

*Day and night do not share the sky. They take turns with it
and are on opposite sides of the same coin. One precludes
the other, but they are both needed to complete the natural
order. This opposed but complementary relationship between
day and night is also expressed in the way people have
talked about the Sun and the Moon.*[1]

E.C. Krupp

In order to understand star power in relation to human beings, it
is necessary to go to earliest sources—the stories, hieroglyphs,
and petroglyphs of the Ancients. These patterns and legends,
created to overcome fears and help make sense of mysteries,
evolved into rituals, ceremonies, and religious observances. In our
time, the making of shrines can complement meditation and "formal knowledge."

The cycle of day and night lies at the root of our world's order.
Logically, that cycle was the most common sky phenomenon observed by evolving human beings. For them, darkness and light
regulated time, and ultimately led to the first calendar. All ancient
cultures had their own creation myths, attempts to explain not only
the beginnings of the universe, but also to exemplify the day-night
cycle. There were also stories that helped the earliest peoples interact with their celestial environment and that linked them with the
heavens for all time.

Since ancient times humans have recognized Nature's duality.
The Sun and Moon symbolized and embodied the power of that
duality. They also represented the constant interaction between the

male and female forces from which the universe and all life sprang, and by which both are maintained. They kept time for the people and foretold the future. Locked until the end of time as we know it in their cosmic dance, the Sun and Moon spoke into the ears of the ancestral initiates and told them what could and would be. They gave portents of times not lived, battles not fought, songs not sung, floods not yet rained, and droughts not yet birthed from the rays of an unyielding Sun.

In order to know them better, the Ancients gave the Sun and Moon distinct personalities, though the characters appointed varied from culture to culture. There were myths to explain how the Sun came to be, its name, its function as a sky deity, and its relationship with human beings. Wonderful examples of this type of story come to us from the peoples of India, the Vikings, and the early Greeks, who said that the Sun moved about the heavens because it had wheels. (Krupp, p.47)

Tracing the Sun's attributes through the various myths of both ancient and contemporary societies tells us that they are in relative agreement. Common themes point out the Sun's "rulership" qualities, and assign to it positions of lordship. The Egyptians thought of it as Ra, the ruler of the day and of human affairs. The Babylonians called the Sun God, Shamash, who "stepped through the eastern gate and onto the Mountain of Sunrise at the horizon." (Krupp, p.46) To the Greeks he was Apollo; to the Native Americans he is Grandfather. In Vedic India the Sun was Varuna, the guardian of universal law and order. The Inca of Peru knew him as Inti, their ancestor who possessed supreme divine authority. And to the Aztec he was Tonah Tuih, the one responsible for the world's existence. (Krupp, pp.44-51) To the Cherokee and others the Sun is female, the giver of light and life.

Whether masculine or feminine, it is the role of the Sun as the power of light that is uppermost. Memory of the power embodied by the Sun is contained within our unconscious, and maybe even in our genes. That power has been spoken of down through time in stories told and retold. Humans have always sought to understand life and the world we live in. "We tell ourselves these Sun stories about ourselves whenever we rechronicle the triumph of light over dark. We see ourselves born; we witness our deaths; and we celebrate the new children that replace us. We also speak of another kind of rebirth, a rebirth of the soul, and the crucial episode in that story is death. That's why the Egyptians put a Sun story on the walls of a tomb. They and many other peoples have believed that we complete the cyclical tale and put it in motion again by dying and transcending death through resurrection, reincarnation, or some other transformation of the soul that transports us to heaven, that carries us from darkness into the light." (Krupp, p.53)

Clearly, the Sun has long been associated with birth, renewal, and new beginnings. Awareness of its presence strikes a deep chord within the human psyche. Poets and artists through the ages have sought to convey the feelings inspired by the rising and setting Sun. Who among us has not seen a beautiful sunrise and inhaled the freshness of the dawn? Who has not seen the sky turn to turquoise and gold as the Day Star sinks into the horizon at day's end?

I have seen the Sun turn the snow pink when it rose over the snow-capped Rockies. I have seen it rise in golden splendor over the pyramids on the Nile, and sneak its light between the oaks and pines in the forests of the Great Smoky Mountains. I have seen the big orange beach ball slipping into the sea off Key West, and watched as it changed the colors of the rocks of the Grand Canyon to golds, purples, and blues that defy words. Yet, when the subject of sunrises and sunsets comes up, my mind always goes back to a time at Hopiland in northeastern Arizona. While standing on First Mesa looking out over the desert below, I witnessed a sunset I will never forget: The sky was transformed into layers of turquoise, yellow, orange, gold, and even pink and mauve and purple, as if a master had painted the entire firmament. I have seen nothing like it since.

I have never known a people who have a more intimate relationship with the Sun than the Pueblo tribes of the American Southwest. Though the landscape is beautiful and has its positive points, the desert is also harsh and arid, a place where the Sun imposes itself upon all that lives, oftentimes in the cruelest ways. Staying in harmony with the Day Star and in step with its rhythms means the difference between living and dying. The Hopi and the Zuni are veteran desert-dwellers who share many spiritual and ceremonial traditions. Both have Sunwatchers who note, time, and record what they see on a daily basis. Both have Sun Priests who practice their craft and accept the responsibility of observance handed down to them from the father-priests before them, all for the benefit of the people. They observe everything the Sun does. They watch it rise and climb into the sky; they "call it back" every morning from the darkness it falls into at sunset. They watch its daily journey across the sky. They watch it set. And they pray the Sun into returning from its southwestern place at midwinter during the holiest of all their rites.

Among the sacred rites of these Pueblo tribes, none is more impressive than the Zuni *Shalako*, which is performed every year on the Full Moon near the time of the winter solstice. The event must be timed perfectly by the *Pekwin*, the Sun Priests, the most respected priests in the tribe. Mistakes can result in difficulties for the people in the form of unexpected drought, storms, famine, or other weather-related problems. The Sun Priest has to know his stuff—the right prayers, offerings, and timing.

A vivid description of the elaborate age-old Shalako ritual is given by archaeoastronomer and author Evan Hadingham in *Early Man and the Cosmos*. He provides a clear description of the Shalakos as "long-haired, bearded, great-eyed, and long-snouted, so managed by means of strings and sticks by a person concealed under their ample, embroidered skirts that they seem alive, and strike terror to the uninitiated."[2] What struck me most were their twelve-foot-high headdresses called tablitas, and the birdlike masks worn over their faces. For eight days prior to the ceremony the Pekwin make a pilgrimage to Thunder Mountain to get in touch, through special prayers, with Father Sun. On the ninth day the priests announce the time of the solstice. The ceremony begins ten days later. Father Sun has to be in precisely the right place, and only the Sun Priests are entrusted with determining this time. (Hadingham, pp.131-132) Throughout the performance of their duties, the Pekwin priests fast for the eight-day period and spend that time alone.

Hopi Sunwatchers operate similarly by looking toward the sacred San Francisco Peaks near Flagstaff. The patient priest waits for the Sun to rise at a particular place on the mountain. When it does he knows it is time for the rites to begin. Comparable sunwatching vigils are kept at the time of the summer solstice.

Visual observance is not the only way the priests time sacred rites, or keep track of the Sun's activity for various other purposes. Routine solar alignments are made with houses, distant mountains, and other features on the horizon. Knotted cords and notched sticks for counting are common tools of the Pueblo tribes.[3] It is clear that to the people of the southwestern desert, Father Sun watches over the world of the living by day; at night he takes his light to the world of the dead.

The Sun and Moon are also prominent mythical characters. An example is seen in a Navajo emergence myth that tells of a time when humans came up from the underworld to live on Earth's surface. These First People were in semidarkness and craved more light. They tried many ways to get light without success. Finally, they decided to create light by taking a large quartz crystal and fashioning it into two disks. They decorated the first disk with a mask of turquoise that radiated light and heat, and placed red coral around its outer rim and earlobes. They also placed feathers from a flicker, a lark, and an eagle around the rim to radiate heat and light in the four directions. The first disk, the Sun, was then hung in the eastern sky by bolts of lightning. The second disk was the Moon, which was decorated and hung in the west. It too was made of crystal, but its borders were trimmed with white shells. They put sheet lightning on its face, as well as images of all kinds of water.

But this arrangement soon produced a problem. The east was too hot, the west was too cold. The problem was solved however, when two Elders came forward and offered to give their spirits to the stationary Sun and Moon so they could move in their specific paths across the heavens. First Man gave them each twelve eagle feathers to guide them along their proper paths. The changes in their paths would mark the seasons. The Sun began its journey and the Moon followed. As the Sun reached its place of daily departure, it was moving too slow. To help the Sun move faster, the Wind Boy blew on it. The wind blew the eagle feathers in the Moon's face, and it could not see its way. This is why the Moon wanders across the sky. (Krupp, p.161)

The phases of the Sun and Moon are clearly indicated by this legend. (It should be noted that in Navajo culture the Moon is masculine.) The absence of light is symbolic of the Otherworld, darkness symbolizing the mysteries of life and the unknown, cold the death of sleep, trance, and the physical death that all lives must experience. Similarly, legends about the Sun and Moon tell of an "original time" when there was complete darkness from which light and matter came forth.

Just as the Sun graces the sky by day, the Moon rules the night. In most cultures down through time, the Moon represented the feminine principle in Nature, and in the human psyche. In fact, the position of the Moon in a given culture more than likely determined the position of women in the same culture, their fates inexorably shared. The ancestral peoples, worldwide, knew that crops grew in rhythm with the cycles of the Moon. They knew that women's menstrual cycles were in tune with the lunar cycles, as were the mating cycles of animals. In light of this the Moon was the object in Nature that represented fertility and the continuity of life. Legends tell us that it was synonymous with the Mother Goddess who was known by various names in various cultures. The Mother Goddess is the oldest recorded deity, and has been celebrated since prehistoric times in art and ritual. A common creation myth involves the concept of the world beginning as an egg that cracked into two parts, forming Earth and the Moon, making the two celestial "sisters."

Undoubtedly, the earliest lunar rites were those that involved the drawing down of the Moon's energy to replenish the energy of fertility and growth in the world. The Moon was also said to heighten the emotions, passions, and feelings within human beings. I think it is safe to say that among both the ancestral and modern-day tribal peoples throughout the world, it has been priestesses who communicate with and celebrate the life within the Moon. Priestesses have expressed the power of the Moon on Earth in their daily personal and religious lives.

A solar eclipse occurs when the Moon is directly between Earth and the Sun, producing a phenomenon that is unrivaled in splendor and intrigue. If the lineup is not exact, only a partial eclipse is witnessed. Before completely disappearing, the Sun is an ever-so-thin crescent with sparkly shiny beads produced by the Sun's light shining between the mountains on the Moon's edge. Then there is the single startling, fleeting flash of light that comes immediately before, and sometimes just after, totality. In the precious moments when the sky has no Sun, rare sights may be seen. First there are the solar prominences that are long wispy tongues of solar fire, incandescent gases that appear. A closer look reveals the glorious filmy corona stretching for millions of miles in all directions from the blacked-out Day Star, creating the so-called "diamond ring" effect. At least two total eclipses happen each year, though there can be as many as five. Because the paths along which the eclipses can be seen are so narrow, relatively few people have the opportunity to see them. Sky omens have always played a significant role in tribal spirituality. Meteors, comets, lunar halos, rainbows, and solar and lunar eclipses were all "messengers" of coming events or, as with the appearance of a rainbow after the Biblical flood, of a future promise or state of affairs. Not all omens were bad; however they were always of consequence.

Of all celestial phenomena, eclipses generated the most excitement and caused the greatest concern. Anyone who has witnessed a solar eclipse is familiar with the eerie night that interrupts the day, casting the world into an unnatural darkness. Nothing seems right. Time itself seems to be confused and stopped. Our sense of order is disturbed, and our security is threatened. (Krupp, p.167)

A lunar eclipse is no less awesome. Once in a while, when the Moon is full, it passes through Earth's shadow. A full lunar eclipse can last for up to an hour and 40 minutes. One spectacular reward, which is caused by a small amount of sunlight being refracted into Earth's atmosphere, is the Moon's taking on a red or sometimes coppery color. A full eclipse of the Moon was witnessed in late September of 1996. During this event, not only did the Moon turn copper in color, but it was in conjunction with the planet Saturn, which shone brightly in the night sky with its lunar companion.

Having a scientific explanation for solar and lunar eclipses as we do, and knowing in advance when they will occur, is one thing. The approximately seven and one-half minutes duration of a full solar eclipse is not much time, but the psychological impact upon human consciousness can far outlast the phenomenon. Imagine what it must have been like during the earliest times when there was no such explanation or pronouncement. Eclipses came without warning upon an unsuspecting world. What was happening? What did it mean? Had something fierce and alien devoured the Sun and taken away the light, casting the world into an eerie and uncanny darkness? Who or what had eaten the Moon? Of course the answer would have depended upon the beliefs of a given culture, but such an unnatural and frightening state of affairs must have caused more than one of our ancestors to fall to their knees in awe and fright.

Eclipses may also have given rise to some of the earliest sacred ceremonies. Think about it. If everything had gone wrong in your world once, it could happen again. Based upon the premise of ritual being a way of appeasing the angry forces of Nature, no matter what forms they might take—demons or dragons or wolves—solar and lunar conciliatory rites must certainly have played important ritualistic roles. What these rituals involved would depend upon the nature of a people's beliefs regarding the Sun and Moon in the first place, as well as upon basic religious beliefs and practices. It stands to reason that such rites would have evolved primarily as preventive measures. The fervent prayers of the frightened people for an eclipse to end would never have failed; but the same would not have been true for the ceremonies of prevention. Eclipses continued to happen.

Over time, enough eclipses were recorded that, ultimately, they could be predicted. Humans no doubt measured the time when eclipses would occur by carefully monitoring the movements of the luminaries across the sky. This was no small task, as described by Krupp: "It takes an accurate calendar system of reference stars to do this, and the ancient Mesopotamians were among those who devised such a set of celestial markers. With those stars and constellations in 'the path of the Moon', the Mesopotamians entered a celestial sweepstakes that eventually rewarded them with reasonable success at lunar eclipse prediction and the ability to know when solar eclipses were either possible or out of the question." (Krupp, p.167)

Eclipses may have lost their mystique due to our knowledge of modern science. But they have not lost their psychic impact. Embedded within the depths of human consciousness are the ancestral memories of those times when the world was plunged into enigmatic, unsettling darkness. I am not suggesting that we must become ignorant about eclipse events in order to more fully appreciate their occurrence. That would be impossible. But to view a total or partial solar or lunar eclipse with both scientific understanding and the awareness that eclipses gave to humanity's relationship with the heavens helps us appreciate them on a different and deeper level.

Solar and lunar ceremonies have probably been going on since the earliest times. For life to thrive there has to be an innate sense of rhythm, a pulse within at the base of everything. From the earliest weeks of human life the rhythm or cycle that first becomes familiar is that of night and day, darkness and light. By and through this pulse, time becomes real. We begin to associate, both visually and psychologically, the Sun with the light and the Moon with the darkness. It is just a small step for human consciousness to see the Sun as the "Lord" of light and the Moon as the "Mistress" of darkness. Furthermore, light soon becomes representative of the conscious waking state, while the Moon is the night, the time of sleep and, ultimately, the realm of death. The Sun helps us see our way along the path of life in the external, physical world. The Moon illumines the shadows, whether in the sometimes ominous physical world we live in, or in the nooks and crannies of inner landscape. So life becomes a matter of personal navigation by the archetypal Sun and Moon within the human psyche, ever guiding us along our way.

Swiss psychologist Carl Jung concluded that the human psyche has a built-in subliminal need to recognize and go beyond the mundane. Since earliest times, that instinctive need has been fulfilled by and through ritual. Our ancestors relied upon their dual mental allies, instinct and intuition, because our overemphasis on logic had not yet become dominant. They were keenly aware of the Force around and within themselves, and realized how utterly dependent they were upon it. They sought through ritual to interact with it, to communicate with it, and to appease it. Humans began to wonder what the benefits would be if they could live in harmony with the Force. This gave birth to the sacred ritual.

The earliest rites sought to acknowledge and honor the cosmological and celestial energies and influences that were generated by the Sun and Moon, planets, stars, comets, and other natural bodies, and phenomena such as thunder and lightning, rain, and eclipses. Through ritual humans appeased the forces of Nature, the ancestral spirits, and the Sky Gods and Goddesses. In return they survived. They received abundance. Once this mutual exchange had been set into motion via ritual, ceremony became a necessary insurance

policy for a balanced, prosperous life. Human failure to engage in
sacred rites would lead to eventual disenchantment and bring down
the wrath of the deities. The collective need for dialogue with the
natural forces and deities provided the opportunity for the rise of
shamans, the first specialists. They formed the priesthoods, and in
doing so they became vital to the physical and spiritual well-being
of the people.

As stated, most likely the earliest ceremonies were those performed in honor of the Sun and Moon. In times we know about,
solar rituals numbered four, one for each of the solstices and equinoxes. The Moon was most honored when it was full, and the Full
Moon ceremony remains today as the most commonly observed ceremonial happening. Maybe the oldest solar rites consisted of dancing around a blazing sacred fire. And maybe the first lunar rites
were performed by ancestral women who stood with their arms
stretched up to the Mother of the Night. At any rate, solar and lunar
archetypes became indelibly etched in our collective unconscious.
And their powers continue to affect our psyches. That the Sun,
Moon, and other planetary bodies and phenomena in the solar system influence life on Earth is an important and surviving part of our
celestial legacy.

Of course we have the option of viewing this as so much superstitious nonsense. Or we can choose to be aware of the transitional state that we on Earth are in right now and seek to rediscover the
female principle within and around us, and allow it to reclaim its
rightful place in our lives. We can seek to balance the male and
female within. We can reconnect with the Sun and Moon by erecting solar and lunar shrines and by performing solar and lunar rituals. By our connection with the Sun and Moon we can make our
way into space, and in the process savor the nectar that nourished
the very souls of the skywatchers and Starwalkers of yesteryear. But
the reconnection must come first. The following information is
designed to help facilitate that link.

Intimate knowledge of the Sun and Moon is an integral part of
being aware of the psychic and physical balance in Nature. Sun-
consciousness is awareness of our environment and its workings.
Moon-consciousness is never separate from the human unconscious. Sun-consciousness is active. Moon-consciousness is passive,
a conscious awareness of the subjective realms within each human

being. The subjective side of ourselves, of the world and life, is recognized by the ego, but not always understood by it. Inner experience does not lend itself easily to words. It cannot be transmitted from one who has had the experiences, thoughts, and feelings that accompany it to one who has not undergone the same or similar occurrences. This is why a "masculine" consciousness that relies solely upon logic and reason finds the psychic and intuitive knowledge and experiences born from feminine, or matriarchal, feelings and experiences hopelessly mystical and esoteric.

Beginning in the 1960s, many of us have engaged in a fervent search for the inner self, the psychic and intuitive side of human nature. We have yearned, individually and collectively, for the transcendental experience, and for meaning in our relationships with God, Nature, and each other. We have sought to arouse the latent psychic sensitivity that was so natural to our ancestors. Particularly since the late 1970s, there is an ever-growing interest in the Moon's energy and how it relates to spirituality. Interest in and groups based upon feminist spirituality have sprung up everywhere. The Old Religion, commonly known as Wicca, has made a strong reemergence into our culture. All this implies our individual and collective need to get back into the good graces of the Moon Goddess, and to understand the energy and the powers she bestows.

Knowledge of the Sun and a relationship with the Sun God has its own rewards, not the least of which is a conscious awareness of the power of the life force and the ongoing scheme of evolution. The Ancients had stories to explain such things. In fact, that is the beauty of myth. It is not judged by the need for rationality, not hampered by the boundaries and demands of science. Mythology is free to explain the unexplainable, and in doing so awakens archetypal images that relate humans to all that exists.

Solar and lunar eclipses provide wonderful opportunities for doing ceremonies to honor our celestial Grandfather and Grandmother whom we take so much for granted. A simple ritual will do. Since we know far in advance when an eclipse will occur there is more than ample time to select an appropriate offering—perhaps a sacred herb, flowers, a pretty shell, or a crystal—and make plans to be alone or gather a group to view the event, sing songs, and choreograph a simple but special dance. Aside from the reason of honoring the Sun and Moon, the action will also stir ancient memories within you—memories of times and perhaps even of celestial knowledge that has long been forgotten.

MAKING SUN AND MOON SHRINES

Constructing Sun and Moon shrines on your land is a simple way to seek to reconnect with these significant celestial luminaries. (You may also wish to create a Star Shrine. Construction will be similar to those discussed.) A shrine is an outdoor altar that is used as a ceremonial site to draw down celestial powers. It can also be a monument to honor the Sun and Moon. Shrines are common in the Shinto and Tibetan religions in the East and with Native Americans in the West. Before you erect your shrine, you will need to select a suitable site for it. The Sun Shrine should be placed in the east, and the Moon Shrine in the west. The shrines will not take up much space, and if constructed properly will in no way deface the land.

For the Sun Shrine you will need to collect 31 rocks about twice the size of your fist, one for each day of the Sun's passage through a zodiac sign. As you gather each of the stones, a traditional offering of cornmeal should be left in its place. Should you feel that any stone is resisting being taken or that it just doesn't feel right to take it, select another, until you have gathered them all. Volcanic rock is especially good for a Sun Shrine, but any type of stone will do. Take the stones to the site you have chosen. It is good to construct it during the day, preferably at noon when the Sun is at its zenith and therefore at its full power. When you are ready, take the stones one at a time and arrange them into a cairn (pile). You may also wish to

Sun Shrine

place a crystal on the cairn and an effigy of the Sun on top or nearby. Ceramic and brass solar plaques can be purchased at most garden shops. Some people like to place small wooden benches near the shrine. Flowers or other small plants can also be placed around the cairn, turning the area into a little meditation garden. Making the area beautiful and serene is a wonderful way to honor our Day Star. You can also set a larger circle around the central cairn for doing your ceremony. At the Sun Shrine place your offering at noon on the first day the Sun moves into a different sign in the zodiac on the twenty-first or twenty-second day of the month.

The Lunar Shrine is built in honor of the Moon, and should be placed in the western part of your land. Prior to construction, gather 28 stones, one for each night of the Moon's cycle, about the same size as those used in the Sun Shrine. Or you may wish to use large shells, as these have long been associated with the Moon. On the evening of the New Moon or Full Moon arrange your stones in a circle, placing them about six to eight inches apart. If you wish to have a larger or smaller circle, space the stones or shells accordingly. If you prefer, you can form a crescent with the stones reminiscent of the crescent moon. You might like to place a crystal or some other mineral in the center of the circle or crescent. The Moon Shrine is a wonderful place to do Full Moon ceremonies. Suggested offerings for the Moon include flowers, water (especially from a sacred spring or well, lake, or river), crystals, sage or other sacred herbs. Offerings should be given at least twice a month at the New Moon and Full Moon even if you do not choose to do a full-fledged ceremony.

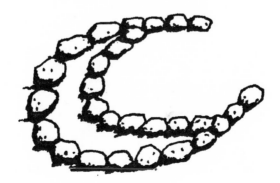

Lunar Shrine

Aside from being beautiful, shrines have a positive psychological impact on us and serve a useful ceremonial purpose. After all, if we are going to reconnect with the heavens, part of our work must be physical. Ceremony inspires us, and solar and lunar shrines help to link us both psychologically and spiritually to the source of that inspiration.

Star Shrine

CHAPTER TWO

CONSTELLATIONS AND THE FIXED STARS

*Why did somebody not teach me the
constellations and make me
at home in the starry heavens which
I don't half know to this day.*[1]

Thomas Carlyle

This book is about gaining knowledge of and forming a relationship with the heavens. That involves a journey, and every
journey begins with the first step. Our destination is Sky
Country. It is a jaunt I invite you to take with me so that together
we not only learn the facts about the night sky, but experience it as
well. In order for our trip be a fulfilling and enlightening one, we
must acquaint ourselves with where we are going. It therefore
behooves us to make learning our way around the night sky our
first priority.

Dividing the sky scene into seasons and knowing what constellations are visible between the hours of eight and twelve midnight make our task easy and fun. Star maps are provided to help
you become familiar with the seasonal constellations and individual stars. For more advanced stargazers, the maps will provide a
good refresher course. Since the brightest stars are located within
the constellations, using these to help spot a given star group is
quite helpful. Our journey will take us around the dome of the sky
where we will encounter many interesting "places" and "characters"
along the way.

From our vantage point on Earth we can see about 20,000 stars with the naked eye. When we realize that there are over 200,000,000 stars in our Milky Way galaxy alone, that 20,000 really isn't many. But it is enough to dazzle us as it has humans since the beginning of our existence. Because of our relatively short life span, the night sky seems unchanging, every star in its place night after night. In truth however, the stars are not constant. They move. As Earth rotates on its axis from west to east, the rotation produces movement which we do not feel, giving the illusion that everything we see in the sky is doing the moving, not us.

Of the stars we can see, 110 of them have gained special prominence. These are the so-called *fixed* stars, those we count on to be in their places. Among them are some of the most well-known stars and some of the most obscure; some of the brightest and the dimmest; some of the closest and the most distant. Some have familiar names: Polaris, Arcturus, Sirius, Castor, Pollux, Rigel, and Antares. Others seem hopelessly foreign and mysterious: Vertex, Unu Kalhai, Alpheratz, Zavajava, and Khambalia. I have chosen to pay detailed attention to the more familiar stars and constellations, so not all 110 stars are listed.

Fixed stars are believed by some to be divinely appointed, to serve the purpose of shedding light upon the karmic condition and debts of individual humans. (Staal, p.2) This allows for an interchange between heaven and Earth that has been part of moral philosophies and religions since the remotest times.

We have to understand that ancestral people did not view stars the way we do today. They saw them as living beings or entities. They sensed the power inherent within each and every celestial body, no matter what kind it was. They gave every body a "personality" to correspond to its inherent power, which they determined intuitively. An example is seen with the star Algol, which some thought of as the "devil" star due to perceived evil properties. Sometimes the name described and/or defined a star's power. In other cases it was the time a star appeared in the sky that determined and revealed its power. An example of this is the Pleiades, which is a calendric star group that marks the time for planting and reaping. The point is that people believed that stars had power, and that star power affected all else, including human beings. Decentralizing the Sun,[2] the Moon, and the planets can go far in helping us come to know our true point of origin—the stars—and in doing so to discover our individual and collective human destiny.

It dawned on me early on that much of what I wanted and needed to know for a "textbook" on the nature of the fixed stars was spread out in numerous cultures all over the world. And that some cultures paid more attention to particular stars than other peoples did. It became a matter of discovering what I could about individual stars, though getting a little bit here and a little bit there was slow going, but rewarding. The key was that different cultures had their own interpretation of the energy emitted by the various stars and that stars were assigned to different ranks of importance within the different societies. But, while they do differ, many interpretations are surprisingly similar. An example is seen with the star Sirius: Both the ancient Egyptians and the Dogons in Africa associated Sirius with females.

In addition, we should keep in mind that ancient societies recognized and honored the dual nature of the universe. This led star priests and priestesses in varying times and cultures to classify all the celestial bodies (and phenomena), including stars, as having both positive and negative qualities. When we, individually and collectively, evolve to a point where we can respond to the positive or soul nature of a given star, that star's power will have a completely positive effect. Until then a given star's adverse power cannot be sidestepped, and any attempt to do so is futile. The same applies to our ability to respond to comets, eclipses, asteroids, and planets.

Those missing pieces have often brought my search to a dead end. So I began to "make" pieces to fill in the gaps. I made them out of common sense, logic, imagination, my knowledge and personal experience with indigenous peoples and their cultures, my knowledge of astronomy and astrology, and my intuition. The picture has slowly become clearer. Much of the information that follows discusses the value and meaning placed upon specific stars by various peoples globally, as well as what has been kept safe within the annals of fixed-star astrology and the astronomical history of various archaic cultures. Along with the information, I will explain ways by which stellar power can be accessed and how it can be used for purposes of individual personal and spiritual growth, as well as for the benefit of the planet and all that lives.

Stellar power is emanated in "streams" that come to Earth as rays, waves, or beams of pure star force. These rays affect all that lives on Earth, as well as the planet herself. Star power is the *activating* and *transforming* power in the cosmos. Through it human beings are connected to the Star Nation and ultimately to the entire universe. It bequeaths us life. It can also enter our consciousness via dreams and visions that are sometimes induced by the use of sacred plants, sacred rites, meditation, and through the telling and retelling of star myths. In most instances humans are not conscious that they are being influenced by star energy. If we accept that incoming stellar energy influences us, and we pursue a study of that truth, we will begin to see a profoundly effective system of knowledge that originated within various cultures, and that still exists worldwide.

It is important to understand that stellar energy is released or directed to Earth at varying times. Stars and/or constellations radiate energy all the time, but different stellar emanations are only let into Earth's aura at intervals. Incoming stellar force is being regulated by highly evolved Galactic and Systemic Beings whom I refer to as the *Regulators.* They allow in those energies necessary for the ongoing process of evolution of life on this planet.

It is their work of regulation of cosmic and stellar forces from other parts of the solar system, galaxy, and beyond that constitutes my primary objective here. Keep this objective in mind while reading the information about specific stars and constellations. An equally important point is that while the work of the Regulators is of tremendous significance, there is another way that a particular star, or stars, can affect humans on a purely individual level: if a star appears in the natal horoscope. These placements only occur when a lesson needs to be learned through working on personal karmic responsibilities that only a certain star can teach. Some stars that show up in the birth chart have a positive effect and are a blessing; others present obstacles and adverse energies that must be overcome over the course of one or more lifetimes. (See detailed information on fixed-star astrology in Appendix Nine.)

Many interpretations of the power inherent within the fixed stars have proven to be quite useful and insightful. A study of the various interpretations has increased my stellar awareness of the complexities involved. Therefore, rather than relying solely upon what I have learned from others, I choose to offer information about the energy inherent within specific stars that I have intuited through meditation and ceremonial work. The validity of what is presented as intuited can be determined by and through your own experience with the stars, or gained in the various ways suggested to connect you with the stars. Each individual must test the validity of the information for her- or himself. Whenever possible and if necessary for clarification, I have coupled my intuited information with the historical and religious significance the stars hold for various cultures.

I have grouped the stars in the traditional constellations in which they appear to reside for ease in learning the night sky, as well as for clarity in interpreting and understanding stellar energy as it applies to the individual and to the masses.

There are 88 constellations; the ones discussed are those in which a fixed star is located. Star maps to help you determine the visibility of each constellation by season are provided. The degree and minutes and sign for each fixed star are also provided in the reference section at the back of the book. This data will remain the same through the year A.D. 2000. Note that constellations constitute apparent groups of stars that have been linked into arbitrary patterns. The patterns have nothing to do with the stars' actual proximity in the heavens. However, because they have been seen to form certain images over many millennia, they do indeed exert a unified or concentrated energy that affects and influences lives on Earth.

Star energies unleash specific forces that come to the planet in starwaves that manifest as principles, inclinations, potentials, conditions, and events within the consciousness of the planet and the lives in all kingdoms. Only human beings can deal with star energy consciously.

Being able to sight and identify the fixed stars is an important step in familiarizing yourself with the starry vault and coming to feel at home in the night. It takes time, but it is time well-spent. Knowing where in the heavens these all-important stars are, and learning how to draw upon their power is of significant benefit in learning how to become a Starwalker.

All of us are dealing with planetary energy all the time. But those working with fixed-star energy are dealing with a very human and very karmic relationship with the stars. Stars embody powers that in turn represent and transmit spiritual truths to those who are open and ready to receive them. All lives on Earth are vessels through which star waves flow. In this way stars and planets are our teachers, serving as tools of self-understanding and aiding in our individual and collective spiritual growth.

Books that offer additional information about interpretations of fixed-star energies are available. It is important to point out, however, that interpretation—whether of a planet, a star, or other celestial body or phenomenon's presence in a birth chart—is an art that is highly dependent upon the ability to grasp, both intellectually and intuitively, the nature of a given body's energy. Over time, as you learn the ceremonies to draw upon star energies (see chapter 3), and meditate upon them, the stars' true natures will be revealed. Patterns created by the planets and stars are guides that show which planetary and stellar waves are influencing us at any given time. We always have free will to succumb to these influences, or to make conscious use of and allowance for their energy in our lives.

Some additional comments regarding the Regulators are in order here. I hope to inspire you to pursue a deeper understanding of these Enlightened Ones. I have focused purely on their regulating of incoming and outgoing stellar energies, but their work with the planet and all the kingdoms that live here is far more extensive. Working through the Law of Karma, it is their duty to assure that Earth's life is maintained until all lives have reached a point of God consciousness. Intuitively, I understand that there is a particular function of the Regulators that is not discussed or explained in any detail in other teachings. It concerns the regulation of various terrestrial, systemic, and cosmic energies in a synthesis of pure cosmic force that plays upon all lives, including that of the planet herself. In part, this regulating power determines the source and degree of incoming stellar and planetary energies.

The type of knowledge I am presenting involves what might be called "esoteric astronomy." Both astrology and astronomy are valuable tools for helping us pursue a more in-depth, conscious knowledge of ourselves and the powers that are inherent with the Star Nation. After all, the stars are influencing us whether we are conscious of it or not. Even if and when we become conscious of stellar influences, we cannot control the fact that the influence is there. But we can determine our response to it. So let's begin our journey through the night sky. Along the way, use the sky maps to help you locate the various constellations by season.

AUTUMN

CONSTELLATION	FIXED STAR
Cetus	Menkar
	Difda
Pegasus	Algenib
	Markeb
Andromeda	Alpheratz
	Vertex
Pisces	Al Pherg
Aries	Sheratan
Perseus	Capulus
	Algol
Aquarius	Sadalmelik
	Skat
	Sadalsuud

WINTER

CONSTELLATION	FIXED STAR
Taurus	Aldebaran
	Elnath
	Al Hecka
Pleiades	Alycone
Hyades	Prima Hyadum
Orion	Rigel
	Bellatrix
	Betelgeuse
	Alnilam
Auriga	Menkalinan
	Capella
Columba	Phact
Carina—Argo Navis	Foramen
	Canopus
Eradinus	Achernar
Canis Minor	Procyon

Canis Major	Sirius
Gemini	Propus Tejat
	Dirah
	Wasat
	Propus
	Castor
	Pollux
Vela	Markab

SUMMER

CONSTELLATION	FIXED STAR
Cygnus	Albireo
	Deneb Adige
Aquila	Altair
	Deneb
Sagittarius	Polis
	Facies
	Pelagus (Nunki)
	Ascella
	Manubrium
	Terebellum
Lyra	Vega
Capricorn	Giedi
	Dabih
	Oculus
	Bos
	Armus
	Dorsum
	Nashira
	Deneb Algedi
Corona Borealis	Alphecca
Serpens—Caput—Serpentis—Ophiuchus	Unukalhai
	Rasalhague
	Lesath
	Sabik
	Yed Prior
	Sinistra
	Han
Scorpio—Scorpios	Antares
	Graffias (Acrab)

	Isidis
	Aculeus
Libra	North Scale
	South Scale
Boötes	Seginus
	Arcturus
	Princeps
Virgo	Spica
	Vindemiatrix
	Caphir
	Zavijava
	Khamballa
Corvus	Algorab
Centaurus	Agena
	Bungula (Toliman)
Leo	Zosma
	Denebola
	Algenubi
	Al Jabha
	Regulus
Cancer	Praesaepe
	Asellus Borealis
	Asellus Australis
	Acubens
	Labrum
Hydra	Alphard
Canes Venatici	Copula
Crux	Acrux

The information on the fixed stars is, with the exception of the astrological implications, which are clearly stated as such, my own. Again, you must weigh what I have said carefully, apply the interpretations to your own natal horoscope, and work with drawing down the various stars' power through the meditation and ceremonial techniques that will be given later in this writing. Remember, the information represents an effort on my part to "fill in the gaps," if you will, of what has been lost of the vast body of esoteric stellar knowledge, and is presented here in the spirit of the desire to make a contribution to the evolution of all that lives.

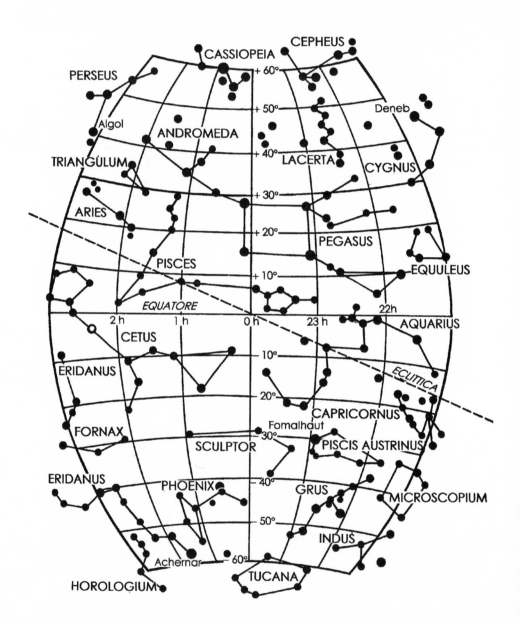

Autumn Star Map

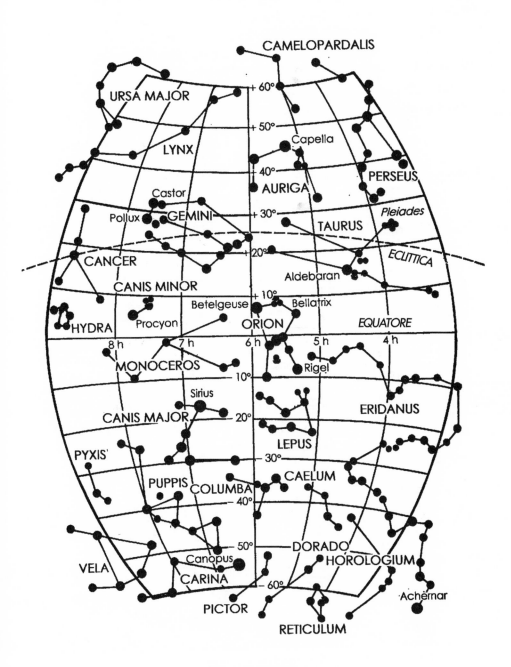

Winter Star Map

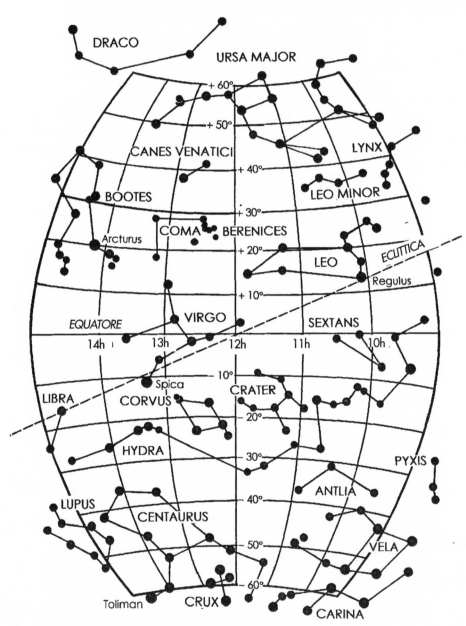

DRACO

URSA MAJOR

+ 60°

+ 50°

CANES VENATICI

LYNX

+ 40°

LEO MINOR

BOOTES

+ 30°

COMA BERENICES

+ 20°

Arcturus

LEO

ECLITTICA

Regulus

+ 10°

EQUATORE

VIRGO

SEXTANS

14h   13h   12h   11h   10h

10°

Spica

CRATER

LIBRA   CORVUS

20°

HYDRA

30°

PYXIS

ANTLIA

LUPUS

40°

CENTAURUS

50°

VELA

60°

Toliman   CRUX

CARINA

Spring Star Map

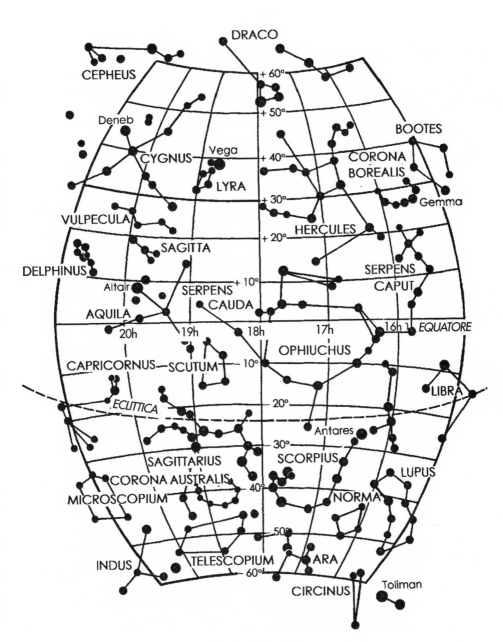

Summer Star Map

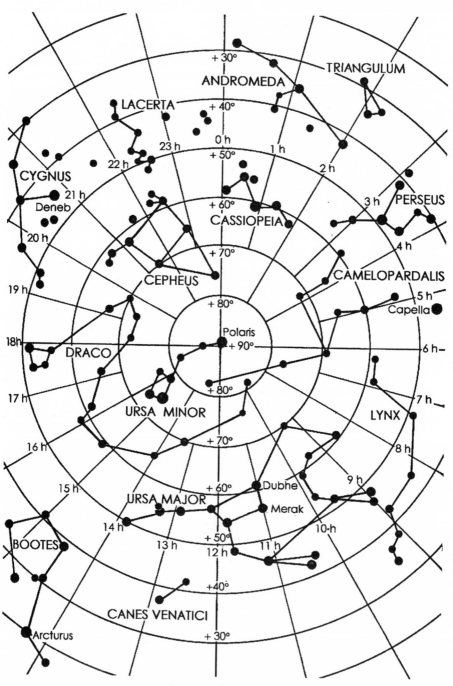

Circumpolar Star Map

CHAPTER THREE

STAR POWER FOR PERSONAL GROWTH

Kings may enforce heaven's commands on Earth, but shamans travel to the sky and consort with the celestial gods in person.[1]

E. C. Krupp

To a large extent the study and interpretations contained within this chapter are based on the research and practice of astrologers, to whom we owe a great debt of gratitude for preserving this arcane celestial knowledge. Our exploration of the stars thus far has been primarily from an esoteric, a scientific, and spiritual perspective.

How far are various stars from Earth? How big are the different stars? How do other stars compare with our Sun? To what constellation does a given star belong? The answers to these and other questions help us balance the cultural and spiritual and physical information about stars. Astrology should be accompanied by, if not preceded by, a basic knowledge of astronomy. Together, the two form a foundation of information and awareness upon which you can grow and expand.

There are ways we can gain knowledge and personal experience of stars and their energy. *Meditation, visualization, prayer,* and *ceremony* are used for "drawing down" stellar power. The power drawn upon in turn may be used for varying purposes, depending on the nature of the star from which it comes. A deliberate conscious attempt to work with our celestial counterparts not only can serve to benefit and enhance our spirituality, but also goes far in facilitating a personal relationship with the stars, which has been almost completely lacking for modern humanity. We must be mindful that how we respond to and choose to use the energies we have consciously drawn down makes all the difference. We must accept full responsibility for our motives. I should also point out that dealing with star energy, regardless of what methods are employed, is quite different from handling the types of energies we encounter from sacred sites, mountains, the Moon, the planets, or even those of spirit forces, with the exception, of course, of the Star Spirits themselves.

DRAWING DOWN STAR POWER FOR PERSONAL USE

I find that the average amount of time involved in the drawing down process need be no more than fifteen minutes. The time may vary however, depending upon which method you are using at any given time. Keep in mind that your motivation must be clear. *There must always be purpose involved.* The quality of that purpose will not only embody and determine the motivation behind the attunement, but will also determine the quality and success of the drawing-down process.

From personal experience I know three ways that star power may be tapped: *ceremony, meditation,* and *visualization.* For me, the most efficient is ceremony. Ceremony is a sacred rite designed to celebrate and/or connect and communicate with the invisible forces in Nature and with spirit entities.

A star ceremony is performed so that a participant might place himself or herself in the proper frame of mind to receive star power. Unfortunately, few such ceremonies survive today, and those that do are part of secret tribal rituals not, as a rule, open to the uninitiated. The star-related ceremonies about which I know personally have to do primarily with stars serving as "timers" to determine when a sacred rite will begin. An example is the Hopi Soyal (winter solstice), which involves the three belt stars in Orion. (see chapter 10)

Since precious few accounts of star-oriented rites are available to us, we are basically on our own. Over the past several years, under the tutelage of my Spirit Teacher, Albion, using my intuition

and my study of astronomy, and the study and ceremonial assignments I have worked with among my private students, I have frequently performed star rituals. To illustrate these experiences and
for the purpose of instruction, the following is a description of work
I often do with the North Star, Polaris.

The purpose of my ceremonial work with the North Star has
always been the same: *to invoke the power of stability, practicality,
and perseverance into my consciousness and subsequently into my
life.* Because we are living through times of major planetary change,
and because change is often the cause of uncertainty and insecuri-
ty on a personal and collective level, I have felt a need to solicit
help from the stars. I call upon Polaris during times when I feel fear-
ful due to some circumstance that made me feel unsteady, or when
I have needed help in making a commitment. I find that being able
to literally fix my eyes on the star with which I am working not only
helps my concentration, but also enables me to relate better and
more easily with that star.

However, star energy can be tapped without physically sighting
the stars. If it is cloudy or the Moon is full, it does not mean that
you must postpone your ceremony. I do, however, recommend that
your rite be done outdoors whenever possible. This way you can at
least face the general direction of the star or constellation with
which you will be working.

Obviously star workers must know their way around the night
sky. As stated earlier, the simplest way to gain this knowledge is by
learning what constellations are visible during the various seasons
of the year. This also helps simplify a voluminous amount of information. I recommend that you check your local newspaper, since
many publish weekly or monthly columns that provide the dates of
the new and full moons, eclipses, comets, planets currently visible,
and other pertinent astronomical data. There is also *Astronomy* magazine, a monthly publication with a centerfold showing the night
sky for the month, with information regarding current astronomical
events. *Astronomy* is particularly useful to amateur astronomers as
well as others interested in pursuing a more in-depth knowledge of
the general field.

Books and posters showing the constellations and seasonal star maps are available, particularly in bookstores and gift shops connected with planetariums and museums. As for books, I especially recommend *365 Starry Nights* by Chet Raymo (see Bibliography), but any basic planet and star guide will do.

There will be occasions when you will be working with a particular star or constellation that is not visible or, if it is, not during a convenient time of night. On these occasions, you must rely upon drawing-down methods that do not involve physically sighting the star(s).

Prior to the actual ceremony, a circle should be drawn on the ground, either using creative visualization or literally. It may be outlined with carefully selected stones, shells, crystals, or other desired objects. The size of the circle will be determined by what feels comfortable to you and by the number of people who will be participating. Once drawn, the circle should be consecrated with incense or herbal smoke, sacred water, prayer, or some other method you feel comfortable with and are accustomed to using in ceremony. This cleanses the ceremonial area, and gives it away as an offering to the Sky Gods. If you wish, a specially designed robe or garment may be worn during the rite, as can a star mask. Instructions for making both are provided later in this chapter. You may also wish to use other sacred tools, chants, music, jewelry, a wand or staff, and/or a headdress.

Let me pause at this point for some comments concerning the wearing of a star mask or headdress. First, if you choose to wear either or both, they should be made by you or for you and worn only during star ceremonies. Second, they are ceremonial objects and are therefore sacred tools, just as much sacred objects as a chalice, wand or staff, drums and rattles, pipes, or feathers employed for ceremonial use, and should be respected and cared for in the same way. As is the case with all ceremonial objects, the sight of and the wearing of the star mask should help a wearer get into the proper frame of mind for doing ceremonial work. Otherwise, it isn't really a tool, and serves little more than a purely decorative purpose. The star mask should be worn by its owner and no one else. It should be smudged or passed through the smoke of a sacred fire each time before being worn for psychic cleansing.

Regarding the use of a star mask specifically: My Spirit Teacher says that the human face we wear is but one identity. Each of us has had many faces. The making and wearing of a star mask during star ceremonies, he says, is a way to present one face, every time, to the Star Nation, one face that sums up and represents the soul's, not the ego's, identity. Of course you are free to design your own star mask. It can be as simple or as colorful and elaborate as you choose.

Though I have seen several star masks my students have made, one impressed me most with its simplicity and subtle silent beauty. The mask was constructed from thick cardboard or matboard cut in a general mask shape (see figure 1) and was slightly curved to conform to the contour of the face when worn. Spaces for the eyes were cut out, but none for the nose or mouth.

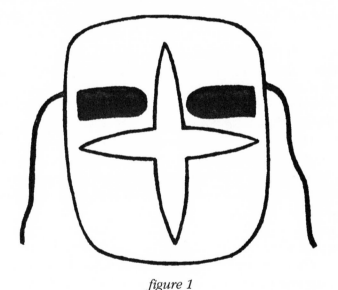

figure 1

The entire front side of the mask was then painted white. Next, a simple four-pointed star was fashioned from styrofoam that was painted gold and glued to the face of the mask. (See figure 2.) Note the elongated bottom spike of the star-figure design. Leather straps were attached to each side so that the mask could be tied onto the head comfortably.

figure 2

The star mask is also an object of art. When not in use, it may be hung on the wall behind your star altar (to be discussed later) or propped up on the altar as an offering/gift to the Star Nation.

A robe or some other type of ceremonial garment should also be designed and made by or for the wearer. My suggestion is that the garment be plain white, perhaps trimmed around the sleeves and/or hem with a gold-colored braid or fabric. Gold or white fabric stars might be sewn onto the fabric, or you might wish to select the material from the celestially designed cloth that is currently popular and widely available. Like the star mask, the star robe is a sacred object and should be worn only during star ceremonies and meditation to help you enter into the proper mindset and to empower the ceremony.

The headdress, too, should be designed by, made by or for the wearer, and worn only for star-oriented ceremonial occasions. A simple headband will do, perhaps one with metal star studs attached to it. Feathers, beads, or other decorations found in craft stores might also be added. Be the creator; let your imagination soar.

After adorning yourself with the star mask and ceremonial garment and headdress (should they be chosen), step inside the star circle. Look up and face the star or constellation you will be working with or face the general area of the night sky where they are located. When it is time for the drawing-down ceremony to begin, remember: *your eyes and breath are your most useful tools.* Begin to inhale, deeply and slowly, filling yourself with star energy. Repeat the inhaling process seven times, each time allowing the starlight and its power to flow into your body and fill your consciousness . . . feel it empowering you. This is the drawing-down process. Then greet the Great Star Nation. A simply worded salutation will do.

As you draw in starlight, you may experience some physical and/or emotional reactions, especially when you first begin to work with star power. These can range from mild lightheadedness, to a moderate electrical current that seems to pass through your body, to slight changes in breathing, minor elevation of the blood pressure and/or heart rate, to elevated body heat. While focusing on a given star, I have experienced visions of the indwelling star spirit, single or multicolored energy patterns, and other visual effects. I have also heard sounds psychically. All stars, planets, and other celestial bodies emit an audio quality sometimes called the "music of the spheres."

Once the inhaling process is complete, observe a moment of quiet stillness to allow ample time for the energy taken in to be absorbed by your mind and the more subtle bodies. The energy drawn from a constellation, such as the Pleiades or Orion, will last longer than that drawn from a single star, unless the star is particularly potent, such as Sirius and Antares. You will, over time, get a feeling for the energy of certain stars and stellar groups, in terms of the amount and the quality of power they possess. Antares' energy, for example, lasts longer than that of Polaris. This is due in part to their being two different types of stars in terms of general makeup, age, and distance from Earth, as well as to the natural power of each. I have found, incidentally, that the invoked stellar energy stays with me and is available for twenty-four to forty-eight hours, depending upon the quality and potency of the star or stars involved.

Once the ceremony is finished, and before leaving the circle, remember to give thanks to the star(s) for sharing power. I have made it a practice to spend time alone after doing star work for the purpose of grounding and centering myself. It is also a good idea to eat moderately for at least one or two days before and after star work, and to refrain from any intake of drugs, alcohol, red meat, caffeine, and refined sugars, since these substances are highly electric and therefore stimulate the body and consciousness. Because star energy is itself extremely stimulating, additional stimulation is neither needed nor advised. Also, keep in mind that when you are working with a variable star, it is best to perform your ceremony when the star is at its most potent cycle when its luminosity is greatest.

The following information is offered to give you a basic understanding of variable stars. Stars are as different in terms of their physical makeup and behavior as human beings. Like us, they also come in various sizes and, of course, differ in age. An example is the so-called *cepheid variables,* named for the astronomer who discovered their unusual behavior. These stars display variations in brightness, therefore, in their luminosity. It is assumed that they are actually expanding and contracting in size in a rhythmic cycle. The time between the peaks is known as the star's *period.* Such a period varies from variable to variable, and can range from one to one hundred days. (Raymo, p.156)

To date, some 700 variables are known. The most familiar of these is Polaris, the North Star. I feel that a variable star is at its full power when it is in its peak period. Which of the fixed stars (the ones with which you will be working more frequently) are cepheid variables may be determined from most texts about fixed stars. (See Bibliography.)

Over the years I have developed a way to draw down star power when there are a number of participants in a group. (I used this method with some four hundred people during a medicine wheel gathering several summers ago.) Once the group has assembled and selected the individual star or constellation that will be worked with, the reason and purpose for doing the work must be determined and agreed upon by all. A human circle is then formed. If it is an exceptionally large group, circles within circles work well.

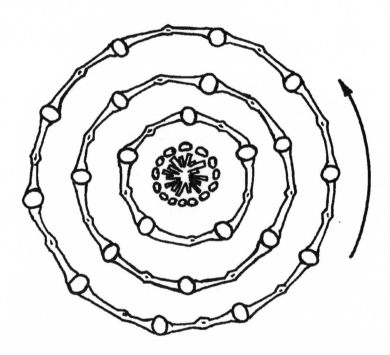

Drawing-Down Ceremony (with many participants)

If conditions are appropriate, a central fire may be helpful for providing light and for ceremonial inspiration. A group offering or individual gifts for the star are also proper.

Once the fire has been lit and the circle or circles formed around it, participants should join hands and begin moving, slowly, clockwise. At the same time everyone should repeat, in unison, an incantation designed to draw down the star's power. Energy-wise, the moving circle focus on one star or constellation makes a gigantic cone of power. The following is a verse I have used often. You may use it or write one of your own.

Star light, Star bright;
Work our magic with your light.

Repeat the chant over and over again, beginning slowly. As it goes on, the motion of the group and the rhythm of the chant should be increased until the motion reaches a brisk clip and the chant becomes louder. Upon a cue from the designated leader, and when the movement and voices have reached a peak, participants should release hands, sink to the ground, and lie still for several moments to allow the star energy to be assimilated into their bodies and consciousness.

Sometimes an individual or group may choose to draw down star power and release it to a person or place to help accomplish some magical end. For example: Polaris' power does well in helping stabilize the collective energy of a group, business, or organization. Antares is useful in helping a person or group meet a particularly difficult challenge. The energy of any of the prosperity stars may be drawn upon for financial well-being, or when some other form of abundance is needed. In all these cases the same star ceremony may be used to draw in stellar energy and, at the peak of the raising of the cone of power when hands are loosed and everyone sinks to the ground, the power may be transmitted. On these occasions, the individual involved should be notified in advance and his or her permission requested as the recipient of the stellar energy and the benefits of the sacred rite.

Another method of drawing down star power is through the use of a Star Shrine. This is something I have used frequently, finding it to be both simple to construct and effective. I define a shrine as an outdoor altar that, in this instance, is constructed and used solely for drawing down celestial power. The shrine, if it is left intact once it is built, will continuously attract stellar energy from the entire Star Nation.

The Star Shrine is built of stones and can be put in any area of your property or some other selected site you feel drawn to and have permission to use. The shrine should be approximately two to three feet in diameter unless of course you wish to use it for large groups. The stones should be arranged in a circle with a four-pointed or five-pointed star, also made from stones, in the center.

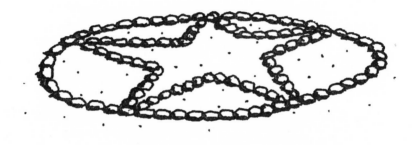

Star Shrine

When completed the shrine should be consecrated and given away as an offering to a specific star or in honor of the entire Star Nation. Making best use of the Star Shrine involves standing inside or just outside the stones and setting your sight upon a given star. Next, begin drawing in the starlight and power with your breath. Each time you inhale, stare at or visualize the star. Then, exhale the breath into a piece of quartz crystal. Repeat this procedure seven times. Place the crystal in the center of the shrine and leave it there. The mineral will continue to draw in star power and store it, serving as a sort of "stellar battery." Holding the crystal later will release the star energy into your body and consciousness. When you sense that all the energy contained within the crystal has been drained or faded, it should be cleansed in salt water before being replaced on your Star Shrine to store more stellar power.

Another method of star attunement is a form of *meditation.* This is a good way to work when viewing conditions are poor or the night sky is otherwise inaccessible to you. It is also the first step that must be taken to begin to cultivate the skill of the ancient Starwalkers. I do not find this method as satisfying personally, since I prefer being out under the stars because of the magic the night sky imparts to me. However, it does work, particularly for those who are especially adept and comfortable with mental imaging. The process works best when done at night, and may be done alone or with a group.

The actual procedure involves sitting in a comfortable position on a chair or on the floor or, if you choose to work outside, on the ground. First, go through a process you are accustomed to using to relax your body and mind. Next, visualize a bright star and "see" yourself traveling toward it. See it getting closer to you, feel its heat, see its sparkling colors. While holding the image, imagine that you are inhaling the star's power, breathing it in slowly and deeply, seven times. It is also helpful to repeat, to yourself or aloud, the name of the star with which you are working, like a mantra.

After completing the procedure once, determine whether you feel the need to repeat it, for better, more powerful results. This may be done as often as you like. The star energy you have drawn in should be effective for twelve hours. When working this way, I find the power tends to last a shorter time than when I have employed other methods.

As we have seen, certain stars, usually the brightest ones, have played important roles in the practical and ceremonial lives of human beings. Grouping stars into constellations helped our ancestral peoples arrange the night sky into "parts," and thus to bring order. In addition to the usual constellations, a notable star arrangement is the four Archangel Stars.[2] These stars were considered highly significant by the Babylonians, and at one time were used to mark the solstices and equinoxes. The number four is the sacred number for many cultures, both ancient and modern, representing the four directions and the four corners of the world. The Archangel Stars were known as the four *Watchtowers* or the *Watchers* in the Kaballah, watching over Earth and its inhabitants.

The *Watcher of the East* is assigned to Michael, whose stellar counterpart is Aldebaran (Morse, p.36), the great ruby-red giant in Taurus. Michael has long been considered a sort of "general" who slays the dragons that imperil human life. The *Watcher of the South* is aligned with archangel Gabriel, and is said to be the great star Formalhaut in Piscis Australis. (Morse, p.175) Respected for its power over change, this star is also a "messenger" who announces important forthcoming events. The *Watcher of the North* is symbolized by archangel Raphael. Its stellar alter ego is Regulus, the Star of Kings in the constellation Leo. (Morse, p.56) No star more than Regulus has been credited with the powers of kingship and rulers. It is surely a fitting companion to the other three Watchers, the last of which is the *Watcher of the West*. This is related to archangel Uriel whose star is the red giant Antares in the tail of the Scorpion. (Morse, p.83) Among its many attributes, Antares is credited with bestowing the virtue of courage. In light of the antiquity of the recognition of the Archangel Stars and their strategic positions in the night sky, I recommend that all star ceremonies begin with an invocation to the Watchers. This recognizes the *Spirit Keepers of the Four Directions* as is done in other ceremonies, and relates the four directions to star wisdom, to the Medicine Wheel and other sacred traditions, and to the timing of the equinoxes and solstices. It also helps to orient you so that you will begin to realize the star spiral that is *precession*. Precession is the passage of time due to the "wobble" of Earth's orbit. The names of the archangels themselves, and/or the actual stars with which they are associated, may be used in your invocation, which may be voiced in your own words, beginning with the east and proceeding to the south and west, ending with Raphael and Regulus in the north.

Another interesting group of stars is the Hyades in the constellation Taurus. Actually a small pseudo-constellation, the Hyades is composed of six stars that the Greeks viewed as the daughters of Atlas and Aethra, whose daughters actually numbered seven. In ancient times these stars were thought of as the messengers who warned of the Great Flood. They have been identified as the bringer of rain to farmers and seafarers. Morse discussed the attributes of two of the Hyades stars: Prima Hyadum and Ain Hyadum. He relates both stars to the qualities and powers of communication. (Morse, p.37) His book is an excellent guide for learning about specific stars and constellations from an esoteric perspective, and a useful handbook for fixed-star astrologers.

The famous astronomer Copernicus once wrote "what is nobler than the heavens, the heavens which contain all noble things."[3] This statement clearly reveals Copernicus' personal view of the heavens. If our own attraction to and love for the night sky grows, the impact it can and will have will run into the deepest depths of our individual and collective consciousness. Even Socrates, who cared little about astronomy, believed that it was good for the soul to study the sky. (Ferris, p.20) By studying the sky, from both a scientific and an esoteric perspective, we will come to know ourselves better.

However, our knowledge of Nature may always be inadequate, and never complete. Why so? One reason may have to do with the immensity of the cosmos. Can we ever hope to know the nature of it all? Another reason is its complexity. Yet, even if we, through technological leaps (and we have taken leaps in the last few decades) gather all the physical data necessary for *intellectual* awareness, will we ever come to a complete *understanding of the implications* of what we have learned? Only time—much time—will tell. It is certain that every answer we receive and every cosmic riddle we solve will bring more questions. The universe is as simple as it is complex, as normal as it is weird, as peaceful as it is violent. Unless we study and ponder the stars and all our celestial relations, we will never know even the most basic of its mechanisms, never know its inhabitants beyond our own planet or system, never hope to gain any real insight into its highways and byways, much less take the first step to walk among the stars.

CHAPTER FOUR

COMETS AND METEORS: MESSENGERS OF THE GODS

(Y)ou must address the stones as grandfathers, for Tirawahat first made gods of the stones and placed them in the heavens.[1]

James Murie

On an ordinary morning, while I sat leisurely over a cup of coffee, tuned into "Good Morning America" in the background, my ears caught an extraordinary comment on the news: "The comets are coming!" It immediately got my attention for two reasons: It was a complete surprise, and the newscaster had said comets—plural.

I was aware of the increasing excitement regarding the appearance of comet Hale-Bopp in the latter part of 1996, a comet that astronomers claimed could be as big and bright as a full moon! Hale-Bopp (named after the two backyard observers who first spotted it in July 1995) was little more than a faint fuzzy patch when it was sighted. However, a few calculations quickly informed astronomers of an anticipated orbit that predicted the comet would be a significantly bright visitor in our skies for eighteen months.

Additional research on Hale-Bopp revealed some of the comet's unusual features. It is big. The dust cloud that surrounds it "stretches over 2.5 million kilometers, so that the comet has a volume larger than the Sun. The nucleus itself, the icy ball slowly giving up its gases, may span several dozens of kilometers."[2] Another incredible feature is that Hale-Bopp is spewing "luminous jets" of comet stuff because its nucleus is cracked due to the Sun's heat, which allows the warm inner gases to escape. If predictions are accurate, Hale-Bopp will provide many hours of viewing pleasure and intrigue, particularly in the spring of 1997, when it makes its closest approach.

Now, though, I had heard that *comets* are coming! Aside from the obvious fact that still another comet had been sighted moving in our direction—a rather unexpected interloper, I might add—we would not have to wait to see a comet streaking across the night. Comet Hyakutake would see to that!

Comets have been getting a lot of press lately. From time to time, we have been primed by the scientific community to expect memorable light shows: comet Kohoutek in 1973 and 1974, the much-anticipated and touted return of Halley's comet in 1986; but these fell far short of the hype that heralded their arrivals. The events that were to "wow" us were little more than faint fizzles, not the firecracker types we were expecting. Comet astronomers had the proverbial egg on their faces. In 1994, however, astronomers were redeemed when comet Shoemaker-Levy 9 crashed into the giant planet, Jupiter, providing photos that testified to the spectacular collisions (the comet was broken into pieces) that occurred over seven days.

Now, a comet is again in the news. With Hale-Bopp, astronomers expect a wonderful show, although they are being exceptionally cautious in order to avoid disappointing the public and embarrassing themselves again. Missing the mark on just how sensational a given comet is likely to be is a touchy subject, especially after the fizzled appearance of Halley's comet in 1986 led to a congressional inquiry. "Why?" you ask. It seems that forecasts of comets the size of full moons with marvelously long tails briskly improve sales of telescopes and other paraphernalia of astronomy in a big way. Congress began to wonder if the comet predictions were a ploy to boost sales.

Why all the fuss? Clearly, the phenomenon of a huge comet generates a tremendous amount of comet-related activity in observatories, planetaria, and amateur astronomy groups nationwide: setting up field trips away from cities to get a better view of the comet;

printing posters that track its course; setting up "home pages" on the Internet; and even, in the case of comet Hyakutake, bringing its discoverer to the United States for a hero's welcome that included honorary Chicago citizenship! Since the Hyakutake appearance was an event that sneaked up on everyone, the swirl of activities surrounding its appearance was almost frantic. This is testimony to the fascination comets have held for humans since the dawn of civilization.

One of the most provocative of all sky apparitions, comets both fascinate and frighten us. Remnants of the formation of the solar system, comets were no strangers to the ancestral peoples worldwide. Their images were painted on cave walls and etched into stone, where they remain as witness to what ancient eyes beheld in the night. Modern times have not diminished our fascination with these mysterious and beautiful trespassers into our field of view. We know a lot about comets today.

A "dirty snowball" made of debris left over from the formation of the solar system, a comet is a big—sometimes colossally big—chunk of dust and ice trailing various gases that weighs tons and can be up to ten miles wide! Its much-acclaimed tail is formed when the solar winds, caused by the Sun's intense radiation, blow off the gases and dust from the nucleus. Although the nucleus orbits the Sun, it is far too distant and faint most of the time to be seen. But when the comet comes close enough to the Day Star to respond to its heat, it begins to put off jets of gas and dust due to the melting of its core. This results in the comet's tail, which sets these bodies apart from all other heavenly objects.

As we might guess, comets have hit Earth. Some astronomers, in fact, strongly suspect that eons ago, comets brought water to form oceans and lakes. A cometary collision with Earth is credited with the disappearance of the dinosaurs some 65 million years ago. As many as four other mass extinctions have happened,[3] and it may be scientifically sound to attribute these to major impacts. Needless to say, these past impacts lead astronomers to believe that such can and will occur again.

Although comet crashes are rare, they result in severe alterations to our planet that, if the impacting body is large enough, produce a dramatic environmental change, including severe meteorological imbalances. Just how vulnerable are we? Recent speculation, regarding not only comets but also asteroids and meteors, suggests that the probability of their colliding with Earth may be higher than previously thought.

Thanks to modern technology, we on Earth got a bird's-eye view of a collision when comet Shoemaker-Levy 9 fell onto Jupiter's surface, creating a spectacular and revealing sight for professionals and laypersons alike. It was the first time that we were able to actually witness this kind of event, which was anticipated sixteen months in advance. Astronomers had ample time to arrange observational time on the largest telescopes. Repairs made to the lens of the orbiting Hubble telescope enabled astronomers to make detailed studies of the collision and the phenomena that accompanied and resulted from it.

The impacts exceeded all expectations. They threw up visible dark clouds that were entirely unexpected; from their color, we "infer that the dark material is composed chiefly of organic compounds." (Spencer/Mitton, p.ix) In addition to the visual rewards of the comet's crash, the event provided a unique "deep-space" laboratory for interpreting the makeup and behavior of comets, particularly their relationship with our planet and the possibility of future collisions.

That the comet's dark material produced by the impact with Jupiter might be primarily composed of *organic* materials is of tremendous interest. Sir Fred Hoyle, astronomer and physicist, and Chandra Wickramasinghe, internationally recognized authority on interstellar matter, in the 1970s proposed a radical theory: that life arrived on Earth from interstellar space. This was a stretch not all that well received in the world's scientific circles. In a new age of our understanding of the universe, particularly the origin of life, Hoyle and Wickramasinghe's theory may turn out not to be so far-fetched after all.

We know that the basic chemicals of life have long existed within interstellar dust clouds and that they have survived long after the initial stages of creation. These biochemicals evolved into primitive lifeforms on comet-sized bodies that most likely existed over the first few hundred million years in our solar system's history.[4] It is believed that, when comets struck our young planet some four billion years ago, Earth received some of these biomaterials, and was thus given the gift of life. In short, living cells from space impregnated Earth, so to speak, and all that exist here are the descendants of those first cells.

In a later book, the two astronomers furthered their theory by suggesting that viruses and germs also came to Earth from space, and these have been responsible for plagues and diseases throughout human history.[5] Although the theory has its detractors, it is now being given careful consideration to determine whether or not it has any validity. Should it be deemed probable, such a revelation will completely readjust our current understanding of the relationship between the stars and lifeforms on Earth.

Technically, comets are members of our solar system. We know they number in the hundreds of thousands, all revolving around the Sun, but out beyond the planet Pluto in a region called the Oort Cloud. Named for its discoverer (the general rule of thumb in astronomy), the Oort Cloud is composed of comet cores of varying types and sizes. The cloud exists as a sort of shell or halo around the solar system.

What we know as comets are pulled from the inner belt area by the gravity of Pluto and Neptune or by collisions between the comets themselves. Such bodies in turn can veer toward the Sun and settle into their own elliptical orbits. The Sun's stronger gravitational pull causes a comet to speed up, slingshotting it around the Sun and toward the outer solar system. Orbits can range from a few years to millions of years. One periodic comet is the famous Halley's that returns to our solar system every 76 years.

It is easy to imagine why these celestial vagabonds captured the minds and eyes and struck fear in the hearts of our ancestors. The unexpected appearance of a truly brilliant "star" certainly would have stirred anxiety. It would have made a clear impression on a primitive mind: This is no star, or no *ordinary* star. Where did it come from? Why is it here? How long will it stay? And, logically, what does it mean to the lives on Earth? What message does it bring? What event does it signify and/or foretell? Since the sky is the abode of the gods, the comet must bring a message from them.

It seems feasible to assume that whatever happened during, or just after, a comet's appearance would have been linked to the comet: What it "caused" was thus the message it brought. One message often associated with a comet's appearance was the impending fall and/or death of a great leader, or even an entire country. In ancient Babylon comets were first associated with the deaths of kings and with governmental instability, a belief that spread to ancient China. While Nero fiddled during the decline of the Roman Empire, a comet was blazing across the sky!

A great story related to what a comet might mean to a king is recounted by Vincent Cronin. It seems an unknown astronomer named Astronomus was summoned by King Louis the Pious around Easter in A.D. 838 to interpret the appearance of a comet that was disturbing the monarch's peace of mind. After studying the portent carefully, Astronomus went to the king, but he could not find the words to convince the monarch that the comet would result in doom, so he said little. Convinced that the astronomer's silence signaled his death, the king became quite concerned. Astronomus tried to reassure his master by saying that the comet's sign of death was only a heathen superstition. Something must have worked because Louis lived on for another two years before dying of natural causes. However, the ruler didn't just trust the fates. He spent the night in fervent prayer, and the next day he gave generous gifts of money to the clergy and the poor![6] Talk about covering all your bases!

The presence of a large comet in the night sky is a sight I eagerly awaited. Although I saw Halley's through a good-sized telescope and another periodical comet in the night over northern Arizona, they were both less than impressive. In 1996 my wait was over. The comets were arriving in *pairs* no less. When a large comet appears it brings a "message" from the Regulators that I would classify as highly spiritual in nature. It is calling our attention to something extremely important, something that concerns the entire planet and all that live upon her skin. I get a sense that comet Hale-Bopp heralds an acceleration of planetary changes, particularly meteorological changes in the form of wind and water activities and events that will occur at least until the year 2000. These will constitute a true global cleansing. I feel that wind and water are the keynotes of the comet's appearance. We shall see. I also think that souls who come into physical incarnation during the time a great comet is visible from Earth are souls with specific "missions" having to do with a change in the course of human evolution.

While we are more knowledgeable today about comets and the heavens in general, we have to wonder if there is something to the age-old belief of comets as harbingers of doom. A case in point is comet Kohoutek in 1974. Although visibly disappointing, Kohoutek did appear at the time of the infamous Watergate scandal that resulted in the resignation of then-President Richard Nixon. And, there is no rule that suggests that human events are the only ones brought about or prophesied by a comet's eerie appearance. Floods, droughts, killer winds, and other natural disasters have been foretold by these celestial messengers, as well as such disastrous human events as war, famine, and plagues. Is it any wonder, therefore, that over time comets have become unwelcome guests.

Because the span of a human life is so short in astronomical terms, we tend to think that, because something hasn't happened in millions, thousands, or even hundreds of years, it won't happen again. We forget and go on living, allowing ourselves to be lulled into a false and dangerous sense of security. This illusion, however, is changing. Lately, there has been increasing concern about the possibility of Earth being hit by an extraterrestrial visitor. In *Rain of Iron and Ice,* author John S. Lewis presents a provocative look at what he terms the very real threat we face should Earth be struck by a sizable comet or asteroid.[7] It is a clear enough danger that scientists are beginning to determine the likelihood of such an event and to seek ways to actually prevent such occurrences. Though the threat we face is not considered an imminent one, it *is* real. Until we find a way to deflect that threat, there is solace in the fact that the potential is recognized and taken seriously.

However, threats and fears aside, can anything be more beautiful or intriguing a sight than a comet racing silently through the night, weaving its way ever so gracefully among the stars? We have now found the answer with comet Hyukatake.

Like the stars (see chapter 3), comets give of their power to humans beyond the natural way they influence life on Earth. Although we may not be visually aware of the presence of comets, they are frequent visitors trekking through the night. Of course, the ones that receive the most attention are those that are visible and predicted to provide the most spectacular show.

I view celestial bodies from the perspective of their energy. Through photographs and visualization, I have come to feel that comets are tremendously powerful, and are thus empowering. Because of their origins and ages I see them as "memory keepers," and the memories they keep are of the formation of our solar system and of all that had occurred in the system, including on Earth. On an individual level, I feel that comet energy is useful in propelling us into the depths of the personal and the collective unconscious of the human psyche. This means that when a comet is around a lot of our "stuff" comes up, individually and collectively, for us to face, process, and cleanse.

When a comet is coming, we usually have enough advance notice to be able to design and prepare a ritual to draw upon its power. You might prepare by fasting for six to twelve hours prior to the ritual, spending time alone and, for a couple of hours before beginning, doing a quiet meditation during which the comet is visualized in order to "feel" its energy, see its light, and hear its sound as it races through space. The comet ceremony may be done to honor the comet's spirit, as well as to draw upon its power.

You may or may not choose to wear your star mask or other ceremonial objects. You might even wish to make a special comet mask for the occasion. Such a mask might be designed with a comet drawn or sculpted on it. Another idea might be to make a streamer of white goose feathers as these are easily procured and legal. The feather streamer could be affixed to a simple headband or some other type of head piece.

Permit me to divert from the comet ritual to share a story with you. Several years ago (1984 or '85) I received a telephone call from Jerry, a friend in Colorado. While on a trip into town he came upon a Native American man thumbing a ride. The man was clutching a large brown paper bag. Jerry picked him up, and during the ride they engaged in small talk. When they got into town the young man asked to be let off at the bus station. As he got out of the truck he said he only had enough money for a bus ticket, but that he wanted my friend to have the contents of the bag as a gift. Before Jerry could refuse, the man put the bag on the truck's seat and walked away.

Arriving home, Jerry opened the bag and discovered what he thought was a beautiful, though obviously old, Native American warbonnet. At first he was pleased to have such a wonderful gift, but before long he began to feel very uncomfortable. He knew it was a traditional artifact of some religious significance and it did not belong in his possession. So he decided to telephone my husband and me, figuring that since we knew a lot of Native people we might know someone we could pass it on to, or otherwise know what should be done with it. I suggested that he send it to us and we would send it on to a medicine man we know. When the package arrived and I saw the object, I was astonished! I knew immediately that it was a *comet bonnet* such as those worn by the Skidi Pawnee people of the Great Plains!

We shipped the treasure to our medicine man friend and that is the last we saw of it. I have often wondered about how and why it came to us, and have wished I had kept it long enough to validate its origin. It was as if the Skidi were speaking to me across time.

When you are ready to do the ceremony, go outside if conditions permit, gaze at the comet and welcome its presence. You may wish at this point to give an offering to the comet's indwelling spirit. Choose anything you like, or I suggest a piece of flint, moldavite, or meteorite; an herb such as sage or sweetgrass; or, if you prefer, a flower such as a stargazer lily or a single white rose. If you cannot actually see the comet, you can still honor it and tune into and communicate with it. Keeping in mind that a comet's energy is beneficial in helping you look back into time—both your time and universal time—you should draw in the comet's power and allow it to take you on a time journey, back into a past life, or back to the beginning of the cosmos. Let yourself flow . . . with time . . . spiraling back . . . ever back . . . to feel and experience within your innermost self . . . let yourself go back to a time when the ancestral Starwalkers made their treks into the heavens . . . see them . . . feel their presence . . . be with them. When your journey is completed and it is time to bring your ceremony to an end, give thanks to the comet spirit and to the Star Nation of which it is a part. So be it.

While not everyone has seen a comet, almost everyone has seen a "shooting star." If the night is clear and moonless, observers can see things that would otherwise remain obscure. Looking up into the sky can give you a kink in the neck in a relatively short time so, on just such a night, lie on the ground to make viewing more comfortable over a longer period of time. Soon the night sky will draw you like a magnet; and it is relentless in its grip!

I remember well my first experience of looking up into the desert sky over Sedona. The atmosphere was crystal clear and unusually dark. The viewing conditions were perfect. As I settled into a relaxed state physically, my mind quickly followed suit. My vision was soon fixed only on the night sky above me, a sky that seemed so close. Thousands of stars lay before my eyes, so many that it was almost impossible to pick out even the most familiar constellations. As I scanned the night sky, I noticed a particularly brilliant light. It was Venus, the Evening Star, its light strong and steady. I also spotted Jupiter. Then I noticed something I couldn't recall ever seeing before. Stars come in different colors—red, yellow, blue and ever-so-slightly green—and the longer I looked, the more vivid their colors became.

Suddenly, my visual tranquillity was interrupted by a radiant object that streaked across my field of vision! It was gone as quickly as it had appeared. I had seen a "shooting star." The light trail that accompanied the streaking object was so bright that it left its imprint on my eyes, the kind of imprint that occurs when a flashbulb goes off, only milder. I felt a tingle race up my spine. Still, I lay there and, after a while, perhaps fifteen to twenty minutes, my thoughts drifted away from the stars only to the quiet of the night. The world, it seemed, had gone away. Then it happened again. Another meteor, this one much smaller and less brilliant, zipped across the corner of my vision. I felt the sky was giving me a gift.

When I decided to end my viewing session, I gave a heartfelt thank you to the Star Nation and let a special feeling of gratitude flow from me to the meteor spirits making their fiery flight at moments when I could see them. I have seen many meteors since that night. All of them were beautiful, and each triggered a now-familiar tingle up my spine. None of them, however, has excited me quite like those I saw that night when I lay upon the ground and looked up, really looked up, into the night.

Like comets, meteors and meteorites have played an important role in the star-centered religions of the ancient peoples. Pieces of interplanetary debris, meteors are large enough to survive their entrance into Earth's atmosphere. Their size ranges from nearly microscopic dust-sized particles to those weighing many tons. On a clear dark night, an average of six meteors per hour can be seen streaking quickly across the sky. Sometimes there are many more.

Meteorites have been called stones from heaven. The fall itself can be quite spectacular: "a fiery mass appears in the sky; shooting down, it sometimes leaves a luminous trail, and its fall is accompanied by what is often described as 'thunder.'"[8] The fire of a meteorite is caused by the object's entering Earth's atmosphere at a tremendous speed, then being slowed down by the air's friction and the heat around the object's body. As the heat is released, the meteor's body ignites, resulting in its fiery appearance. The shock waves produced by the body's rushing through the air often sound like thunder. (Bauval/Gilbert, p.201)

Meteorites are classified into three types: *stone, iron*, and the composite *stony iron*. Iron meteorites are heavier and stay intact when they hit the ground. All the largest known meteorites are iron due to the fact that they are the sturdiest. They are, in fact, virtually indestructible because of their high nickel content.[9] Stony meteorites, on the other hand, are more porous and more plentiful; most of those recovered have been of this type. Stony meteorites do not come through their encounter with and journey through Earth's atmosphere as well as their iron relatives. As a rule, they are hard to distinguish from ordinary rocks. Composites, as the name suggests, are stone and iron compounds.

The largest meteorite ever found (of iron) was located in southwest Africa. It weighs almost 60 tons and still lies where it fell. (*Meteor Crater*, p.35) When huge meteorites hit Earth, they leave their marks in the form of impact craters. One such gigantic hole lies in the northern Arizona plateau some 45 miles east of Flagstaff. The crater's rim rises 150 feet from the flat desert floor that stretches as far as the eye can see in all directions. The crater's 570-foot depth is startling, particularly the first time one sees it. Its 4100-foot circumference is almost perfectly circular, and the footpath around the rim measures three miles! What is even more astounding is that the colossal hole was made in mere seconds by the collision between Earth and a large body from space. Now called "Meteor Crater," it is the first to be positively identified, thanks to the large number of individual meteorites found at the site over the years. (*Meteor Crater*, p.6)

There is no doubt that the Ancients saw meteors and fireballs and that they valued meteorites. They knew they had come from the sky. Bauval and Gilbert offer evidence of the existence in times past of so-called meteoritic cults, whose religions were based upon sacred stones from heaven. (Bauval/Gilbert, p.201)

The ancient Greeks, for example, possessed a stone that they believed was cast down from the sky by Kronos, the god of time. They named the stone Zeus-Baetylos. The stone had the appearance of an oval-shaped cannonball. (Bauval/Gilbert, p.201) Another was called Zeus-Kappotas. Still others, said by Pliny the Elder to have existed in A.D. 23 to 79, were worshipped at Potidae, Argos-Potamus, and Abydos. Meteoritic cults were known in Phoenicia and Syria, and many of the sky relics were described as "black, conical stones." (Bauval/Gilbert, p.202) Often, these stones symbolized deities, as in the case of the goddess, Cybele in ancient Turkey, and the god Amun in Egypt.

It is easy to see why many cultures considered the heavenly stones sacred: They fell from the sky, the abode of the gods. Meteorites had power. In many cultures, they were carved into ceremonial objects and even weapons. In China, right up to the twentieth century, meteorites were ground into a powder and eaten,[10] presumably for medicinal and/or religious purposes. It was a fairly common practice among early American Indians to bury meteorites with their dead or to carry small pieces in a medicine bundle, which was worn and used for both ceremonial and empowerment purposes.

As far back as the Pyramid Age, meteoritic iron was known to the ancient Egyptians. It is repeatedly mentioned in the Pyramid Texts, where it is referred to as "the 'bones' of the star kings." (Bauval/Gilbert, p.203) Egyptian religion taught that the pharaohs became stars when they died. (see chapter 7.) Bauval and Gilbert report that "such cosmic iron objects were the only material evidence of a tangible land in the sky populated by star souls, and it was easy to see why the stars were thought to be made from *bja* (iron). Since the souls of departed kings were the stars, they too had bones made of iron." (Bauval/Gilbert, p.203)

Ancient Egyptians and other Middle Eastern cultures were not the only peoples who revered meteorites. American Indian star cults of the Great Plains included the now-extinct Skidi Pawnee and the

Lakota Sioux. Of these two, the Skidi must be counted among the world's meteoritic cults. They knew that objects sometimes fell from the sky. These sky stones were considered sacred, collected, and kept in individual bundles that were, in turn, used for healing, personal empowerment, and protection. Finding a meteorite was therefore an event of some significance both individually and collectively. The Skidi's view of meteorites was unique, as is clearly attested to by their belief that stones heated and used in the sacred sweat lodge possessed the same power as meteorites and held the power of the gods of heaven. (Chamberlain, p.142) Also, to the Skidi, a meteor shower was believed to signal the end of the world!

The Skidi's view of meteors was equally interesting. These they thought were "visiting stars" bringing messages from friends who lived in the direction from which the meteor came. (Chamberlain, p.142) As for the power inherent in meteorites, the Skidi have given us a valuable clue. "When the Skidi found it [the meteorite] and gave native tobacco to it, they were successful in their raids among the enemy." (Chamberlain, p.146) Meteorites were "children" of the Creator, *Tirawahat*, and were carried in sacred medicine bags that were opened only when one had a dream about them. (Chamberlain, p.146)

A Skidi story recounts a dream experienced by a man named Osage Sky-Seeing. There was a warrior who, while out on the prairie, fell asleep and dreamed about a flying star. He awakened at just the moment to see the star fall close by. He went to search for it, found it, wrapped it up, tied it to his belt, and continued on his journey. Later, while sitting atop a hill, the warrior fell asleep again. This time he dreamed of a young long-haired male who had a star painted on the dark skin of his forehead. The youth spoke to the dreamer and identified himself as the meteorite the warrior had found. He said it had come from a star in the southeast, and that the warrior should take it with him everywhere he went for it would serve him well. He was also to smoke to it, and when the meteor shone brightly the warrior would know that the "star man" was with him. The warrior followed the instructions and took his precious stone to an elder. Together they made a sacred bundle for it. The stone fulfilled its promise and assisted the warrior in many successful hunts. (Chamberlain, pp.146-148)

Another story attests to the Skidi belief that meteorites possessed

special healing powers. This one concerns a great being called
Pahokatawa who made himself known to the people by falling
from the sky as a meteorite, then promising that he would stay with
them. Pahokatawa was a prophet who told the people not to fear
when the stars flew around the sky for it would not signal the end
of the world. He predicted that one of the meteorites that fell would
be very big and would have many colors and be in the shape of a
turtle. Years later a party of buffalo hunters came across a curious
spot where no grass was growing. In the center a strange multicolored rock was sticking out of the ground. It was the meteorite that
had been predicted. It was so big and heavy that they had to get
ponies to help pull it out of the ground and drag it back to the village. Priests offered sacred smoke to the stone first and then all the
villagers gathered around it and made smoke and prayers to it. The
stone was said to have given the people many blessings. It protected the warriors in battle, brought successful hunts, and warded off
disease. The Indians say that when they moved to Oklahoma they
placed the sacred stone atop a high hill from where it disappeared.
(Chamberlain, pp.144-149)

I suppose this story is my favorite because of the turtle-shaped
meteorite, which has tremendous significance to me personally after
an incident that occurred some years ago. At the time I was deeply
involved with my study of archaeoastronomy and had only recently learned about the Skidi. I was also enrolled in an astronomy class
at Northern Arizona University. One day the professor gave the class
an assignment that entailed making a visit to Meteor Crater. After
viewing the crater, and being the gift shop junkie that I am, I spent
time browsing among the astronomy and NASA-related books and
souvenirs, posters, and gifts. The shop also contained an extensive
mineral section.

I had been looking for a piece of meteorite to use for the star
bundle I wanted to make for myself. I asked the Visitor Center
ranger about any meteorites that might be for sale. There were only
some small pieces, which he brought out to show me. I told him
that what I really wanted was one about the size of my fist, having
no idea at the time just how expensive meteorites can be. His eyes
lit up and he began telling me about a piece he had at home that
he had found a couple of years before. "You would really like it,"

he said. "It's about fist size and shaped just like a turtle!" I was floored! Yes, it was for sale: $500.00! That brought me back to earth quickly enough; but what a curious thing to have happen. The ranger didn't know me or of my interest, especially in the Skidi. I told him about the legend of the Pawnee meteorite, which he found most interesting. At the very least I considered the incident a powerful synchronicity, the kind that lets you know that you are in the right place at the right time, whether you know why or not.

I have had more than one mystifying experience regarding meteorites and the Skidi legends about meteorites. One legend said that if you put a meteorite on a high hill, it will fly back into the heavens. Another told of personally owned meteorites the Skidi kept in sacred bundles. It seems that when a bundle's owner died, it was opened and placed on a hill so the meteorites could return to heaven. When I first learned about the meteorite bundles and how they were put together, I decided to make one for myself to use during star ceremonies. I got a piece of buffalo hide, some sage, a small chunk of meteorite that was a piece of the one that fell on the Arizona desert eons ago, and two large tektites I had been given as a birthday gift a few months previously. (Tektites are mysterious glassy objects found in various places on Earth. Their origin is unknown but most astronomers relate them to meteorites.) I put my bundle together and began using it. A few weeks later, after opening my meteorite bundle during a sweat, I left the lodge, leaving the bundle and its contents behind. Realizing my oversight an hour or so later, I asked a friend to go to the sweat lodge and retrieve it for me. All he found was the hide and sage right where I had left it. The tektites and the piece of meteorite were gone! Nowhere could they be found, not until this day. I have often wondered if they flew back to heaven!

Comets, meteors, meteorites, and meteor showers are certainly among Nature's most celebrated phenomena and objects. They have fascinated, frightened, puzzled, inspired, predicted future events, and served as sacred objects in ceremonies in cultures and times long past. This doesn't mean, however, that these, our celestial relations, must lose their power and intrigue for us today. We can make our own sacred bundles and place a piece of meteorite inside. We can do ceremony in honor of the appearance of a great comet. We can peer into the darkness of space in hopes of catching a glimpse and cherishing the experience of a fiery meteor shooting across the sky. We can read how some of the ancestral peoples regarded these objects, including the magnificent event of a meteor shower, many of which have been recorded for thousands of years. Since the earliest times, humans believed that meteors and meteorites were the business of the gods, sometimes the storm gods hurling bolts of thunder and lightning, other times the thunder gods giving voice to their will for the children of Earth.

Among the meteor showers, the Leonids that appear in mid-November have been widely acclaimed for both the sheer numbers of meteors usually seen, and for the incredible "storms" that sometimes occur. "The next Leonid peak is due on November 17, 1999. The tendency of the Leonids to (approximately) commemorate centennial and millennial years will undoubtedly be much discussed as the end of the current millennium approaches." (Lewis, p.41)

While I am not suggesting that the Leonids or any other meteor shower will signal Earth's demise, I could easily agree that they and other celestial occurrences, such as the appearance of an unusual number of comets and large meteors, may herald a most, if not *the* most, significant time in human history.

The Bible tells us that there will always be signs in the heavens. Learning to read those signs is an integral part of the ancient skill of Starwalking. It would behoove us, as we go through these times of planetary change, to be in step with Nature, to be aware of the signs, which I firmly believe are appearing in the heavens as they have since the beginning of time. It was the heavens that predicted the birth of a savior whom the Wise Men sought, the heavens that guided the ancient Hopi to their home on the desert mesas almost 2000 years ago, where they still remain today.

It seems perhaps ignorant and superstitious for me or anyone else to suggest that we, the masses, should put stock in what the heavens tell us. "Look for signs?" you ask. "Today, we are far too sophisticated for that. We're educated. How can we be expected to act like primitives again, we who live on the cusp of the twenty-first century at the epitome of the Age of Reason? We who know how the sky works better than any others in human history?"

Do we now? Is it that we know the *workings* of the sky, the mechanics of the cosmos and the various celestial bodies from stars to comets, but not the sky itself? That is like knowing, as a physician knows, the anatomy of the human body and how the body works, yet knowing nothing about the rest of the human being, the personality, the feelings, the heart.

Mother Nature can and will speak to us if we will only listen. She will show us signs if we will but open our eyes to see. We have shut off our intuition in so many ways and stifled our imagination. In doing so, we have closed our eyes and turned deaf ears to the heavens. Maybe it is time for us, individually and collectively, to wipe the sleep from our eyes and take the cotton out of our ears, time to look skyward to see what the Sky Gods, the Thunderers, and the Star Spirits are showing us, and to listen to what they have to say. What, pray tell, do we have to lose? Maybe, just maybe, we have something to gain, an *intimate connection* with a place that is part of us, that gave us life: Parent Space, the Home of the Creator, the source of the power that moves us. Can we afford not to ponder the sky? Can we ever fail to let it take us beyond Earth, beyond ourselves, into the worlds up there that can only be understood by the world inside the human heart?

As I write these words, I hear the voice of a news commentator speaking about the imminent appearance of comet Hyakutake— "the one that really surprised astronomers; the one that crept up on us so unexpectedly." Now how could that have happened to us? We who know so much, who are so technologically sophisticated? Well it did. The sky surprised us. It let us know, once again, that there are still mysteries to be solved, things to be learned. Hyakutake, moving through space at 90,000 m.p.h., has not been seen in our neighborhood for more than 10,000 years. Yet, here it is again, unexpected, unannounced.

Let's consider, then, the *time* it was last here. Ten thousand-plus years ago would have been the time, we are told, when Earth was in the throes of a major cycle of change, a time of the destruction of Atlantis, when earthquakes and volcanoes shook the very foundation of the planet. When the migrations began and the survivors of the cataclysms spread over the globe, carrying with them their cultures, religions, and knowledge of the sky, Earth, and Nature. The rise and fall of civilizations is a fact. There is more than ample archaeological proof. This time around, Hyakutake again visits the neighborhood of a world in the throes of geological, meteorological, social, religious, and political change, of cyclic rises and falls.

All of the prophecies and prophets, ancient and modern, tell us of this time—the Hopi call it the Great Day of Purification—when again Earth will tremble. In virtually all of the prophecies, we are told that in the heavens there will be *signs*. Let the comets speak to us; let the fireballs trigger the inner voice.

Of course, it might be an exercise in futility, accomplishing little more than being considered a bit on the weird side! But that is only *one* possible outcome, is it not? We might also employ some of the skywatching techniques of our ancestors, open ourselves to the language of the sky, consider the spiritual or esoteric nature of what we see and what occurs. We might awaken and reinstate our individual and collective imagination and intuition to combine with the value and use of the intellect. We might also reinstate something modern society seems to have lost, something that may be the greatest loss of all in light of the state of global human affairs today. We might regain our *conscience*.

CHAPTER FIVE

THE ANCIENT ART
OF STARWALKING

*Nowhere else in nature—not in the comings and goings of
the birds, the blossoming of trees, nor the arrival of the rains
—do we find a more reliable environmental reality in which
to frame the drama of life than the celestial backdrop.*[1]

Anthony Aveni

I magine what it must have been like to live in an earth lodge built
as a model of the sky, or in a tipi that was a hologram of a star.
Imagine knowing you were watched over by a protective star
that would help guide you through life's course as you grew?
Imagine if you had been taught to go out into the quiet of each
morning to give an offering to the Sun, to thank the Sun for the light
of a new day, for another opportunity to live and for the breath of
life itself. Imagine being lifted up to the stars at the time of your
birth into this world, and proclaimed by the strong, bold voice of
your father to be a child of the universe. Imagine your mother and
all the other women in your family gathered around you when you
were a small child and dedicating you to Grandmother Moon. How
would you be different?

What if scientists and intuitives worked together in seeking to
understand our world and the worlds beyond our own? What if we
accepted the reality of dimensions beyond what our intellect tells us
exist? What if we, as a society, realized that spaceships are not the
only way to travel into space? How would we be different?

Ancient peoples knew, intuitively, many of the things we know intellectually now. To them the heavens were no less inspiring. If we want to reconnect with the heavens and make ourselves complete, there are steps we can take that will draw us closer to that goal. Today, in our modern world we have tools that we have developed, and in some cases perfected, that will take us into the sky. Modern astronomers have telescopes that enable them to see to the edge of the universe, spectrographs that reveal what stars are made of and how old they are. We have spacecraft that can take us aloft, and communication satellites that have made our world shrink. We can breakfast in London and lunch in New York.

Our ancestors had "tools" too. Granted, they were different from ours. They were drums and rattles, chants, sacred geometry, gods and goddesses, and sacred rites. The Ancients kept life simple. Their view of the universe was simple. Yet they were able to know much of what we are only now "discovering" about the cosmos! Mayan and Egyptian architects combined intellect with intuition and built monuments that today we can reproduce only with heavy machines. We can't even figure out how they accomplished such feats. These are of course a far cry from spacecraft and computers. But do our tools serve us any better?

The sacred rites designed to honor and appease the Sky Gods were the unifying tool, the act that united the people with the worlds above. But, we don't do ceremony anymore. Current interest in shamanism and the spiritual traditions of the ancestral peoples seems to suggest that we are hungry to fill this lack in our lives. Many of us seem to feel the need to reinstate ceremony, to reconnect with Mother Earth and Father Sky. Ceremony is a tool by and through which we can take a step in precisely that direction.

Ceremony, ritual, and rite may be aptly defined as procedures followed regularly whose purpose is to unite the practitioner with the sacred. The "sacred" on the other hand is that which is associated with God or a god or goddess, that which the intellect cannot apprehend or comprehend, which logic cannot interpret, and which reason alone cannot discern. Ceremony is enhanced by sacred tools. Ordinary objects can be transformed into sacred objects by certain magical processes employed by trained shamans. But, by following instructions carefully, we can all accomplish the same thing.

Sacred objects are often personalized by their owners with sacred symbols, words, and designs that depict a special feature in the user's local landscape or that represent the holy. These give the objects meaning, which is in turn empowering to those who use them. Such symbols and designs might include a sacred mountain, a totem animal, or a special mandala. Holy objects may also be engraved with symbols of the Sun, Moon, planets, and/or stars. Rattles and drums are often decorated with star designs or other celestial objects compatible with and complementary to the rites in which they will be used. The ceremonial garments, jewelry, head-dresses, and masks discussed in chapter 3 serve the same purpose.

At this point I would like to offer some instructions for creating two special kinds of ceremonial tools: the Star Shield and the Star Bundle (incorporating a piece of meteorite). The shield is based upon the familiar traditional one most often associated with the Native peoples of North America. Though a shield is usually thought of as a tool of defense from bodily harm, it does have another purpose and use that involves the sacred. Such purpose and use transform a shield into a ceremonial object. As a sacred object, a shield is in no way used for or associated with battle. Shields are in fact fairly common medicine objects and can be used for three basic purposes: *stimulator, focal point,* and *magnet.*

First, *all* ceremonial objects stimulate the imagination. The imagination is the mind's tool for getting beyond the confines of the intellect and into the realm of freedom required for an intuitive, spiritual experience to occur. How often our intellect gets in our way and blocks us from taking mental flight! Secondly, the Star Shield is a mandala that draws us into it, that serves as a focal point for concentration and meditation. Thirdly, it can be used as a magnet to attract star energy.

The Star Shield is a representative of the Star Nation. It can be a useful tool in ceremonies we do to reconnect ourselves with our stellar relations. As with all sacred objects, the shield should be kept in its own special place, perhaps on the wall or as part of a personal altar, when not in use.

MAKING A STAR SHIELD

Before you make a Star Shield, materials must be gathered. First you will need a metal hoop (the type used for macramé or embroidery projects, or it can be made from a willow branch if you prefer. It can be any size you choose. If you make a natural one you must soak the wood overnight. Then, strip the bark and use the bark strips to fasten the branch into a circle. Next, you will also need a piece of hide or chamois leather large enough to cover the space inside the hoop. You will then decide how you wish to put the star or other celestial symbol(s) of your choice onto the hide. If you choose to use paint, acrylics are best; ink will also work. If you prefer to burn the symbols into the hide, an inexpensive wood-burning tool is available at most craft stores. You will also need a hole punch used for leather. Any other decorative materials such as beads or feathers are optional and left to individual taste.

Once the materials have been collected, select a time to create your shield. I feel that this is best done at night, preferably on a new or full moon. You may work alone or with a group. I also think it

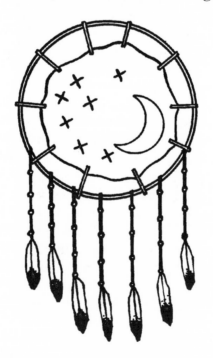

Star Shield

is very important to be in a positive, relaxed frame of mind when you are going to do ceremony; and making the shield is a ceremony. If you are ill or in a negative space it is best to wait. When you are ready to proceed, smudge all of your shield materials, including the tools you will be using to make it, by passing them through the smoke of sage, sweetgrass, or natural tobacco. Then smudge yourself. Smudging is a traditional cleansing ceremony employed by Native Americans. Next, cut part of your piece of leather (or whatever you are going to use) into a dozen narrow strips to tie the edges of the leather piece onto the hoop. Make streamers of the remaining strips to hang from its bottom edge. Your leather need not be perfectly round. Any shape can be used for a nice effect. (See illustration.) Next, punch twelve small holes 1/2" to 1" from the edge of your leather piece, spacing the holes about 2" to 3" apart. Lay your hoop on a flat surface so you can work with it easily. Loop your strips, one through each hole, and tie them to the hoop. Next, tie leather streamers across the bottom of your shield by making a simple loop knot. You may wish to add feathers and beads to several or all of the leather streamers. Pony beads usually fit the streamers nicely, and these are easy to come by at craft and discount stores.

When completed, the Star Shield should be "given away" as an offering to the Great Star Nation. Do this out-of-doors. First, offer the shield to the Spirits of the Four Directions, beginning in the east and moving clockwise to the south, west, and north. Next, hold your shield up to the heavens and make a prayer that tells the Star Nation why you have made it. Offer the shield to the heavens as a gift. It is not yours anymore. It belongs to the Sky Gods. You may wish to honor these deities in your prayer. Ask for their assistance and guidance in your work with the stars. Ask them to help you to connect yourself with the stars and the universe. From then on the Star Shield can be used on your indoor altar or at an outdoor shrine when you are performing a ceremony. It may also be placed on a pole or laid in the center of your ritual circle. As with any sacred object, it will increase in power each time it is used.

MAKING A STAR BUNDLE

Sacred bundles were common to the Skidi Pawnee people of the Great Plains. The Skidi may have had a special secret ceremony

that accompanied the making of a bundle. I feel that satisfactory results can be achieved on our own as long as we have respect for the people from whom the bundles originated, and if we are motivated to use and care for our bundles properly. Traditionally, any type of medicine bundle or bag is worn about the neck or carried on another part of your person, unless it contains objects that are too large. The instructions offered here have a Native American flair of course, but if you feel more in tune with the Celts, Egyptians, or some other culture and time you can easily adapt your bundle to meet that criteria.

To make a Star Bundle you will first need a piece of animal hide. The Pawnee used buffalo, but deer, elk, or cowhide will work fine. Buffalo hide can be obtained if you check with trading posts that do mail orders and/or a local taxidermist or tannery. I advise you to be careful that the hide you use has not been taken from an animal that was killed for sport or in some other improper manner. The hide can be about 7" to 9" square, or make the bundle any size you wish. You will also need some fresh sage, a small piece of meteorite, and some leather strips or red yarn to tie the materials into a bundle. Everything should be smudged, including you. (Again, I suggest that the ritual of actually putting the bundle together be done at night, inside or out, on a new or full Moon. Lunar energy is most conducive to enhancing constructive ceremonial work.)

Lay the hide, hair side down, on a flat surface. Place a "bed" of sage in the center of the hide. Take the meteorite in your hands and visualize it as a brilliant meteor traveling through space. Think about how old it is. Remember that it has been in existence since the birth of the solar system. See it coming, as a ball of white, red, and orange light, into Earth's atmosphere . . . streaking across the night sky. Fly with it . . . feel its heat . . . and its power. Then place the meteorite on the bed of sage. (Incidentally, you may choose to use a piece of moldavite or a tektite in your bundle instead of a meteorite. Moldavite is green meteorite, but the origin of tektites is unknown though they are thought to be pieces of Mars or some other systemic body. Both are similar in energy to meteorites.) Wrap the hide around the contents as you would wrap any package, or make it pouch-like by tying the corners and edges at the top. (See illustration.) When the bundle is finished it, like the Star Shield, should be "given away" by following the same procedure described earlier.

Should you prefer to put together a Star Bundle that has an Egyptian energy, the same general procedure may be followed with a few minor exceptions. For example, instead of using buffalo hide you may wish to use a sheet of papyrus or heavy parchment. Paint one side of the paper with whatever celestial symbols or figures you choose. Let it dry thoroughly. Place the paper on a flat surface, and add a bed of sage or some other herb in the center. You may wish to use a high-grade incense or a perfumed oil instead of an herb. If you have a small rock or object from Egypt or something that represents it to you, that may also be included. Along with these, add the meteorite. The papyrus can be wrapped into a neat bundle, and tied with a simple strand of colored yarn, twine, or some other material such as gold braid or ribbon. You might wish to decorate your bundle with a piece of jewelry that has an Egyptian design, a single earring or pin perhaps. For a Celtic bundle you could choose a piece of deer hide, as the deer (stag) was a prominent totem to those ancient people. The hide can be painted with stellar and/or celestial objects. Since the apple was sacred to Celtic Druids, you might lay your piece of meteorite on a few slices of dried apple or even a few leaves or some bark from an apple tree. The hide and its contents can then be tied into a bundle, and used for ceremonial purposes and/or worn on your person, or be kept on your altar to honor the Star Nation.

The Star Bundle is a power object, a star amulet if you will. Having it on your person keeps you in touch with the Star Nation. I am sure you will intuit the appropriate uses for your Star Bundle in addition to what I have suggested. If you wish, the bundle may be opened during special star ceremonies.

STAR RITUAL

To the best of my knowledge there are few star-related rituals being performed today. In our country those that are occur among the American Indians. Most are secret tribal affairs that are not open to the public. Non-Natives who live in the Southwest or perhaps in some areas of the Great Plains, and those who are personally acquainted with Indian people, stand a better chance of being invited to attend such ceremonies. The best way to find out about these rites is to visit a reservation and make inquiries. If you are fortunate enough to be acquainted with Native Elders or medicine people or know someone who is, it will be easier to find out about rituals. Never show up at any ceremony if you have not gotten express permission from the tribal Elders or the medicine persons in charge to attend.

If you cannot gain entrance into a traditional ceremony you can do your own. Within each of us there are deep-seated archetypes and ancient memories . . . Sun, Moon, thunder, clouds, lightning, Morning Star, Evening Star, God, power that will motivate and guide us along our way. By reconnecting with the Star Nation we reconnect to our environment . . . all of it . . . to Earth and to the sky. This helps us take the first steps toward understanding and reclaiming our rightful place in the universe. *We can experience the sky. We can respond to what our senses and reason, together, tell us.*

Chet Raymo says we can make "a personal pilgrimage into the darkness and the silence of the night sky in quest of human meaning. It is a quest rewarded with fleeting revelations, intimations of grace, and brief encounters with something greater than ourselves, a force, a beauty, and a grandeur that draw us into rapturous contemplation of the most distant celestial objects."[2] Occasionally, if we are lucky, the quest is rewarded with a special transcendent moment when the grandeur that abides in the night flares out "like shining from shook foil." (Raymo, p.x)

THE MOST IMPORTANT TOOL: THE MIND

When the ancient Starwalker left on a journey into the sky he or she had help. We have explored several of those sources of help: ceremony, sacred objects, sacred herbs, and the Sun and Moon shrines (see chapter 1). However, for the ancestral Starwalker, there was ultimately but one true "tool"—*his or her mind*. The mind knows no boundaries of time or distance. With the mind as a vehicle, Starwalkers went to the stars and brought their power back to Earth. They did not call upon the intellect alone to help with this task, for the intellect is bound to Earth by the same chains that bind the physical body. The intellect would surely have told them, as it will tell you, that they could not accomplish what they set out to experience and achieve. So, they opened themselves to intuition and its gift of freedom and imagination, and used these to explore and experience, firsthand, worlds beyond their own.

Opening and developing the intuition takes practice. It also takes patience. We must learn how to be open and visualize to become able to "see" into and beyond the physical world. Creative visualization is a way we can begin to loosen our mental muscles. This must occur before we can go where the mind can and will take us.

Sometime ago I intuited the following guided journey that is designed to help us imagine and experience what the intellect and the physical body cannot permit. I have used this journey in workshops and in small, intimate groups and found it well-received and successful. For best results I suggest that the visualization be put on cassette tape so that it can be played back to help carry you on your Sky Journey. This exercise can be a valuable tool to get you out of your body and into the heavens. When making your tape, speak slowly and leave some gaps to allow yourself or your group ample time to visualize the images and enjoy the fullest experience possible. When you are ready, sit or lie down in a comfortable place and position.

* * *

Imagine yourself standing in a meadow at the base of a great mountain . . . the mountain is very high, with steep grassy slopes . . . its summit is covered with snow . . . and glaciers . . . the glacial ice as pale blue as the day sky. It is an earthly mountain . . . a sacred mountain. The trees on the slopes are glistening with morning dew . . . it is dawn . . . you can feel the coolness of the newborn day . . . you can smell the grass . . . you can hear the morning sounds . . . the softly cooing dove . . . the gentle waters of a nearby stream. As you stand in full view of the majestic mountain, you know that within it there dwells a spirit . . . the soul of the mountain . . . an ancient spirit whose task it is to send out the living force of the mountain to the people . . . to the animals . . . to the plants . . . to you. The mountain sustains the people . . . it gives them strength in times of need . . . it gives security in times of fear. You smell the fragrances around you . . . the morning dew . . . the little ferns and mosses at your feet . . . the grass . . . the moist trees . . . the air . . . the soft aroma of the snow. You have come to the mountain to begin an important journey . . . one for which you have been preparing for a long time. In your dreams you were told of your journey . . . you were told to come here . . . to the mountain. Now you are here . . . and you know you will be met . . . and for the first time you will be borne on the wings of a Great Spirit Bird . . . a bird that will come from within the sacred mountain . . . one who will come forth to meet you when the time is right. You have made your prayers . . . you have done your fasting . . . the time is now. To your right . . . in the quiet of the morning . . . you hear a rustling . . . it rudely invades the still, quiet sanctity of the dawn. As you look in the direction of the sound . . . you see that it has come from the flapping of great wings . . . the wings of the Spirit Bird . . . a magnificent Winged Being. His feathers look like sheer gold. As the Sun comes up over the mountain . . . its rays shine on those feathers . . . spun gold feathers that glisten in the morning's virgin light. The eyes of the big bird are as golden as his wings . . . from his beak he lets out a call . . . a shrill call that pierces the silence. He becomes airborne now . . . he lights at your feet. He is so big . . . when he stands before you he can look into your eyes . . . one look . . . and you know he is ready for your flight . . . to take you into the sky. Slowly . . . with ease . . . you climb onto the back of the Great Bird . . . you wrap your arms around his strong neck so you will feel secure. At once the Spirit Bird springs into the air . . . and together you soar . . . higher . . . higher . . . and higher. On the back of the big bird . . . you can feel his feathers . . . and the strong muscles in his giant body . . . higher, you fly . . . leaving Earth. Looking down . . . you can see the mountain below you . . . the sacred mountain . . . getting smaller and smaller . . . the features of Earth are slowly fading away . . . it is as if the planet is enveloped in the stillness . . . and in the quiet . . . of the dark time . . . the dream time. You are free. You trust yourself now to look away from Earth . . . to look heavenward . . . trusting the big bird . . . the bird that is helping you cross the bridge . . . the bridge that links Earth with the vastness of interstellar space . . . the Milky Way . . . the Spirit Path that leads into the Great Star Nation. As you travel through the night sky . . . you look to your left . . . and then to your right . . . there are stars . . . everywhere there are stars . . . above you . . . below you . . . thousands of sky lights . . . some bright . . . brilliant . . . sending forth their golden rays . . . white rays . . . some are red . . . like glowing embers . . . these are the Ancient Ones . . . the red giants . . . the wise stellar elders . . . some are yellow . . . some are green . . . all are warm . . . and bright. Now you see that you are coming to the end of the Sky Bridge . . . the Spirit Bird slowly begins to alight . . . to come down ever so gently. He lands now . . . his great body slowly comes to rest . . . you slide off his back. Ahead you see the gates . . . the star gates . . . they begin to open . . . and as they open you see the Star Being . . . Melha . . . the Keeper of the Sky Fires . . . the Igniter of the Flames of the Heavens. As you look upon the Star Being . . . you know he comes in peace . . . in love . . . emitting the power of the Star Nation. It is a privilege that the star gates have opened before you . . . it is as if you were expected . . . Melha is your host . . . he gives you entry. As you go through the star gates . . . you look at the Star Being carefully . . . from his head down to his feet . . . you see his face . . . his features . . . you notice his hands . . . his garment . . . you look into his eyes . . . you see his hair . . . his expressions. What do they tell you about him? As you stand before him you make eye contact with him . . . you speak your name softly . . . "I am _____." He replies: "I am Melha, the Star Gate Keeper." You tell him that you have come to visit a star . . . to see it up close . . . to feel its heat. You look into his eyes . . . what does his expression tell you about your request? You hear him ask what star you would like to visit . . . you answer . . . Polaris (or any star you choose). As you are standing with Melha, you lift your eyes toward him . . . from the tips of his fingers you notice that there flows a cobweb-like substance . . . it shines ever so brightly . . . as if from a light within every fiber . . . the substance comes toward you . . . the web wraps you in a safe, protective cocoon . . . you can see out of it clearly . . . not a star is dimmed . . . it protects you . . . tiny, shiny fibers made from his wisdom and his love. Now, accompanied by the Star Being . . . you glide through the heavens

with ease . . . without fear . . . filled with wonder and expectation
. . . you see through the stars . . . some big . . . some small . . . some
bright . . . others dim. One star looms closer . . . brighter . . . you
have come to Polaris . . . closer . . . closer you come . . . you feel
its gentle warmth . . . it penetrates your body . . . warming you from
within, without . . . the cocoon protects you so that the star's great
heat cannot burn or harm you . . . you are safe . . . you can and
will survive. As you come closer to the star it loses its whiteness
. . . it becomes a massive sphere of orange light . . . penetrating light
. . . hot light. For a moment you imagine the intensity of its heat. All
of a sudden . . . you begin to roll in your cocoon . . . head over
heels . . . rolling . . . tumbling in space . . . you hear what sounds
like the winds of a thousand storms . . . the howling star wind . . .
for a second you fear you might panic . . . but the image of Melha
stabilizes you . . . you know you are safe. The winds begin to blow
past you . . . you smell the heat of the great star . . . you see its
powerful, almost blinding light . . . its brightness uplifts you . . . then
you hear the very heartbeat of the star . . . throbbing . . . pounding
. . . pulsing . . . it sounds like your own heart . . . beating with the
rhythm of life. Now it is time to go . . . to pull away . . . you must
go back . . . and you slowly begin to pull away from the star . . .
you get caught again in the star wind . . . it gently carries you back
. . . slowly . . . Polaris assumes its white, twinkling state again . . .
the sound of the solar wind dies away . . . fades away . . . the star
recedes . . . becoming smaller . . . smaller . . . ever smaller. You
remember the sight you have seen . . . the heat . . . the sounds . . .
the smells . . . the light . . . the cocoon fades slowly away. The Star
Being . . . Melha . . . is there to meet you . . . he leads you to the
star gates . . . you walk through the gates . . . they close gently
behind you. The Spirit Bird awaits you . . . once again you climb
upon his back . . . and you feel his muscles tighten as he leaps into
flight. Before you is the Sky Bridge . . . like a great road paved with
sparkling diamonds . . . star diamonds. You can feel the coldness of
space . . . you see the blue Earth come into view . . . it gets bigger
. . . bigger . . . bluer . . . white clouds whirl in its aura . . . you see
the sacred mountain. The Spirit Bird lights . . . his talons getting a
firm grip in the soft, warm soil that is Earth . . . the planet's smells
once again fill your senses . . . you are home . . . you have changed
. . . you have been to the stars . . . you have crossed over the Sky

Bridge . . . you now know what it truly means to be a child of the universe.

It is important for us to be able to "communicate" with the stars. To do so we must get in touch with the Star Spirits who are the indwelling energies within each individual star or any other celestial body. The following instructions are designed to help us do precisely that.

GETTING IN TOUCH AND COMMUNICATING WITH THE STAR SPIRITS

Stars are alive! They, like Earth and all other celestial and planetary bodies, are living, evolving entities. We cannot think of stars in human terms, literally, because the type of lifeforms they are and the evolutionary path they are on are obviously different. But, we can personify our stellar relations. Personification allows us to attune ourselves more easily to them and in turn communicate more freely. Personification is a useful and powerfully effective tool that assists the human mind in putting the members of other kingdoms, both on Earth and beyond, into a frame that helps us understand their true nature. When we personify something we are in essence giving that something, be it a planet, a tree, a mineral, a river, or a star, a form and a personality like our own; "humanizing" it if you will.

When we use this age-old technique to get better acquainted with the stars, we will soon be able to perceive a star's indwelling life, which I call the Star Spirit. Personification also allows us, as individuals, to free our minds to "see" and/or sense the star spirits as they choose to appear to us. I for example see the stellar entity that resides within, and thus embodies the power of, the star Polaris as a young male rather like an Apollo figure with golden hair and piercing sapphire-colored eyes. You might see the same star spirit in a completely different form, perhaps as an aging female or crone with long bushy gray hair! One image does not invalidate the other. I find it interesting, however, that when I am teaching, several students "see" one star spirit or another in the same way. I take this as confirmation that Star Spirits do indeed reveal themselves to humans, and oftentimes in an image that is consistent and recognizable. The form may very well represent an archetype or image within our collective unconscious.

As I see it, a star myth is often but a method ancient peoples used to personify the energy contained within a certain star, constellation, or other heavenly body. After all, in constellations the patterns of stars rarely resemble the gods or goddesses, the animal, human, bird, or other figures for which they are named. Scorpio is one of the few exceptions. It looks like a scorpion. And the Big Dipper does look like a dipper. But if I asked you to point out to me the hunter in the sky, and you knew nothing about the stars or how they have been grouped, who among you would point out the Orion constellation? Or if I asked you to show me the virgin in Virgo, or the bull in Taurus, could you see these? Nonetheless, the Ancients perceived those figures in the sky.

I believe that they designated specific stars as specific mythical people and animals and objects because they sensed the nature of the energy of the stars involved. They detected the similarity of the stellar powers and the power inherent within their various cultural heroes and deities. Again, it is the tool of personification that, through these types of myths, gives us a frame of reference and a clue to the energy contained within various stellar groups. Virgo could be said to possess a feminine force, whereas Scorpio might have a bit of a sting and therefore an exceptionally intense male-like power to its nature. The great Antares, a major force in the Scorpio constellation, I call the Warrior Star.

To see an image of an indwelling Star Spirit within a given star, it is easy to use the simple process of creative visualization. Ask and you shall receive! Ask the star to show itself to you in humanized form. In other words, if the star was a human being, how would it look?

Always sit in a relaxed, quiet state and allow the image to appear in your mind's eye. I advise doing this visualization prior to working with drawing down the power of any given star. If you are working with a constellation, I suggest you work with seeing the Star Spirit of the brightest star in the group. Remember, constellations are not necessarily stars that are close to each other. They only appear to be against the backdrop of space. If you focus upon the major star in a designated group you will eventually wish to form a relationship with the entire group. There is also the distinct possibility that a given constellation will show itself to you as a group of Star Beings right away. In any case, the objective is to take a step toward forming a relationship, both personally and spiritually, with the various members of the Star Nation.

These relationships, like our human ones, create a feeling bond between an individual and the star(s). Feeling is the "glue" that holds the bond together. The union formed will bring human and stars closer, making the communication with one another, and the ceremonies performed for drawing upon each other's power (yes, it works both ways), much easier and more fulfilling.

My study of archaeoastronomy has taught me things that have baffled me, things that have inspired me, and things that have activated my intuition. One involves the vivid images and visions many of the ancestral peoples had of the Star Spirits. Of these, one that came from a small band within the great Pawnee Nation, the Chawi, impressed me in a powerful way. Von del Chamberlain tells a Chawi story about a mythical woman identified as a comet who appeared to a male member of the tribe. The description of this Comet Woman that so dazzled me reads:

> About her throat she wore some glittering object which looked like a star. Her head was in darkness, but down feathers stood up straight from it, signifying that she was in reality a comet . . . the bird in the center represented Tirawhat (the power and the fire); the owls represented the four gods in the west . . . In the spring he planted the two grains of corn near their grass lodge. These two grains represented the moon and a comet . . . another woman appeared before him and said, "Mother Moon promised you many things, but I cannot promise you much for I am a comet; that is why I wear down feathers on top of my head. Mother Moon is second only to Tirawhat in power. I have power only to increase your people. My corn is white and has a tassel on the top.". . .[3]

My intuition, triggered by this description, revealed an image that I would like to share, the vision of an entity whom I will sim-

ply call Star Woman. I invite you to "see" her in your mind's eye as
you read and to use this guided meditation as an exercise to assist
you in getting in touch with the Star Spirits.

A bronze-skinned star woman stands before me. Her well-
formed body is evident because I can see the firm muscles in her
arms and legs. Her hair is long, black, and straight; it is silky and
shines with the kind of softness that comes from moonlight. Her
face is that of an American Indian, but I know it is but one of many
guises she can take. Around her neck is a gold-colored symbol of a
four-pointed star. Her dress is fashioned from white buckskin speckled all over with the same kind of tiny, black star symbols. I know
that the dress is a "robe of stars." Her feet are bare. Around her right
ankle is a circlet of white corn kernels. On her head is a nest of
down feathers that stand up in a beautiful delicate "spray." Her dark,
piercing eyes peer out over her high cheekbones; her full mouth
and strong nose bridge complete an ageless face. I sense that she is
a "collective image" of the female star gods who come into the
dreams and visions of the women on Earth. She brings the powers
of the feminine stars . . . the kind of power the Dogons know is
inherent within their *emme ya* star, the one they call the "Sun of
Women."

Making intuitive-visual contact with Star Woman can assist us in
crossing into the initial stages of Starwalking. The following is the
visualization I use in order to make contact with her.

First, quiet and relax yourself both physically and mentally.
Then "see" the great Star Bridge, the Milky Way, like a roadway of
sparkling diamonds arcing before you, for it is the celestial span that
links you and Earth to the heavens. Standing at its terrestrial base,
slowly step onto the bridge and begin to walk into the sky. Walk up
and up the archway, each step bringing you closer to the realm of
the Great Star Nation. As you walk skyward, feel when you have left
the bondage of Earth . . . when you are more star than human. Feel
the transformation taking place . . . feel your body lightening . . .

becoming weightless . . . becoming free. See your human body glowing now . . . from the inside out . . . glowing . . . radiating in pure brilliance. As you come to the apex of the Sky Bridge, see the tall stately figure looming before you . . . awaiting you. It is Star Woman. Feel her power, and as you move closer, feel it with even greater intensity. Soon you are close enough to feel the heat radiating from her body and being, then look into her eyes . . . and see black pools of interstellar space. Those pupils . . . each is a silent, whirling galaxy suspended in the watery space of her eyes. Her necklace begins to glow in a soft, pulsating golden glow. As you move closer, she extends her arm and hand to you. Move still closer to her . . . offer her your hand. As your hands join, you can feel a tingling current of pure cosmic electricity flow into you . . . activating every cell in you . . . filling and nourishing you in a way you have not experienced before. Feel the current bonding you for this precious moment . . . a moment that opens for you a glimpse of eternity. She has welcomed you . . . accepted you . . . she has bonded with you . . . and you are one. From her mind you can access the power of the stars . . . you can know the wisdom of the Ancients who have gone before you on this very journey into her domain. Whatever question troubles you . . . whatever solution you seek . . . she telepathically reveals answers to you. She renews you . . . she suckles you in her depths . . . the depths known only to those who have "walked" this walk . . . who have trod this time-worn star path.

Now, it is time for you to leave. Star Woman releases you . . . your light body is freed . . . your mind is again your own. Begin to walk away, feeling her heat fade into a balmy, comforting coolness. When you have descended halfway on the diamond star path, turn and look up to her . . . see her being slowly fade from sight. Return home . . . back to Earth . . . renewed . . . strengthened . . . nourished. Feel the sense of wonder beating inside your chest as your light body gives way to physical flesh once more. You are enriched . . . so very enriched. You now know she is always there . . . that she has always been there . . . for you . . . for all women . . . for all time. She is your Celestial Mother . . . your Star Sister . . . your Stellar Counterpart . . . the Great Star Goddess . . . the Eternal She. She is you and you are she. You are one.

* * *

Creative visualization is but one tool we can employ in our quest to connect with the Star Nation. Divination is another, the art of foretelling future events or discovering hidden information about a person, place, or object. Throughout history humans have devised various methods for accomplishing this task. Some of the most familiar include the use of a crystal ball, cards such as the Tarot, palmistry, dowsing with pendulums and divining rods, and of course the use of so-called psychic ability without the assistance of any "props." Others that might be less familiar are aeromancy or "reading" the clouds; geomancy, "reading" the earth; and pyromancy, "reading" the forms seen in ashes.

Among the Navajo Indians of the American Southwest there exists a unique form of divination known as *stargazing*. Used by medicine people (for lack of a better term), stargazing involves divining the cause of illness or the source of trouble in a life, locating lost objects, or discovering the identity of a witch who is causing someone difficulty. It could be said that stargazers are diagnosticians; but they are more than that. Because they draw their power from and through personal contact with supernatural spirit forces, and perform their rituals while in a trance state, they are clearly shamans. Stargazing techniques vary. The basic Navajo practice involves the stargazer's looking through a quartz crystal at a bright star. Questions that concern the problem at hand are then posed to the star. The answers are determined by the colors refracted through the crystal. The stargazer can then diagnose the problem as well as determine the rituals and sacred sand paintings that must be done to correct it.[4]

Upon learning about this unusual method of divination, I decided to try it. Receiving "information" was not the most intriguing part. I have done that for so many years I have trained myself to receive in whatever circumstances or from whatever "tool." Rather, it was the act of holding the crystal, a fairly large piece of clear quartz, up to the star (I chose Antares the first time) that really interested me. I noticed several things, the first being the "feel" of the crystal in my hand. It fit; it felt solid and heavy . . . like a real "tool." My initial experience was on a particularly clear, star-filled night, as is typical in the desert of northern Arizona where I was living at the time. Then I noticed that the star's light became somewhat distorted, like a candle flame when you look at it with your eyes slightly squinted. Its rays became elongated, and were white and red in color. Even blades of blue showed through. It was beautiful and very empowering. It made me feel somehow "closer" to Antares, as if in some strange way the crystal blocked out the world and there was no distance between me and the star! It was a good and positive sensation that is difficult to put into words. I have experimented with this form of stargazing numerous times, and I teach it to those who study with me.

The world the Ancients lived in might just as well have been in another universe when compared to the world we live in today. In many ways our world is smaller than theirs. No place on the planet is beyond our reach. We can jet across the oceans at the speed of sound, and dine on two continents in a day. We have seen Earth from space. We have sent our personal cameramen to photograph Earth rising over the lunar horizon. It may very well be that, because our world is getting smaller all the time, we feel the need to travel into the sky and the spaces beyond more than ever. We have fine-tuned our brains and developed computers that put a global information network literally at our fingertips. The mystery of the atom has given way to the mystery of its parts. We send out space probes that speed past planets and moons in other parts of our solar community, and they in turn send back images of strange and wonderful worlds so different and distant from our own. This is our world, and it is a good world, an exciting and dangerous world, this world outside and around us.

Yet, questions may be asked: What archetypes empower and guide us in today's world? What unconscious memories direct and influence our path? What models form the foundation of our society? What are our values? A clue, at least in part, may come from those among us who are our heroes and villains: Mikhail Gorbachev, Nelson Mandela, the Dalai Lama, Mother Teresa, General Schwarzkopf, Charles Manson, Saddam Hussein, Manuel Noriega, the Ayatollah Khomeini, various scientists, statesmen, musicians and poets, mass murderers, dictators, and politicians. This cross section of humanity represents an "archetypal personality profile"—the best and worst in all of us.

The world of the ancestral peoples was small too, but for different reasons. They only knew the small part of it where they lived.

It was a quiet world and, in the night, a dark world. Campfires lit the caves and warmed the shelters made from the hides of the same animals that fed the family. Storytellers chronicled what had been. Prophets foretold what might be. The night . . . ah, the night . . . opened up a whole other world, the world of the Moon, stars, the Sky Gods. The Great Sky Bridge sliced the night in two, and stars . . . millions of stars . . . lit the heavens like sparkling diamonds in the night. Yes, it was a different world. It was a good world and, like ours, an exciting and dangerous world. The primordial realities it was based upon were the animals, community, climate, life, death, and ceremony. The archetypes were the Ancient Ones: Father Sun, Grandmother Moon, Earth Mother, stars, Sky Gods.

The most comprehensive definition of archetypes I know is that of Dr. Carol S. Pearson. She views archetypes as "energy within the unconscious psychological life of all people everywhere; they exist both inside and outside the individual human soul."[5] I think of archetypes as individual "powers," somewhat like cells, that embody a specific energy. The God archetype embodies the power attributed to God down through time; the mother archetype the powers of woman—nurturing, protective; the Merlin archetype embodies all that is represented by shamans and magicians; and so on. Nature's powers—thunder, lightning, water, fire, air, wind, and others—are archetypes, as are the Sun, Moon, stars; and what might be called "life powers," birth and death, are too.

Jung said the archetypes reside within what he called the collective unconscious, that reservoir of collective human memory, if you will, that each of us "inherits." In short, we have all inherited, like "consciousness genetics," the same archetypes, so the content of our collective unconscious is identical.

Within the minds of our earliest ancestors, the archetypes were primitive, basic. As the evolution of our species and life on Earth has progressed, the archetypes have increased in number because human knowledge and experience have expanded and become more complex through dreams, fantasies, visions, and through our behavior and values. They become evident in society through art, literature, myth, religion, and according to Pearson in "the *constellations* [italics mine] and the birds and animals of the Earth." (Pearson, p.6) She also says that archetypes "leave the same or similar traces over time and space," and that they are the "invisible patterns that control how we experience the world". (Pearson, p.6) This is the key.

From Jung's work we can determine which archetypes are "active" and are therefore influencing any particular nation or culture at any given time in history. It is clear that archetypes can and do both *awaken* and *slumber*, becoming active and dormant if you will, determined by what collective stage we have reached along the evolutionary journey. The archetypes dominant at any given time will have tremendously powerful influence, as is clearly evident in today's modern world, movies and television programs, fads, fashions, and even interior designs and accessories. (Pearson, p.7)

In this writing I am of course viewing the matter of archetypes from a collective perspective in the outer world, in society, religion, art, and so on. So the question becomes: Which archetypes are awakening that will influence us now and into the future? In light of the fact that we are approaching a major change of time—the turn of the millennium—and are progressing through a time of planetary change, we are open and vulnerable to the "energies" that are and will be dominant. "How we view the world is defined by what archetype currently dominates our thinking and acting." (Pearson, p.7)

I am reminded of a channeling given by Albion in 1985. I now realize that the subject being discussed involved the "awakening" of an archetype. It was evident to me that Albion was talking about the stars . . . the Great Star Nation. He began with the subject of Earth and our present environmental condition, which is at best troubling. The Teacher reminded us that, during the 1970s and '80s there had been an increasing interest by an increasing number of people in ancient and traditional Earth-based religions, particularly the Native American. He explained that this interest was due to the relationship with Earth and Nature that these teachings espouse. It seems that Albion was saying that we and the planet are in *big* trouble, but learning these teachings and adopting the philosophy and values they embody can and will show us a way to right the wrongs we have done and continue to do to ourselves and our Earth Mother. Also, it became clear that the Mother Earth archetype had awakened within individuals and in society as a whole.

Evidence of this awakening can also be seen in the founding of environmental groups and organizations like Greenpeace, Friends of the Earth, and the Nature Conservancy, whose concerns are much the same as those addressed by the religions of the indigenous peoples. The Earth Mother archetype has permeated our lives in numerous other ways: art, concern for the endangered species, movies based on Native American history, religion, and in culture, general public education regarding various environmental issues, sacred ecology, interest in Earth mysteries (ley lines, grids, and vortexes), interest in sacred sites, and the feminine force in Nature as it manifests and expresses itself through women, matriarchy, and the goddesses of ancient times.

Albion said, *You have all the information and tools you need to reconnect yourselves to the Earth. There is nothing more to be said, nothing more that can be taught. It is up to you, individually and collectively, what you do with the knowledge you have gained. You know what you have lost, and you know the way things are. You know the changes that must be made. Otherwise, the severity of this cycle of planetary change will come to pass in the ways foretold by the various prophecies.* He went on to say that at the beginning of the 1990s, the focus of his teachings would shift to the primary concern of spiritual seekers throughout the '90s and into the next millennium: *star knowledge, both exoteric* (astronomy) and *esoteric* (ancient spiritual stellar wisdom). Albion concluded, *It is time to reconnect yourselves with Father Sky. All of our teachings will now center on the stars. It is time.*

I cannot honestly say that I grasped the full implications of Albion's words that night, but they soon became quite clear. I guess it's like buying a red car. You don't really notice red cars until you get one, then you suddenly see them everywhere! In the years since that channeling I have noticed many things concerning the stars that would otherwise either have escaped my attention completely, or have had less meaning had I not known that the star archetype was awakening. Seemingly insignificant things may not appear to have any real or spiritual value. When viewed from the archetypal perspective, however, the trend they represent and the energy they embody and transmit is clearly evident. Examples I have noticed include the ever-increasing interest in extraterrestrial life and Uf-ology, expanded space travel and exploration, the ever-widening market for books and articles on archaeoastronomy, the advent of the popular Star Trek movies, new Star Trek television series, and even celestial themes in home decorations and Christmas orna-ments. Telescope sales have skyrocketed. On a personal level, the workshops and lectures I have offered on the astronomy of the ancient peoples and the stars have been increasingly well attended.

In 1995, *The Orion Mystery*, a book about the star religion of the Egyptians, became an international bestseller! This is only one book. *The Pleiadian Agenda, You Are Becoming A Galactic Human,* and *Bringers of the Dawn,* to name a few others whose themes involve the wisdom of extraterrestrial beings, are steadily gaining in popu-larity and acceptance. Albion mentioned in April 1993 that, due to the intensification of Earth changes, we would begin to see Elders and medicine people from several American Indian tribes come for-ward to speak to all races about their traditional teachings. He specifically named the Cherokee, Navajo, Hopi, Sioux, and the Potawatomi of the northeastern woodlands. The Teacher explained that there was at that time an outpouring of star energy on these nations, and that the sources of that stellar power were the constel-lations Orion and the Big Dipper, and the star Sirius.

Not long after the channeling, some rather significant events occurred within some of these tribes that called attention to them in one way or another. One concerned the fulfillment of ancient instructions given to the Hopi, when a small delegation of tradi-tional Elders was allowed to deliver a message to world leaders at United Nations headquarters in New York on November 22, 1993. Their message concerned the Hopi prophecies warning that the time of purification is at hand. The Hopi were joined in their effort by members of the Mic Mac, Maya, Huichol, Lakota, the Algonquin Nations of North America, and the Six Nations of the Iroquois Confederacy. Another important "sign" was the birth of a rare white female buffalo calf on a farm in Wisconsin. The white buffalo, sacred to the Sioux, is representative of White Buffalo Calf Woman, the spirit woman who brought the gift of the sacred pipe to the peo-ple long ago. Furthermore, in the fall of 1995, the Eastern Band of the Cherokee elected the first woman to the position of Principal

Chief. Though not directly star-related, these are highly symbolic events with profound social, political, and spiritual/religious implications not only for these peoples, but for us all.

In the spring of 1996 I received a communiqué from a devout supporter of Native American peoples. It concerned a conference scheduled for June of that year in Wagner, South Dakota. The purpose and theme of the conference caught my attention immediately: *Star Knowledge Conference.* The message was synchronistic to me in a way that is hard to put into words, but the following excerpt said it all: "From all over the hemisphere medicine people from various tribes are gathering to share for the first time secret oral traditions about generations of Star Nation (extraterrestrial) contacts and messages with the Native Americans." The initiator of this effort identified himself as Standing Elk of the Yankton Sioux Reservation. The Elder's words indicated his willingness to accept full responsibility for his decision to share the star knowledge with all peoples of the four directions, and cited as his reasons for doing so, "the closeness and the fulfillment of prophecies that are vital for our existence as a human race," and the need for "strengthening the foundation of nations that are sincerely interested in being that element that will be the foundation of the 'thousand years of peace'." He also revealed the importance of the Star Nation when he stated: "The Lakota/Dakota Medicine Men are now being instructed to share the spiritual knowledge of the Star Nations because of the contamination of Mother Earth and the pollution of the air."

I now know beyond any doubt that Albion was right in his prediction concerning the coming out of the Indian Elders, and in his assessment of the influence of the awakening of the star/Star Nation archetype. It is my sincere hope that you will become more consciously aware of this ever-expanding trend and its subsequent effect upon collective humanity and planet Earth.

Two different worlds? Indeed. And the two cannot exchange places. We cannot go back there; the ancestors cannot come here. Although the ancestors, long gone, can learn nothing from us, we can learn something from them. We can learn simplicity . . . survival . . . self-reliance . . . a love for Earth . . . and the route into the sky. As long as we are bound to the forward, on-going rhythm of time that our intellect and the physical world demand, we move farther from our ancestors and our freedom from intellectual dominion. This kind of freedom will unlock our intuition and allow our souls to take flight into the heavens to reconnect with the stars.

If Carl Jung was right, the ancient human view of their world and how they responded to it is imprinted in our individual and collective unconscious. The same archetypes that made our ancestors what they were still lie slumbering at the very root of our beings. We can still pray the Sun up and draw down the power of the Moon. We can still walk across the Milky Way and warm ourselves at the campfires of the gods. So doing would change our perspective of the outer landscape, of course, and that would be good. Maybe we would come to value it more. That would change our individual inner landscape, too, unlocking doors behind which will be found the power of the indwelling spirits of the Sun and Moon, the planets, and the stars. Comets can once more stir the Voice of Caution within us; meteors can again send a chill down the spine of the night . . . the inner night. The sunrise can once more be the daily miracle. The star shaman is not extinct. He/she is only slumbering within each of us. The Hopi still dance; the Navajo still chant; the Big Starway song is still being sung. The Sun God is still alive. The Moon Goddess is still fertile and feminine. She still brings growth and change.

A pilgrimage to the stars is one that we must ultimately make alone. It is a journey into outer space, to other galaxies, and to the very boundaries of the universe . . . "to that boundary of space and time where the mind and heart encounter the ultimate mystery, the known unknowable. It is a pilgrimage in quest of the soul of the night." (Raymo, p.6)

It is also a journey into *inner* space . . . a pilgrimage into the depths of you . . . and me. What we will encounter depends upon why we go in the first place. We will find what we seek. As we make our way past the layers of self, we will eventually come to a clearing. Within that clearing we will meet ourselves. We will see how and who we really are; who we have been, and who we can become. Somewhere among the many faces that comprise the totality of a self, one will know the way to lead us where we must ultimately go. "Where is that?" you say. Back to the stars. Back into the cosmos . . . into wholeness . . . into freedom. It is a long, sometimes frightening, sometimes painful, but always rewarding journey . . . a journey of self-discovery we all must take . . . sooner or later. Bon voyage, fellow Star Children. God speed.

"When all the stars were ready to be placed in the sky First Woman said, 'I will use these to write the laws that are to govern mankind for all time. These laws cannot be written on the water as that is always changing its form, nor can they be written in the sand as the wind would soon erase them, but if they are written in the stars they can be read and remembered forever'."[6]

Trudy Griffin-Pierce

CHAPTER SIX

PATHWAYS TO
THE GODS

Astronomy was lived as intently as it was practiced, and much of what our predecessors viewed was devoted to purposes that, today, we would regard as religious rather than scientific.[1]

Anthony Aveni

When the archaeologist lifts a potsherd out of the soil where it has lain hidden for centuries, he or she knows it has a story to tell about the human being who used it so long ago. The archaeologist is a scientist, and science concerns itself with only the facts: How old is the sherd; how long ago did the people who made it live; what did they eat; what does the evidence tell about their physical lives? Science does not address the heart.

I wouldn't make a good archaeologist. It would be difficult for me to separate myself from the dreams and aspirations, successes and failures, the romances and the celebrations of births and deaths of the people into whose long-gone world I was literally digging. They were human beings who surely suffered the same losses and savored the same victories we do today. Their world was a place of beauty and hardships too. Their lives unfolded under the same canopy of stars we see. Their day began and ended with the rising and setting of the same Sun. The same Moon illumined the dark nights. In fact the only thing that really separates us from them is time, an immense amount of time.

Like the archaeologist, the astronomer is also separated from the

91

objects studied, divided by time and by mind-staggering distances. Unlike the archaeologist, the astronomer can't put "finds" under a microscope or on display in a museum. A star can't be held in the hand. A comet or a quasar can't be brought into a laboratory. The worlds these scientists pursue are almost unfathomable to those same laypersons who label the ancestors as primitive and the stars alien. However, both worlds hold a special key: the key to the origin of human beings.

At the time of the creation of the universe, the heavier elements, which our bodies and other physical matter are composed of, were not created. These came from the explosion of a great star, a supernova event. The immense heat generated by a supernova resulted in fusion that, in turn, resulted in carbon, iron, and so forth. How paradoxical that the unimaginable *destruction* of a star resulted in the *creation* of the ingredients of physical matter. We are star-born, literally.

Our roots go far beyond the ruins uncovered by archaeologists. Physicists define the Laws of Nature, and do a very good job of speaking to us about atoms, particles, and models of matter. However, more often than not, scientific theories that seek to explain Nature change long before the rest of us gain any real understanding of what is being proposed. Modern cosmological speculations too often are explained in the foreign language of calculations and formulas understood only by an elite few. The lay public does not comprehend what is being proposed, so that exciting promises fail to deliver our longed-for understanding of the universe.

Philosophers suggest that the cosmos is not really accessible to reason, that we will never understand it with our intellectual prowess alone. Working solely with reason has its limitations. Certainly reason and logic are valuable tools and represent an unmistakable part of the human experience. The Age of Reason has yielded incredible knowledge and benefits, but one must wonder, at what price?

With picks and shovels, the archaeologist goes about the business of reconstructing a world lived in long ago. Each time the archaeologist discovers a piece of pottery, a cooking implement, the statue of a god, or a doorstep leading into a home long gone, we learn something more about ourselves, something more of the evolutionary path that has led us to where we are today. This makes the ruin of each ancient village a piece to a puzzle.

As each new world is found floating in space, it too is a piece of the riddle of existence. With technological devices and mathematical formulas astronomers explore alien starscapes that fill interstellar space. Yet, does the discovery of a newborn star really affect us? Is the death of a great star mourned? Does the eerie appearance of a comet streaking across the night speak to the inner human consciousness in the same way as a golden idol or the puzzling pyramids? If not, why?

Perhaps some blame lies with scientists, in their commitment to facts and "laws," who refuse to or cannot even attempt to impart the simple awareness and knowledge of the universe's role in human existence. Maybe the jargon spoken by scientists and academicians masks any real understanding of the universe and robs us of our sense of wonder about the stars. Or maybe the clergy, in their role as mediators, create a separation between us—Creation—and the Creator. We cannot afford to approach a matter of such profound importance as understanding the cosmos and our place in it with any less than all the human faculties and resources at our disposal.

We have evidence that the ancient peoples pondered such things. They observed the order in the heavens that, in turn, gave them a tool by which time could be measured. They devised mathematical systems that assisted them in building monuments that served both a religious and secular purpose. Many of these still stand today in mute testimony to that ancient human intellect, ingenuity, and physical prowess. They figured out that Earth revolves around the Sun, and learned the art of predicting solar and lunar eclipses. Yet, what they learned never separated them from a direct experience of the universe. They never saw themselves as separate from the sky. Through their myths, the Sky Gods came to life. With imagination, our ancestors took flight into the heavens. The rewards of their inner visual experiences linked them with the sky and the Star Spirits that, to them, were the source of life. The Star Journeys they took provided far more than mere flights of fantasy, or means by which crafty shamans could win the respect and favor of a gullible following. The journeys provided *purpose to human life.*

THE ANCIENT ART OF STARWALKING

There are many roads into Sky Country. We can and are surely encouraged to take the road of the sciences, of astronomy and physics. In doing so, we can take full advantage of our intellectual ability to reason. We can also tread the path of observers, seeking not only to broaden our knowledge of the physical universe, but also to experience the wonder, beauty, and excitement of the day and night skies. With the aid of telescopes, we can watch the Sky Bridge spanning overhead. We can watch our Day Star sink slowly into turquoise and golden sunsets. We can gaze at the mysteriously beautiful rings of Saturn, and wonder about those fuzzy patches of light that are distant galaxies drifting in space. We can puzzle over quasars and marvel at neutron stars.

At the same time, we can listen to star myths born in minds long gone, myths that give the breath of life to the spirits of the cosmos. We can learn about ancient cultures and what they knew about the stars. And there is one other choice, a very important choice indeed: *We can go in our minds into the heavens to dance with the stars.* This is what Starwalkers did . . . and do. For them space travel was not limited to a few. Space was accessible to all; time and distance were no obstacles. The Starwalker's spaceship was his or her mind. Intuition and imagination were equal in value with logic and reason, making use of all our human faculties. The scientific picture of the universe is not the *only* picture.

Over time humanity's view of the cosmos has changed. But our need to know about it, and about ourselves, has not. Modern cosmology is the sum of what we know about the beginning of the universe. But what does it really tell us? What *experience* of the cosmos does it offer? I am *not* saying that science and the world picture that has evolved from its efforts should be devalued or abandoned. I *am* saying that such a narrow view of reality does less than justice to our need to relate to the whole of Nature and our own spiritual side. Collectively, humans have an innate need to know about the universe and how we fit into it, and that need is in some way vital to our evolution as a species.

Ancient peoples certainly watched the sky, the risings and the settings of the Sun and Moon and stars. But, the skywatcher's job was different from the Starwalker, and was done for different reasons. The former was an observer of the sky; the latter a *participant* with it. The skywatcher tried and succeeded in making sense of the world. The Starwalker tried and succeeded in establishing a relationship with and uniting with the stars. Starwalkers broke free of the bonds of earthly limitations and, in their minds, visited worlds beyond their own.

Should these experiences be less valued than the "advanced" knowledge that lies recorded in numbers and computer-enhanced images on the pages of scientific journals? Do the Starwalker's supernatural sky deities have to succumb in favor of the endless modern debates over the workings of the mysterious depths of space? Must we be condemned to forever study and admire the universe from afar? Can we or should we measure ourselves by the rationality of a worldview gleaned solely from the scientific method of experimentation and technology? If we do will our self-view, individually and collectively, not come up short?

The Gemini and Apollo astronauts were space pioneers, our modern heroes who reached for the stars . . . for us. But they were not the first pioneers in space. Starwalkers were the original space travelers. It was they who braved their fears and dared to approach the Sky Gods; they who first traveled around in the solar system and beyond. They could not have succeeded in their efforts if they had not possessed three important and necessary "tools": *imagination, willingness,* and *vision.*

Using imagination ancient Starwalkers gave the stars and planets, the Sun and Moon, comets, meteors, and even thunder and lightning, personality and character. To them no part of the universe was inaccessible. They allowed the heavenly bodies to come to life in their own minds, and saw them as powerful beings, not mute and lifeless bodies created by some unknown, unnameable creative force. Using the power that comes with willingness, they overthrew the limitations brought on by the innate fear humans have of unfamiliar realms into which their imagination might lead them. With the vision of purpose and meaning, Starwalkers not only discovered and explored the abode of the gods, but they fitted themselves into the Great Whole. They ascended to participate in the immortality known by the shining star worlds above. They *became* the gods at the end of physical life.

The skywatchers of yesterday gazed up into the night, into the face of infinity. Astronomers today, equipped with the tools of logic and the looking devices they invent, stare into the same face. Their reaction is surely also one of respect and wonder. But with all the modern-day technology at their disposal, astronomers cannot explain infinity. Yet, the concept of infinity exists . . . *out there* . . . in the sky. Thinkers often find themselves in the position of the mathematician Pascal, musing: "I see these frightening spaces in the universe which enclose men, and I find myself attached to one corner of this vast universe, not knowing why I have been placed here rather than there, nor why I have been destined to live my short life at this point of eternity rather than another." (Aveni, p.123)

I don't believe that reason alone gives answers, gives us the understanding we need and seek. I believe we have to dig deeper inside ourselves, individually and collectively, and free our intuition and imagination, valuing them equally with reason and logic. Working together, they can give us the experience of the cosmos. Reason cannot explain the human need to escape terrestrial bondage. Imagination cannot solve a mathematical problem. We cannot define the Creator by merely thinking.

Revealing what is hidden is not just a matter of thinking, it is also a matter for the heart. Not the heart of sentiment, but the heart that is the seat of the immortal soul. That mechanism within us that puts us in touch with and is absolutely essential to our knowledge of who and what we are, and from where we have come. To intuit is to *know*, not merely to feel or suspect or have blind faith that something is true. Starwalkers, staring into the face of the infinite, devised sophisticated systems of astronomy and mathematics. Star shamans were hampered neither by reason nor by the fears and restrictions born from the zealous passion it often generates. They viewed the gods as models, much like physicists today view the atom. Upon these, all was built and all depended.

Starwalkers went beyond the threshold of earthly time into the infinity of Sky Country. They saw the stars first with their eyes, then with their hearts. They crossed the Sky Bridge. They stood fearlessly before the star gates, which they then coaxed open with sacred songs, dances, and incantations. They rode the sometimes nauseating waves induced by holy plants, propelled into a state of spiritual ecstasy that allowed them an awareness of the pulse of Creation.

Starwalkers knew the heavenly zones and the great suns that marked their intersections. They knew how to unlock the starscape's powers that bestow good fortune, health, wealth, guidance, protection, and even fame. They knew the warrior stars like Antares, whose powers they tapped for success and victory in the conflicts in their human world. None of this was accomplished with their ability to reason. They were in fact only able to do it by their willingness to be unreasonable! By allowing their intuition to open and their imagination to soar.

Our first step toward gaining the knowledge and experience of the Starwalkers involves embracing the darkness. To do that we must go out into the night, literally. Sometimes it seems as if we try to escape night's vastness, and its silence. It is the Great Unknown, and we humans fear the unknown, don't we?

At times, we also have trouble being alone with ourselves and with listening to the voice of silence. The first time I stood on the rim of the Grand Canyon, its beauty was magnificent, even overwhelming. But, what struck me most was its silence, the silence that offered no response to my awe, no explanation for being here, no sound—only the vast, deep silence. The silence said it all. All I had to do was to drink in the beauty and listen, to know the power of the great chasm intimately. I became a part of the canyon and it a part of me.

The night sky is silent too. Oh, its peace is interrupted occasionally by a speeding meteor slamming into Earth's atmosphere; and there are the sounds we cannot hear, the hissing and undulating static emitted by the radio waves of stars, planets, and nebulae. To our physical ears, Antares and Betelgeuse burn red in silence. The Big Dipper and Polaris revolve around the roof of the heavens in the quiet. We hear no hissing and static, only the deep silence.

Everything around us is constantly changing. We are forced to adapt again and again to the countless circumstances of our fragile lives on Earth. But, in the short span of a human life, it seems it never changes up there! How then do we learn to accommodate our lives, our thoughts, and our feelings to a universe that seems so quiet and impersonal, so unresponsive to us? How do we cozy up to stars and galaxies so distant that a language just to define those distances is necessary? How do we rid ourselves of our modern tendency to view the heavens as little more than millions of mindless stars and our own planet as planet-dust floating aimlessly around an ordinary star in the suburbs of an ordinary galaxy? How do we reinstate the Milky Way to its prominence as the path that leads to the star gates, behind which reside the great Star Beings? How do we come to believe in the powers inherent in the stars, and to savor the living presence of their indwelling spirits?

The answer is simple. We must go into the universe willingly and without fear, on the wings of intuition and imagination. We must approach our learning with logic and intuition working together as equal partners in a synchronized effort to understand. We must value and trust what they tell us. We must watch and listen to the silent music of the spheres. We must open ourselves to the voices of Arcturus, Aldebaran, and Vega. We must watch and listen. In our deepest archetypal memories we know how to do this. When we investigate what the Ancients knew about the heavens, and how they drew upon the power of the stars and integrated them and the entire sky into their daily lives, we not only can learn a lot, we can also awaken those slumbering memories deep within us.

The purpose of the next several chapters of this book is to inform you about our ancestors, what they knew about the stars, and how that knowledge made them who and what they were, how in some cases, it is reflected in their descendants today. Together we will take a journey back into time, and more often than not into times and cultures that have long since vanished. For that reason, details regarding some of the cultures we visit will be scant. Some of the earliest peoples and the world they lived in may be familiar to some readers, and alien to others. However, I promise you a fascinating and fruitful journey.

To benefit the most from this journey, we must unleash our imprisoned sense of wonder about the universe. We must be willing to speculate, to reason and intuit together and independently. In fact, if there is but one ultimate aim in writing this book, it is my desire to inspire all of us with the wonder of the heavens and to help insure that none of us ever again loses the magic that wonder and awe bring. It is time to become conscious that we are children of the universe, to truly take our place in the cosmic scheme of things.

We *can* lift our praise once again to the Sun and give thanks for its warmth. We can sing to the Moon and let its light illumine the shadows of our dreams, our fears, and our spiritual quests. With our intellect and our intuition working together in harmony, we can remember what we have forgotten, and reunite with what we have abandoned. If we do this we can . . . *and we can* . . . we will come to know the *whole* universe as home.

Yes, I am a child of the Milky Way. The night is my mother. I am made of the dust of stars. Every atom in my body was forged in a star. When the universe exploded into being, already the bird longed for the wood and the fish for the pool. When the first galaxies fell into luminous clumps, already I was struggling toward consciousness. The star clouds in Sagittarius are a burning bush. If there is a voice in Sagittarius, I'd be a fool not to listen. If God's voice in the night is a scrawny cry, then I'll sit back on a dark hillside and wait and watch. A hint here and a trait there. Listening and watching. Waiting, always waiting, for the tingle in the spine.[2]

PART TWO

WHEN THE SKY GODS CAME DOWN TO EARTH

CHAPTER SEVEN

MIGHTY SIRIUS!
MONARCH OF THE SUNS

What we see in the lights overhead is the itinerary of cosmic order. Because it governs everything, it is reflected in the entire world. It is the core of our consciousness. It defines what is sacred and makes the sky the domain of the gods.[1]

E.C. Krupp

Egypt! I well remember my first time in Egypt. After flying for what seemed like days, our group arrived in Cairo at two in the morning. My husband and I were invited to serve as teachers for a group of almost two hundred members of Astara, a spiritual community from all over the world. Riding through the streets of Cairo for the first time was an experience: dark side streets, thick pollution that cast an eerie greenish haze around the streetlights, and unfamiliar sounds and smells. It reminded me of scenes right out of an old Humphrey Bogart movie!

Daylight brought an even greater culture shock. I awoke to the early morning call to prayer that rang out over a very loud speaker, blowing horns—millions of horns—roaring traffic, and the ever-present donkeys and camels, dust and haze . . . and people . . . everywhere there were people. I felt like I was right in the middle of a Middle Eastern Los Angeles! Taxis rushed around buses filled with people on the go. Those who didn't have seats on the buses leaned out the windows, hung onto the doors while standing on the entry steps, or perched like monkeys on the roofs. Bicycle riders with fresh-baked bread piled high dodged in and out. Shops with fresh-butchered meats stacked out front in the open air contributed to the smells of a city that thrives, as it has for centuries, with life unique in the world. Coffee vendors poured their thick, black syrup on every corner, while hibachis cooked bits of lamb and chicken. Construction workers huddled in small groups around their hookahs (pipes for smoking hashish) that belched spiraling hypnotic smoke into the air of dawn. Then, suddenly, there they were . . . the ancient pyramids of Giza! And there was the Sphinx!

As our two-week tour went on, the ancient past unfolded before us. Site after site brought images so clear they seemed to come from only yesterday: the great stepped pyramid at Saqqara . . . the Temple of Karnak . . . the wonderful Luxor Temple . . . the West Bank tombs in the Valley of the Kings and the Temple of Isis on the Isle of Philae . . . the Dendara Temple, so well-preserved . . . the Temple of Horus . . . the ancient storyboards on walls and tombs with colors as vivid as a canvas painted merely a moment ago. I felt keenly the strange, powerful energy at the Temple of Kom Ombo . . . as if the life force of the African continent was flowing into my veins. And, there was the Nile . . . always the Nile, the ageless life-giving artery of the land whose flowing waters seem to defy time itself. I realized I was experiencing *two* Egypts, one modern, the other ancient; both existing side by side, spanning the bridge of time together like few places on Earth.

No one visits Egypt without witnessing first hand the vital role the Nile serves. The river was and is the main artery of the land. It pumps life blood in the form of water through a spreading network of irrigation canals, nourishing the fields and crops today as it has done for ages. Formed by two streams known as the White Nile and the Blue Nile, the river flows north in its ever-steady journey toward the Mediterranean.

The three Egyptian seasons are determined by the river's behavior. They were known in ancient times as Inundation, the time of the annual flood (June through September); Emergence, when the fields came out of the water (October through February); and Drought, the dry period (March through May). This represented the first calendar around which life revolved. Hapi, the God of the Nile and the supplier of water, was predictably of tremendous importance to desert dwellers. Having lived in the great Sonoran desert myself for almost a dozen years, I quickly learned to make peace with and sought out ways to remain in harmony with the water spirits!

Ancient Egypt is woven into the fabric of modern Egypt, which depends largely upon its past and the tourists it draws for its life today. Together, the present and the past emit a power whose effects extend far beyond the bounds of the Egypt of this time. Legacies from the Egypt of old are the timetable from which came our present 365-day calendar and our 24-hour day. The ancient style of art puzzles our minds and pleases our senses, a mystique that draws us into a time and place deep within us, deep and powerful, a faded but not-forgotten time filled with precious ancient memories. It gave to the world that lasting symbol of arcane knowledge, the Great Pyramid, and all the other incredible monuments. All the priceless treasures represent and embody the wisdom and will that empower humanity's search for meaning and place in the universe.

It is clear that the ancient people of the desert were preoccupied with the eternal cycle of birth and death, a cycle they saw reflected in the sky. A close look reveals that their knowledge of these cycles and the sky cannot be separated from their religion, a truth supported by the fact that there are 81 monuments throughout Egypt that are known to have astronomical and ceremonial significance. There can be little doubt that the Egyptians' knowledge of astronomy and their skywatching techniques made an enduring contribution to our understanding of them as a people and of the heavens. Surely the lifestyle and beliefs of this mysterious ancient society made an indelible imprint upon the human psyche.

The god, Osiris, represented the land and the people. The Osiris myth embodied both exoteric and esoteric beliefs. Depicted in hieroglyphics as a mummy, Osiris was the god of continuity and of the renewal of life via resurrection. He ruled the dead and presided over the judgment of departed souls. He was also the god of fertility, kingship, water, the cycle of vegetation and, most especially, of the river Nile.[2] However, it is the great god's celestial attributes that unveil his truest nature and identity. He was the Sun, the Moon, and the stars in the constellation we know as Orion.

Born from the union of the Sky Goddess, Nut, and Geb, the Earth, Osiris became Egypt's first king. He civilized the country. He taught his subjects the arts of planting and harvest, how to survey the land and to lay proper boundaries. He taught them irrigation.

He made the laws and presided over urban life, fathered the religion by which morality was measured, and revealed the existence of a hierarchy of deities. (Krupp, p.16) The sky was in Osiris' blood, and the stars were his bones—so it is to the sky we must turn if we are to gain any true understanding of the depth of the role the Great One played in the minds and souls of the early Egyptians, and how he molded their view of reality.

The Osirian Cycle is the foundation myth of ancient Egypt. It tells of Osiris' travels throughout the land and of his marriage to Isis, a union that symbolized and embodied the masculine and feminine forces in Nature. All went well until Osiris was captured by his evil brother, Set, who placed Osiris in a coffin and threw him into the Nile, where he drowned. The coffin floated down the river and into the Mediterranean, where it was later discovered by Isis.

Though Osiris was dead, Isis used her magical skills to couple with him and conceive a child. Afterward, she hid her husband's body among the bulrushes of the delta marshlands where, unfortunately, it was found by Set. Enraged, he tore his brother's dead body into fourteen pieces and scattered them up and down the Nile. Again, Isis proved her love and faithfulness, gathering the pieces of Osiris' body. She found all except the phallus, which was to remain lost forever. (The fourteen parts clearly correspond to the days of the waning moon and death.) Osiris was eventually resurrected into everlasting life. (Krupp, pp.16-17)

This ancient myth is written in the stars. Osiris appears in the stars of Orion, a constellation that we shall see was among those most significant to the ancient Egyptians. Isis' heavenly counterpart is Sirius, the brightest star that can be seen from Earth. The Egyptians called it Sothis, the Nile Star. The evil Set, who brought death, the desert, chaos, violence, and sterility into Egyptian life, is seen in the stars of the Big Dipper.

Of these, it was Sirius that influenced the daily life of the people the most. The great star made its appearance close to the summer solstice, in conjunction with the annual flooding of the Nile, upon which life and survival were totally dependent. Before the flood came, it was Sirius that heralded the coming of the water that would revive the land just as Isis had revived Osiris. Sirius also brought the new year, symbolized in the myth as Horus, the son of Isis and Osiris.

In fact, much Egyptian astronomy revolved around the Nile Star. Marking the start of the solar year it was symbolic, too, of the rebirth of time over and over again.³ There are some researchers and Egyptologists who believe that Osiris, indeed all the gods and goddesses, actually came from the Sirius star system!⁴ The great star stood for the creation of the cosmos, and subsequently of time itself. When it rose immediately after the constellation Orion, the two comprised a stellar wedded couple in the sky.

A deeper understanding of the celestial symbolism embodied in the mythology of Egypt is found in the writings of astronomer and pioneering archaeoastronomer, E.C. Krupp: "In Egypt, Orion, like Sirius, is absent from the night sky for 70 days. This period is equated with the time Osiris spent in the transitional underworld." (Krupp, p.22) With the heliacal rise of Sirius and the flooding of the Nile, we are reminded how dependent Egyptian agriculture was upon the river. Without it there would only be arid, sterile land.

As indicated in the Osiris myth, the ancient Egyptians believed that death had no permanent hold. It only led the soul back into life. Death was related to the setting Sun, the waning Moon, and year's end, while birth and rebirth were symbolized by the rising Sun, the New Moon, and the year's beginning. The marriage between life and death resulted in the Egyptian's ultimate reward of eternal life. This belief was also seen in the night sky in constellations like the Big Dipper, whose circumpolar stars neither rose or set. (Other ancient cultures also looked upon the circumpolar stars and constellations as being the preservers of order and permanence.)

The wisdom and power inherent in Egyptian religion rested upon one foundation: When a pharaoh died, he became a star and took his place within the heavenly hierarchy. Inscriptions have been found that describe a pharaoh's ascent into the sky where he eternally regulated the night, maintained the calendar, and regulated the seasons. (Krupp, pp.100-101) Evidence of that belief is found in one of the most colossal monuments ever constructed by mankind: the Great Pyramid. Placed to coincide with the four cardinal directions, as is common with ancient monuments worldwide, the Great Pyramid holds many secrets. Now, after thousands of years, the time has come for many of those well-guarded secrets to come to light, as at least one has. We now believe that the shafts inside the pyramid were aligned to stars! (See appendix 6 for more information.) These stars include Thuban, Al Nilam, Rochab, and Al Nitak, in addition to Sirius.

Other constellations and individual stars played an important role in the Egyptian star religion. Among these were the stars of Ursa Major, the Big Dipper, associated with the god, Set. This constellation, according to myth, was also related to the goddess, Seshat, who attended the pharaoh in a ceremony known as the *Stretching of the Cord.* The rite was a cooperative venture in laying out the astronomical alignment(s) for a temple. Seshat was the mistress of measure whose energy corresponds to the number seven, the number of harmony. She is pictured wearing a headdress composed of inverted cow's horns resting atop a shaft. Within the horns is a seven-pointed star, which may represent the stars in the Big Dipper. Her clothing is covered with spots that may represent all the stars in the night sky.

No figure, however, is a more intimate part of Egyptian astronomy than the Sky Goddess, Nut. It was she who swallowed the stars at night, her star-covered body that formed the skydome that loomed overhead. At dawn, the stars Nut had devoured the previous night reappeared, reborn from her celestial womb, the cycle of day and night being played out time and time again. Nut also swallowed the setting Sun, which was seen as a disk in her mouth. It too, along with all the other stars, passed through her body during the night and was reborn again at dawn. The cyclic activity of the stars was reflective of the life cycles of humans on Earth—what went on in the sky was happening on Earth. In this way the stars explained life and Nature to the Egyptians.

Legends tells of an ill-fated union between Geb, the Earth God, and Nut. Their lovemaking, so it seems, was interrupted by Shu, the God of Air. This interference resulted in the sky and Earth being separated. Nut later gave birth to four gods who lived on Earth: Isis, Nepthys, Osiris, and Set, two females, two males.[5]

Osiris' celestial counterpart was the constellation Orion. Visible from every part of the Northern Hemisphere, Orion is one of the most recognizable of all the starry groups. The Dendara Zodiac, which will be discussed in detail later, depicts the constellation as the god "Horus in a boat surmounted by stars, followed by Sirius, shown as a cow, also in a boat."[6] The famous Pyramid Texts, the oldest known funerary literature of the ancient Egyptians, proclaim that the deceased king "would be reborn as a star and that his soul was believed to travel into the sky and become established in the starry world of Osiris-Orion, the god of the dead and of resurrection." (Bauval/Gilbert, pp.75-76)

It is generally assumed by the layperson that all the pyramids, including the Great Pyramid, were built as tombs for the pharaohs. There is in fact no evidence to support that claim. Bauval and Gilbert get directly to the point: "Why make this prodigious effort to house a dead body? Even given that the pharoahs were autocrats and were revered as living gods, this seems like a colossal waste of time and energy." (Bauval/Gilbert, p.2)

If not tombs for egomaniacal pharaohs, then what was the purpose of the pyramids? The answer is twofold: One, the Great Pyramid, and we have no reason to assume it was different with any others, was used for *initiations*. Two, since astronomical knowledge was an integral part of the ancient initiatory teachings, the pyramids were originally designed as *astronomical observatories*, and certainly in the case of the Great Pyramid were built to detect the true meridian. "In order to create a firm body of astronomical data, the ancients needed a true meridian on the solid earth from which to extrapolate a meridian across the heavenly vault, so as to detect the precise moment when stars, sun, planets and moon transited this meridian in the apparent motion through the heavens."[7] Surely, anyone who has done the least amount of research can no longer accept the assumption that the pyramids were built only as tombs!

That the ancient Egyptians possessed a star religion is clear. This is substantiated in writings ranging from the Pyramid Texts to the Book of the Dead to the findings of modern researchers. The king was believed to have come from the stars and returned to the sky to become a star again at the time of death. That was at the root of Egyptian stellar theology. He didn't become just any star, but one of the stars in Orion. Taking this information in hand and coupling it with his own trusted intuition, Robert Bauval was led to make a most startling discovery. (Bauval/Gilbert, pp.123-124) Looking carefully at the belt stars in Orion, he noticed that, contrary to a first glance, they are not in a straight diagonal line. The top star, the smallest of the three, is slightly offset to the east. Likewise, the smallest of the three pyramids on the Giza desert is offset on the desert floor! Coincidence? Accident? No! Deliberate? Of course! The pyramids were deliberately placed. Clearly, this tells us that the sky, this portion of it at least, was duplicated on Earth. As you will soon see, this practice of duplicating the sky on Earth may have been more common than realized previously.

Stars were important, but the ancient Egyptians also had an interest in the planets, which they thought of as "wandering" stars. (Krupp, pp.11-13) Venus, *Bennu*, was represented by a heronlike bird who symbolized the death and resurrection of Osiris. Mercury, *Sebeg*, was associated with Set. Mars was related to Horus and called The Shining Horus and Horus the Red, while Saturn, also associated with Horus, was called the Bull of Heaven, depicted as a falcon head adorned with horns. (Krupp, pp.69-70) Like knowledge of the stars, the planets and their importance in the affairs of human beings on Earth were known by the priesthood. There were most likely systems of both astrology and esoteric astronomy; a recent discovery seems to point in that direction. To investigate this, we must make a journey to Upper Egypt.

Dendara, the capital of the sixth nome of Upper Egypt, reached its most glorious phase at the end of the Old Kingdom (2575-2134 B.C.) and during the first Intermediate Period (2134-2040 B.C.). All these centuries later, a visitor to Dendara can still see remnants of the ancient city's most celebrated temple, dedicated to the goddess Isis in her guise as Hathor, Goddess of Fertility in women, wife of the Sun who ruled the western portion of the sky. Even though the temple is deteriorated, we can see enough to know that it was once elaborately decorated and very beautiful. Its most unusual features are the painted crypts, situated three stories high and set in the thickness of the outside wall. Also, in the wall, staircases lead to the roof where the ritual of Hathor's union with the Sun was performed.

On the roof, two shrines to the god Osiris were found. There were also two zodiacs, one rectangular in shape, the other circular. The circular one, now known as the Dendara Zodiac, occupied the ceiling of a structure built on the temple roof. It is a projection of the constellations visible from Dendara's latitude. The Pole Star of that time is located in the center. The signs of the zodiac, with a

couple of differences from the one with which we are most familiar, are arranged in the correct order within the eccentric circle. The
sign where the Pole Star is located is a jackal, which corresponds to
the Little Bear (Ursa Minor). The thigh of Taurus represents our
Great Bear, and a female hippopotamus represents Draco.[8] The
five known planets are depicted in their exalted positions in relation to the signs. While the true significance of either of the zodiacs is not known for certain, I may be able to shed some light on
that, at least in part.

Since the early 1970s I have had a special interest in ancient
Egypt, a fascination that has never waned. I feel a "connection" with
the land somehow, perhaps through a past life or lives. For many
years, I have noticed that, when I read or saw something about
Egypt, the same vision would pop into my mind: a vivid image of
a group of women. Always, the words "a holy order of women"
would come to me. I knew intuitively that these women once existed, and I knew they were special. I knew they were priestesses. I
also knew they had male counterparts, that they had belonged to a
priestcraft comprised of both men and women. Over the years,
although I read numerous references to the priesthood, nothing I
read or saw validated what I perceived about these women.

Then in 1987 I returned to Egypt a second time, a special journey with a group of about twenty spiritual seekers, most of whom
had been friends and students of my Spirit Teacher, Albion, and me
for a number of years. We had been preparing for months for what
Albion called our "spiritual pilgrimage." I gave each one personal
"assignments" to be done at particular times and places, assignments
designed to help some remember past lives, or to connect with the
land or a particular sacred site or monument, as well as special
places to go for meditation, prayer, and ceremony, both individually and as a group. Albion channeled a carefully orchestrated ceremony for us to do at the pyramids at the beginning of our journey.

From time to time along the way, usually in the evenings after
dinner, we came together as a group so that Albion could offer
information about the place we were in or going to, or perhaps
something that had to do with a past life of a member of the group.
More often than not, he wished to share something concerning the
spiritual tradition of ancient Egyptian society. These sessions were
always special, especially for me, because they gave me the rare

opportunity to work as the Teacher's "instrument" in the actual places he had spoken about so many times over the years. (I began my work with Albion in 1971.)

During one of these sessions we were given some information that piqued my interest considerably about that "holy order of women." We were docked in Aswan at the time. After dinner, the group gathered on the deck of the hotel ship to enjoy the balmy evening and watch the Sun set on the Nile. I felt Albion's presence within me very strongly, and knew he had something to tell us. The session was relatively brief, but the information made a profound impression on me when I listened to the tape later that night. (During sessions, I do not remember what is said and must listen to or read a transcript of the channeling afterward.) The following information represents the original text. I have taken the editorial liberty of changing his sentence structure in places in an effort to have the text flow more smoothly and to include subsequent information the Teacher has given since then.

THE STAR PRIESTESSES OF ANCIENT EGYPT

I, Albion, come into this vibration at this time and place so that we might share some thoughts with you; thoughts that concern a particular type of magic that was practiced in this part of Egypt, specifically at Dendara, and likewise at the pyramid complex in Giza, and at two other locations in other parts of the land where the ruins of no temple have yet been uncovered from the sands of time. (He later said that these two locations are near Memphis in Lower Egypt and in the Valley of the Kings across the river from Luxor.) *But before we proceed, we wish to make clear our thoughts regarding the terms "magic" and "magician." A magician is one who possesses esoteric knowledge that allows him or her to be in perfect harmony and synthesis with the divine Laws of Nature. Magic is the "enactment," physically, of that knowledge through ritual, invocation, incantation, and prayer. Magic can take many forms and has been practiced by priests and priestesses through time. But in the land of Egypt, during the time between the First and Seventh Dynastic periods, a form of magic that I, Albion, choose to call Starwalking was known and performed.* (This was the first time Albion ever used the term "Starwalking.") *We have chosen this term because it says precisely what we wish to imply. These magicians pos-*

sessed divine knowledge and magical skills that enabled them to walk among the stars!

Many ancient cultures held the natural power inherent within Earth sacred. Some of the terrestrial features . . . a great river, a great mountain . . . were considered to be holy places of great power. There came a time when humans evolved to a point when they were able to tap into Earth's sacred power, and in turn to use that power for varying useful purposes that included healing the human body and mind, prophecy, and divination. But in times long before, humanity focused not on the power of Earth but on the stars. Humans realized that the stars, the planets, and other celestial phenomena that occurred in the heavens were of far greater importance than what took place on Earth. They knew that Earth was but a small, albeit integral, part of a great celestial dance. So humans pursued a knowledge and understanding of that dance, and in doing so sought to determine their relationship with the heavens from their own vantage point in the cosmos, and ultimately with the whole of Creation. It was this pursuit that resulted, in part, in the evolution of a great body of stellar knowledge. Stars, comets, meteors, eclipses of the Sun and Moon, and the appearance of various things in the sky became humanity's roadmap toward a greater awareness and more in-depth understanding of the universe and their place in it.

Stars are distant. The earliest humans intuited this great distance and how it separated them from the stars. So they developed a knowledge and philosophy that concerned the nature of the celestial bodies and phenomena, and how they in turn influenced humans and Earth. It was the Spiritual Hierarchy that determined that humanity should have this knowledge. It was at Dendara (Upper Egypt) *and at a certain place in Lower Egypt that the stellar tradition came out of the realm of secret tradition into the realm of the written word and verbal communication. It was then that the "holy orders" of priests and priestesses evolved. These initiates were the "keepers" of this vast body of stellar wisdom, and it was they who practiced and taught it in the Mystery Schools.*

At this time we wish to tell you about a "holy order of women" who were prominent two times and at two places in Egypt. One of these was at what you would know as the Temple of Isis on the Isle of Philae, the other at Dendara. (The Teacher implied that these were not necessarily the only two places where this order of women

existed.) *Neither of these temples was exclusively female oriented,
nor were they built only for women's rites. But they were temples
where women were accepted into the priestcraft and where they were
specially trained in the knowledge of the stars. They were the feminine counterparts of a special order of what we shall call the Star
Priests. It is these Star Priestesses that we wish to tell you about now.*

*At selected temples there existed "schools" where the Star
Priestesses were trained and practiced their starcraft. Though numbers of young women were accepted into the training, not all grad-
uated, for the training was long and arduous. The actual number
who completed the course of study and who took their place within
the special Order was relatively small. The entire Order would rarely
number more than twelve in any place at any given time. Once a
graduate priestess became part of what we will call the Holy Order
of Nut* (the Sky Goddess), *she was a member for life. The only way
her seat would be vacated was through her death, or the rare occasion of expulsion.*

*Basically, there were seven stages of training, seven degrees or
levels of learning, neophytes went through in order to become a
member of the Holy Order of Nut. Upon entrance into the academy,
they were taught the basic skills of sky observation and simple visual and mathematical calculations regarding the Sun, Moon, and
stars. Much of what was learned in those early stages concerned the
rising and setting of the luminaries (Sun and Moon), the cycles of
the Moon, and precession (slow movement of the starscape due to
Earth's rotation on its axis, a cycle taking some twenty-six thousand
years to complete), matters that concerned the setting of the calendar, you see. This work constituted the First Degree. These were matters that could not simply be taught, they were also to be observed.
The woman were taught their way around the sky. They knew individual stars by name and where they were located, by season, in the
night sky. It was also during this degree that the neophytes became
scribes and were taught how to write in the sacred language.* (I
assume the Teacher was referring to hieroglyphics, although writings have been found that were not written in the familiar hiero-
glyphic form.)

*The Second Degree involved gaining in-depth knowledge of the
Sun, both physically and spiritually. The neophytes were taught
about the Sun God, Ra, and how to "communicate" with the spirit of*

Ra. They were also taught about the "freckles" on the Sun's body, about their appearance, their cycles, and how they should be interpreted for predicting the weather and other significant future events that concerned human affairs. (The term "freckles" refers to sun spots.) *They also learned during this degree about solar eclipses, how to predict them, and how they influenced humans.*

The Third Degree of study concerned the Moon. During this time, the priestesses learned more about the cycles of the Moon and how the lunar body influenced the cycles and tides on Earth. They were taught about the physical and sacred anatomy of the female body; about the sacred cycles that occur in a woman's body cycles of menstruation, ovulation, and menopause. They learned about conception and childbirth, and were trained as midwives. They learned about the Great Female, the feminine force in Nature, the great power of fertility. They learned about the Goddess Hathor; how to communicate with her and channel her energy. They learned about their own feminine power and how to use that power in magical practice. This was also when these young women learned about plants and herbs in terms of their medicinal use, and of the "mystery" involved in germination. They learned about healing. They also were taught a highly secret Full Moon ritual that was known only to this Order of priestesses. This ritual involved learning how to draw down the power of the Moon and store it, like a battery, in their bodies so that it might empower them and be put to use for various purposes that included healing, fertility, and prosperity. During this time they were taught how to work with the power of fertility in ways that could often restore a barren woman to fertility. Barren women were brought to the Star Priestesses for this "treatment."

The Fourth Degree had to do with the Nile Star, the star called Sothis *(Isis), the Goddess Star. During this time the neophytes were taught additional esoteric knowledge of the calendar. They were taught about the Spirit of the Nile and how to communicate with it. This spirit forecast the fertility of the land and the harvest. Neophytes learned the skills involved with what we would call "aquatherapy." This was also the time that the priestesses were taught how to read the Akashic Records by tuning into the Nile Star.* (The Nile Star is Sirius.)

The Fifth Degree had to do with comets. Comets were the cosmic "travelers" who brought "messages" from the Sky Gods to the people on Earth. The fledgling Star Priestesses were taught how to "read" comets and other celestial phenomena as omens. They learned about the esoteric life of comets as bringers of the "seeds of life" to the planet. Comets were considered a powerful "personal" omen too. When a young woman entered into the study to become a Star Priestess, the long process toward graduation could take many years. If during the first three years of her training, a comet was not seen, the neophyte was considered unclean in her heart and was put on probation for a time. If no comet appeared within an amount of time decided upon by the senior Star Priestesses who were already a part of the Holy Order, the neophyte would be dismissed from training. If, on the other hand, a comet did appear in the first three years of her training, the neophyte was considered to have special powers and her training was blessed indeed.

During the Sixth Degree of learning, the priestess trainees were taught about single stars and the constellations. They learned about the power inherent within certain stars, as well as that within numerous star groups. They were taught which stars were the "key stars" within each constellation, which stars could unlock the power of the entire constellation, if you will, and make that energy available to be drawn upon by the priests and priestesses. This study required the students to learn even more about the night sky, the names and locations of the major stars and star groups and, importantly, how to "intuit" the presence of various deep-sky objects such as nebulae and galaxies.

The final, Seventh, Degree was when the neophyte Star Priestesses were taught the ancient art of Starwalking. They learned how to travel into the heavens in order to draw energy from the stars and constellations. At the end of this study, when each priestess had demonstrated her learned skills, a special initiation was held to induct them into the Holy Order of Nut. This was a highly secretive ritual that took place in the Sun Temple in the Holy City and in the King's Chamber of the Great Pyramid. (I assume the "Holy City" Albion was referring to was Heliopolis.) *Further information about these things we cannot speak about at this time.*

Of course, I cannot prove that this information Albion gave about the existence and the training involved with the Star Priestesses is true. At the very least, however, if such a scenario could serve to unlock the age-old memories stored within the depths of the human psyche, then it would serve a useful purpose. One thing I *can* say for certain: The great temple at Dendara stirred feelings within me that the information Albion gave regarding the Egyptian Star Priestesses explained. Now that the Dendara zodiacs have been found, they will someday give us more information about the practices of these priestesses and priests.

As I have said, the Sun and Moon played important roles in the Egyptian star religion. Depicted in art as a winged disk, the Sun was the lord of the sky and was associated with several different gods and goddesses, including his mate, the Goddess Hathor. Each association reveals something about the nature of the Sun God and the qualities attributed to him. We can learn a lot about the Sun by investigating the history of the ancient city of Heliopolis, the City of the Sun. Also known as Annu, this metropolis was located on the opposite side of the Nile and twenty kilometers north of Memphis. Now a suburb of Cairo, Heliopolis was once the seat of a powerful priesthood who were the keepers of the star wisdom at the Temple of Ra. I personally view Heliopolis as the crown chakra of the country, the seat of the soul of the land and of the star religion.

A feature of the temple dedicated to Atum, the Complete One, is particularly interesting. It was there that a "Sacred Mound" once existed, the place where it was claimed that the first sunrise occurred, and where the Sun God first revealed himself in the form of a phoenix. An obelisk once stood atop the mound; at the apex was an object called the *pyramidion* or the Benben Stone. Credited with cosmic origins, it is believed that the enigmatic stone was actually a meteorite. (Bauval/Gilbert, pp.203-204) A star hill! (As you will soon learn, virtually *all* cultures, both ancient and contemporary, with access to that great body of esoteric knowledge and the shamanic skills that accompanied it, built mounds or made use of natural hills, tors, and even mountains in the landscape.)

The Benben Stone intrigued me, especially its reputation as a meteorite (as is the Ka'aba Stone at Mecca). You will recall that belief in the power inherent in meteorites also existed in some parts of North America, Greece, Syria, and other places worldwide. The ancient Egyptians believed that the deceased pharaoh not only became a star at the time of death, but that his bones became iron, the stuff that meteorites are made of! (Bauval/Gilbert, p.203)

The Heliopolis priesthood was indeed a "star cult." Their tasks were at least in part star-related. Mythological evidence of this (and myths are based in truth more often than not) tells about the *priestess* who was also the wife of the High Priest of Heliopolis. The story relates that there was a time when the Sun God, Ra, came down to Earth and seeded the wife of the High Priest. As myths often do, this one foretold a historical event in cosmic terms. (Bauval/Gilbert, p.156)

The importance of the Heliopolitan priesthood cannot be denied. I believe it represents a time and an esoteric "society" that possessed the *complete* body of stellar knowledge upon which their religion was founded. I believe Starwalkers resided within the ranks of the ancient order. I also think that the Egyptian Starwalkers had an intimate relationship with the Sun; they resided in the city positioned to mark the place where the Sun rises east of the Milky Way each day.

Two other cities near Heliopolis were Khem, later called Letopolis, which was associated with Horus, and Memphis, the capital. These three comprised a vast sacred site, a symbolic landscape that had its counterpart in the sky: the star Sirius, the constellation Orion, and the Hyades situated on the banks of the celestial river, the Milky Way. (Bauval/Gilbert, p.217)

Looking into the role the Milky Way has played in various star-oriented cultures is important. Before doing so however, let me digress at this point to share another channeling Albion gave two nights after the information regarding the Star Priestesses. This channeling concerned what the Teacher called an order of Star Priests. Since reading *The Orion Mystery*, this information has come to my mind many times, and it may be relevant to the Heliopolitan priesthood just discussed. The following channeling again has been edited to make the words flow more smoothly.

As we come forward into this vibration, we wish, first, to remind you of what we have told you about the Star Priestesses and the seven levels of learning they had to complete. Each of these steps concerned precise academic knowledge, as well as intuitive and magical knowledge about the stars, Moon, planets, and about the phenomena of the celestial realms such as eclipses, comets, and the rising and setting of the luminaries.

Now the time has come for us to speak to you about a unique order of priests: the Star Priests who comprised the High Holy Order of Osiris. There are several important points that we wish to make at this time about this Order. The first is that Osiris was the god upon which the Order was founded so to speak; the god that embodied, as all gods and goddesses do, specific natural forces of which these priests had knowledge and with which they worked their rituals and magic. The multifacets of Osiris that they knew are contained in myths, the most important of which is the Isis-Osirian Cycle that explains the natural rhythm of life and death. The Star Priests were also Sun Priests. They knew about the physical Sun AND the "spirit sun." They drew upon the power of the Sun for their personal physical and spiritual empowerment. There were very few places, three to be exact, in all of Egypt where the Star Priests had their temples, or what we would prefer to call their "colleges." One was at Karnak. (Karnak is in what is now the city of Luxor, the old Thebes.) *Another was at Saqqara, where they gathered at the great pyramid of Zoser. The third was at Thebes on the west bank of the Nile . . . the only one that was situated on the west bank. This temple was at a place that is still underground, hidden and buried by the sands of time and yet to be found. It is near the southeastern side of the Colossus of Memnon.*

The most important thing we wish to tell you about the Star Priests is, at that time, ONE STAR was the sacred star. To them, it was this star that contained the ultimate power needed by these powerful magicians, the star they often called the Spirit Star. This was Sirius, the Nile Star. The Star Priests knew this star intimately. They knew it as the Great Stargate that was guarded at all times by the god Anubis. Through the Sirius Stargate, the Star Priests gained entry into the Star Nation. They knew this as the celestial route, the route that gave them unfailing access to the stars and their power.

Furthermore, as you know, the star Thuban was the Pole Star when the Star Priests originated in the land of the pharaohs. Now the Pole Star has changed; it is Polaris. It is precisely this change (Pole Stars change due to Earth's "wobble," which is known as precession) *that makes it necessary and valuable for I, Albion, to bring forth at this time under the auspices of Polaris, knowledge of these elite priests. The changing of the Pole Stars, which is an on-going celestial transition, produces a great deal of power that influences your planet. The next Pole Star will be Vega in the constellation of Lyra. When Vega is the Pole Star again, the star religions will have been absolutely reborn and reinstated on Earth. This reinstatement process has already begun.*

When all the degrees involved with the training of a Star Priest had been successfully completed, each of them received a special name that aligned the individual priest with his birth or patron star. This would be a star that was prominent in the night sky at the time of the priest's birth. It was this "star name" that was his own personal secret word of power, the name by which he addressed the members of the Star Nation, if you will. The name was known only to the men who were the Priests of the High Holy Order of Osiris, and it was spoken only during sacred rituals and other events that involved magical practices. Upon graduation the Star Priests were inducted into the Order at one of the three locations mentioned earlier. We also wish you to know that a select few of the senior Star Priests possessed highly secretive knowledge that involved the star Algol (in the constellation Perseus). These were the priests who formed an elite "branch" of the High Holy Order of Osiris and who dwelled within the temple on the west bank of the Nile at Thebes. We cannot tell you much about their "work" at this time, only that they knew how to work with the destructive forces of Algol in order to destroy evil forces on Earth.

Again, there is no *proof* that this information represents a valid part of the Heliopolitan priesthood in ancient times. You must decide for yourself how the Teacher's words "feel," and make your judgment accordingly. Now let's return to our discussion of the Milky Way.

The Milky Way figures prominently in many of the sacred texts and in the minds of the keepers of the star religions, no matter where they existed. Though the rim or edge of the galaxy, which we see as a "bridge" of stars forming an archway in the night sky, has been called by many names and defined in many ways, its degree of importance was the same. To the early Egyptians it was a "river," the starry counterpart to their beloved Nile on Earth. (Bauval/Gilbert, pp.119-120) The Milky Way divides the sky; the Nile divides Egypt. The Milky Way served to link Earth with the sky, and in that way it provided a "bridge" for humans to travel into the sky *and* for the sky gods to come to Earth.

The two suns Albion spoke about in the Star Priests channeling were Vega and Algol. Vega was mentioned in reference to its destiny as the future Pole Star. Well, there was an *earlier* time when it was the Pole Star, from 12,000 to 11,000 B.C.! Called Ma'at by the ancient Egyptians, Vega was known as the Vulture Star, and was the orientation point of several temples, including some at Dendara. *Vega* will take the place of Polaris as the Pole Star in about 11,500 years. (Allen, p.286) We can see by this immense amount of time how slow the transition time for the change really is.

(I found the Teacher's remarks about the "power" that is generated by the on-going transition Earth makes from pole star to Pole Star time most interesting. Since Polaris is in that position now, it is important to know what power is inherent within this star. That gives us a clue as to the nature of the energy that has been, and is, influencing us and our planet at this time. Polaris' power is one of stability; it is an "anchor" that helps create steadiness when responded to positively. If it is responded to negatively, it brings about stubbornness, lack of commitment, and narrowness of mind and purpose.)

The other star was Algol, which Albion mentioned in the context of its power being used by the Star Priests to "destroy" evil influences. It is interesting to note that Algol, located in the constellation Perseus, has been called the Demon Star. Astrologers have said that it was the most unfortunate, violent, and dangerous star in the heavens . . . " (Allen, pp.332-333) This description certainly seems to fit with what Albion was saying.

Algol is a variable star, meaning that its output of energy varies. At 2.3 magnitude it is not a really bright star to begin with, but as it decreases, both visually and in its luminosity or power output, the star becomes even fainter. Surely the Star Priests working closely, perhaps even exclusively, with this star, would have known the variability cycle and would have worked with it accordingly.

Were these Ancients in touch with something that we have lost? Though we will never know for certain what was in the minds of the ancient peoples, the evidence seems clear. They lived in a harmony with their world and with the sky that we have devalued or lost completely.

Remember that the pyramids of the Egyptians served *two* important purposes: They were places for celestial observation and orientation AND sites for the performing of sacred religious rites. Science and religion were not separate as they are today. Possibly this separation caused human beings to lose whatever insights or powers that celestial observations and calculations taught our ancestors in the first place. What was observed and the accuracy of the calendar and the geometry that resulted from the observations must have been in some way a matter of both physical and spiritual survival. There is no more powerful motivator than the desire to exist . . . to live . . . and then to thrive. Ritual was and is the formal method by and through which the connection between the gods and humans, Heaven and Earth, was achieved and maintained.

Can we or should we even try to recapture the intuitive tools we have lost that are needed for a holistic view and relationship with the sky? I believe so. Of course we cannot turn back the clock; we cannot go back into time. Nor do we need to. We can learn, thanks to the archaeologists, astronomers, and present-day tribal Elders, what the ancient people knew about the heavens. We can piece together the clues that survive, and draw upon the precious few practices and the esoteric knowledge that still exist today. We can perform ceremonies of our own making in honor of the Sun, Moon, and Star Spirits. We can learn our way around the night sky through a study of basic astronomy. We can learn astrology and seek to apply its wisdom in a credible and useful way toward helping us understand ourselves and our lives. If for no other reason, this will enable us to understand ancient cultures better. Finally, we can see the value in beginning our journey back to the stars from where we came. The journey may be a rocky one. No doubt we will have to be wise enough along the way to distinguish mere superstition from genuine, productive ceremonial and magical practices that can give us our longed-for reconnection with the sky and the powers that reside there.

CHAPTER EIGHT

THE STARS
AND THE STONES

The stone rings are not mathematical exercises. They are patterns contrived to restate our sense that the universe has pattern. This is achieved by imposing symbolic and visual order on the space enclosed, and the order may be expressed in measurement, geometry, and astronomical alignment.[1]

E.C. Krupp

The wind still sweeps across the Salisbury Plain of England as it has for eons of time. This is land that possesses a secret that for centuries has perplexed, intrigued, and inspired human imagination like few places on Earth. Here stand the great weathered "Stones." Arranged by ancient human hands? A temple? The oldest astronomical observatory on our planet? Only the stones themselves know the answer to the puzzle that is Stonehenge. Only they can speak to the open mind of the seeker . . . and speak they do.

Every day people from all over the world trudge the landscapes of the British Isles, stirred by the mystery of silent circles that stand on the emerald hillsides and moors. Around Stonehenge itself, for miles in every direction there are heather, rape fields, and expanses of fertile farmland. Other megalithic sites are found nestled in bare peatbogs, silvery-green lichen, low-growing bilberry, and the tree groves that dot the land and shade the secrets it holds. Occasionally, the flicker of a butterfly and the swooping antics of the curlews and the call of inky-black ravens and blackbirds greet the visitor seeking answers to questions that have confounded scholar and layperson alike through the ages.

Sometime around 6000 B.C., societies began emerging in the British Isles, gradually evolving from hunter-gatherers into full-fledged farmers who relied on stone and flint to fashion their tools. As time went on these people became more sophisticated. They cleared large areas of woodlands to create their farms, built huge barrows within which to bury their dead, and learned the craft of metallurgy in copper and bronze from immigrants from the continent. It was during the period approximately 2500 to 1000 B.C. that the stone circles appeared and flourished, and that an intriguing class of priests and priestesses and the esoteric "laws" they lived by appeared on the scene. These were the Druids.

The building of Stonehenge has often been attributed to the Druids, but it is now known that the site predates them by as much as 2000 years. (Krupp, pp.214-221) Although the Druids did not build Stonehenge, they did take it over. Until the last two or three years, their present-day counterparts continued to use it annually for ceremony at dawn on the summer solstice. However, increasing concern for the sanctity of the monument has resulted in celebrants being blocked from performing rituals inside the great circle.

Stonehenge, sometimes called the Giant's Ring, has received more attention than the other 900-plus stone rings that exist throughout Great Britain. Since the nineteenth century it has been widely believed that the circles served an astronomical purpose. Early proponents of this hypothesis suggested that the Ancients would seek a suitable site and erect the circle, setting out its major axis toward a place on the horizon where the Sun or Moon, or a particular star crossed the skyline at a specific time on a specific day. Some of the circles seem to have shared similar axial alignments to mountain peaks, hills, or mounds, barrows, and rock cairns. An example is the so-called "heel" stone that stands some eighty-five feet outside the major circle at Stonehenge. It is over the heel stone that the Sun rises on the summer solstice. (Krupp, pp.214-216)

Evidence for the astronomical significance of stone circles existed mostly in the minds of theorists until the 1985 appearance of the controversial book *Stonehenge Decoded* by American astronomer Gerald Hawkins. His views created a stir in the scientific community worldwide that continues to this day. Maybe the book's title was partly responsible for the dispute, for it does smack of an "I have figured it out" sort of arrogance. But Hawkins' careful research, which led him to his conclusions, held water. It is now generally accepted that Stonehenge was indeed intended to be an astronomical observatory and a giant stone clock, used as such by its builders and the generations that followed.

The most notable orientations at Stonehenge are those involving the Sun and Moon. Geomancer John Michell tells us that "[A]s a symbolic model of the universe, [Stonehenge] contained all the numbers, shapes, and harmonies in the original blueprint of creation. Stonehenge is a synthesis of geometric types and proportions, an acknowledgement of all the gods in nature, designed to *attract* [italics mine] and harmonize the forces of the cosmos for the benefit of all life on earth."[2]

Astronomers and nonastronomers alike support the astronomical qualities evident at Stonehenge, but there are still questions around the time-worn legends that purport supernatural origins and ceremonial uses for the enigmatic ruin. In my experience, scientists tend to sidestep the issue of Stonehenge's ceremonial value, while those more interested in the ceremonial use and value tend to know little about its astronomical significance and worth.

One well-known myth centers around Merlin, the magician of Arthurian lore. The reigning monarch wanted to erect a monument to honor 460 noblemen slain by the Saxons. Merlin won the argument over what the architectural design would be. He went to Mount Killaraus in Ireland to the "Giant's Ring," or the "Dance of the Giants," with the intention of ripping off the sacred stones. They were so massive they could not be lifted or moved by ordinary means. With the greatest of ease, Merlin took down the stones and *levitated* them to their present site on the Salisbury Plain!

Built by magical means or not, it is a popular assumption that Stonehenge and other circles found throughout the British Isles were once used as places for pagan rituals. Archaeological evidence reveals the presence of "avenues" leading up to many of the sites, suggesting ceremonial processions moving into the inner sanctum where celebrants communicated with the gods and/or spirit forces they held sacred.

Ancient astronomical observatory or circular temple? The truth obviously rests in both theories. In support of the astronomical argument, it is doubtful that the celestial alignments are the result of mere chance or coincidence. Yet, consider the emotional and spiritual excitement, as I have, that surges through the mind and body when one experiences, even now, the awesome thrill of being within the mighty Stonehenge sentinels.

England is not the only place in western Europe where ancient monuments dot the landscape or where the land tells us the old stories. From Ireland to Scotland, from Spain to Brittany, intriguing structures began to pop up. But it is not the terrestrial features or the mind-staggering presence of the megalithic monuments that is of primary concern in this writing, as interesting as they are. Our questions are: What did the builders of megalithic sites along the coasts of western Europe know about the stars and how did that knowledge influence their lives?

We can begin to answer by looking in our immediate neighborhood in the sky. In *Journey To The Stones*, author Ian Cooke tells us that "[S]o many prehistoric sites have very definite associations with the sun and the moon, and so much of the basic pre-Christian symbolism which affected the shape and situation of these monuments was derived from them, that a brief description of the annual 'journeys' would seem to be justified."[3]

Well that is a very simple assignment. Twice during the year, at the equinoxes, the Sun's activity was of importance to different cultures all over the world. The winter solstice and the summer solstice, the 12 to 13 lunar months in a year and the 28.4 days from one Full Moon to the next were also significant. Also, given the need of ancient farmers for a reliable calendar, and because of their reverence for the luminaries as the embodiments of the male and female forces in Nature, it makes sense that they would align special structures to the Sun and Moon. But as we shall see, the Sun and Moon were not alone, for many sites, not all of them in Europe, were oriented to the stars.

Staying in Europe for the moment, let's take a close look at one of the best known of the megaliths in Ireland, the mysterious Newgrange. Built by an unknown people for reasons we can only guess at, this massive mound dates back to 3300 B.C. The monument has been studied and restudied by amateurs and experts, and some conclusions have been reached. One researcher, Claire O'Kelley, gives a graphic description: "Upon looking outwards towards the entrance, one sees the ball of the sun framed dramatically in the slit of the roof-box and one realizes that in the whole course of the year this brief spell is the only period when daylight has sway over the darkness of the tomb."[4]

This passage stands out for two reasons. It tells about a feature of the mound that is rare, though not unique in the world. And, the word "tomb" expresses the generally accepted theory concerning the reason the monument was built. I don't choose to debate the tomb theory here. But the fact that it was designed, with obvious deliberation, to frame the Sun at certain times of the year is of particular star-related interest.

Newgrange is very old. In some of the earliest writings that tell of the origin of Irish gods, the mound is connected with a *supernatural race of Sky Gods* who came to Earth. (We would do well to remember this theme, for it will be encountered time and time again.) Referred to as the "Lords of Light," this celestial cast was allegedly composed of magicians and wizards who were the earliest residents of Ireland.

Legends are not clear about whether these gods were the actual builders of Newgrange, or whether the mound was already there when they came. What is clear are its "otherworldly" qualities. In *The Stars and the Stones,* Martin Brennan describes Newgrange as an "otherworldly palace or festive hall, existing in a timeless realm of the supernatural and not as a place of human habitation. It is the domain of the gods, a place of perpetual festivities and a wonderful 'land' where no one ever dies."[5] Elsewhere, Brennan's descriptions of "three fruit trees which were always in fruit," "an inexhaustible cauldron from which no company went away unsatisfied," and "hazel trees whose nuts drop into its [Otherworld Well] waters . . . forming 'bubbles of mystic inspiration'," further attest to the magic of the mound. (Brennan, p.10)

Magicians and wizards aside, the most well-known of the Newgrange residents was Dagda, the Sun God. Dagda's connection with the Sun is a major clue to the astronomical significance of Newgrange and other surrounding sites. The Irish Celts divided the year into two six-month parts, *Samh*, summer and the light, and *Gamh*, winter and darkness. As in most pagan cultures, these times were celebrated as high holy days, and were marked by rituals and feasts in early May and early November. These, and other feast days that divide the year into quarters, correspond very closely to the solar alignments at various megalithic sites.

Other ritual and magical practices of the prehistoric Celts, such as the wearing of Sun rings for healing, attest to the significance placed on the Sun.

My personal knowledge of and experience with the Sun's energy has taught me a great deal about its ability to empower. Perhaps the Irish Celts built Newgrange as a "temple" to go to for just that purpose. It is also possible that its light in the darkness symbolized victory of life over death and/or good over evil, or even knowledge over ignorance.

Newgrange, as a tomb, has long been associated with the earliest kings of Tara who some believe were buried there, although there is no evidence to substantiate this claim. More interesting are the astronomical references to the Tara site, specifically the ruins of the Hall of Tara, which are in a north-south alignment with the mound and mark the position of the noonday Sun on the summer solstice. A legend tells of a primitive ruler who used the mound as a place to watch the stars to make sure that no hostile sky beings could descend upon his land without his knowledge. With its solar alignment and the reference to sky beings, it is clear that Newgrange has been linked with the stars since the remotest times. (Brennan, pp.10-17)

Brennan makes it clear that that connection included the planets as well. The early Irish recognized five planets, Mars, Mercury, Venus, Jupiter, and Saturn, and thought of the stardome as a sort of protective shell around Earth. Perhaps their astronomical knowledge came from old Welsh annals that tell of an astronomer, Gwydon-ap-Don, who is buried at the site. (Brennan, p.15)

In light of this evidence, all but the most orthodox astronomers and archaeologists accept astronomical alignments as part of the purpose and use of Ireland's megalithic mounds. There is current revival of interest in these astronomical connections and interpretations. Observations have shown that the Moon (like the Sun at Newgrange) illuminated the inner chambers of certain mounds, and that these places also most likely served both astronomical and ceremonial purposes.

From Ireland we return to England where, in the Winterbourne-Kennet valley near Avebury, stands Silbury Hill, unquestionably one of the most outstanding archaeological (and, I might add astronomical) mysteries on Earth. Built in the Early Bronze Age, Silbury is a round mound, 520 feet in diameter, surrounded by a ditch whose soil was used to construct the mound. Silbury was long acclaimed in folklore as the burial chamber of King Sil (or Zel), who was buried there on horseback and, curiously, who was turned to gold, giving rise to the rumor of the so-called Silbury Treasure.[6] Excavations have proved otherwise. No treasure. No king.

I have visited Silbury Hill many times. Each time I am struck by its imposing presence and size, as well as its strange shape. It has a flat top and a "terrace" that leads partway up to the summit. Since I first saw it I have felt that the terrace is the key to the mystery as to why Silbury was built.

Once, my husband and I were spending a few days in Avebury. At the time I was doing onsite research for a possible book on crop circles. The fields around Silbury are where most of the astounding circles have appeared. Late one night we drove to Silbury Hill. The mound was barely visible in the darkness. Sitting and staring into the night, I soon found myself slipping into an altered state. I began to feel the "presence" of the spirits of people long-deceased, and "saw" a village of thatched huts, in whose center stood the Silbury mound. My vision continued to reveal impressions of the people preparing for a sacred ritual . . . a Moon or Sun ritual, I wasn't sure. It ended with my "seeing" a procession of what I felt were "chiefs" slowly climbing to the summit of the flattened cone.

Since that night there has never been a doubt in my mind about why the mound was built or what it was used for. I *know* it was a ceremonial mound. (I later learned that there is evidence that the low levels of the terrace may have provided a view of the summer solstice sunrise, while the highest allowed viewers to see an encore performance.)

In any case, the builders of Silbury Hill and other megalithic monuments throughout Stone Age Britain placed great importance on the risings and settings of the Sun and Moon.

Let's turn our attention now to a subject that is every bit as interesting and no less puzzling than Newgrange and Silbury. Ancient astronomers the world over left evidence of their trade in the form of symbolic writing printed on and etched in the stones at megalithic sites, on the walls and ceilings of caves, on single standing stones, and on ordinary boulders and slabs of rock. Striking examples of this art are found throughout the world, most notably in Chaco Canyon in New Mexico and on the ancient stones and walls in Britain and Ireland. These designs are perhaps best defined as a form of symbolic writing, not unlike the Egyptian hieroglyphs.

Some of the crude images were produced by painting on the rock, others were painstakingly pecked out. Both types probably served a number of purposes, two of which deserve consideration here.

It is possible that the Ancients simply needed to record their celestial observations for timekeeping purposes, and that they desired to preserve the knowledge for posterity. The calendrical argument is supported when we consider that the symbols show evidence of numbers and counting, an indication that they are almost certainly connected with timekeeping. Timekeeping in turn, aside from its purely practical uses, was necessary for the proper scheduling of ceremonies.

It is my belief, however, that the etchings more likely represented the people's sacred views about the sky and their relationship with the sky. Of those carefully examined by archaeoastronomers, virtually all the megalithic sites were related to the Sun and Moon or some other celestial object(s). Solar, lunar, and other celestial images in fact dominated megalithic art, which in my mind explains much of its purpose. Whatever is true, the investment of time and energy required to produce the symbols suggest that they were too important to be brushed aside as mere meaningless doodles.

Aside from the abundant rock art of western Europe, wonderful specimens are also found in North America. Rock carvings and paintings done by Native southern Californians, the Chumash Indians, are among the most interesting. On the sandstone walls of caves and overhangs, we find countless multicolored images. Most of the symbols consist of simple geometrical patterns and a variety of animal and human figures produced in shades of red, white, and black mineral pigments.

The Chumash had a hierarchy of spirits that held tremendous influence over their lives. The most important of these lived in the sky world. (Hadingham, pp.110-123) John Peabody Harrington, an anthropologist and staff member of the Smithsonian, has done exhaustive studies of the Chumash and their shamanic practices. Harrington believes that the symbols were an integral part of ceremonial acts, and were drawn in honor of certain sky beings. He suggests that the very act of their creation activated supernatural powers! (Hadingham, p.119) Absolutely! When I read this I knew intuitively that he was absolutely right. If we accept this, if only for the sake of argument, it could easily apply to, and thus explain the reason for, such art found throughout the world.

Putting those symbols on those rocks was indeed a form of ritual. Based on my own ceremonial work, I can attest to the power invoked by the performance of ritual. Clearly the Ancients did more than observe the skies and choreograph sacred rituals in honor of the beings they believed inhabited the heavens. By the act of drawing the symbols, they *drew down* the power of Sky Spirits, stars, the Sun and Moon, and other sacred celestial powers and entities. The power they invoked was for purposes ranging from the shaman's journeys, which were highly spiritual in nature, to maintaining a superior position within the tribe, which involved politics, healing the physical body, and predicting the future.

When considering megalithic art, it is of primary importance to determine what the symbols depict astronomically. What celestial powers were the shamans drawing upon? The symbols most commonly seen are simple circles and crescents that look like the Sun and Moon. Frequently occurring wavy lines were probably counting symbols, and most likely marked the risings and settings of the Sun and Moon. Series of crescents and circles may have recorded solar and lunar calendrical computations. Some people have suggested that crescents with the horns pointed downward may represent the skydome in a fashion reminiscent of the goddess Nut in ancient Egyptian art. (Brennan, pp.137-180)

There is one particular symbol however—the quadrangle—that interests me most. In *The Stars and the Stones,* Brennan pointed out something that really caught my attention, so I have chosen to put the entire passage in italics. *"The quadrangle appears very early in prehistoric art and could have originated as a sky symbol when the celestial pole was near the rectangular formation of stars in the con-*

stellation Draco. The pole is always the center around which the stars appear to revolve, regardless of the slow shift in its position as a result of the wobble of the earth's polar axis." (Brennan, p.186) Draco has a quadrangle in its design. I think Brennan has hit on something very significant here. And Draco is a constellation to which one shaft in the Great Pyramid is oriented.

Draco is not the only constellation with a quadrangle. Consider the Big Dipper (Ursa Major), which has been important to virtually every culture who had any astronomy at all, the Little Dipper (Ursa Minor), the Great Square in Pegasus, and of course the Pleiades. A giant square is formed by the four outer stars of the constellation Orion, and we know the importance of that star group in the ancient Egyptian star religion. Point made!

Were the ancient peoples who drew those quadrangles drawing down the power inherent within these constellations, particularly Draco, which contains Thuban, at that time the all-important North Star? There are in fact similarities in all rock art no matter where it is found. Wavy lines, crescents, starlike symbols, hands, and various stick figures, for example, are common. This really excites me, to say the least, for it not only proves—after all, how much proof does one need—that the Ancients had a relationship with the stars, it tells us *what* stars!

While on the subject of rock art, I would like to share a personal experience and the insight that came from it. Shortly after moving to western North Carolina in 1991, I was doing research for my book, *The Spiritual Reawakening of the Great Smoky Mountains.* The indigenous people of the area, the Cherokee Indians, have a lot of legends, some involving people living here long ago. When the Cherokee came to the area over a thousand years ago, they called these the "moon-eyed" people, and described them as a tiny albino-like race who had big moon-like eyes. The Cherokee expelled the "mooneyes" and took over their land.

Although who they were is unknown, traces of the "mooneyes" remain. Most notable is a giant soapstone boulder called Judaculla Rock, unique in that it has been etched with strange images. The rock was named by the Cherokee who have long associated it with the mythical slant-eyed giant, Judaculla. They say he was a "magician," a shapeshifter who possessed that and other magical powers.

The legend tells how Judaculla made the "scratches" on the rock when he jumped down on it from a ridge above. The important point is that the Cherokee do not lay claim to having made the "scratches," but do consider the boulder important enough to have sought to explain it. We can speculate that the "moon-eyed" people were the authors of the mystifying images.

The first time I visited Judaculla Rock I was immediately struck by its size. It suddenly dawned on me that I was seeing only the tip of what is surely an enormous stone, the bulk of which is underground. I wondered if the tip was all that had ever been visible. And if there is more rock underneath, if it is inscribed like the tip. To date, I know of no excavations that might answer that or any other question related to the giant rock. As I stood before the rock I found myself confronted with much more than weird markings, (fairly consistent with others I had seen at Hopi and in eastern Washington state, as well as those in Ireland and England). Because of the rock's shape, I felt like I was looking at a huge open book, a ledger upon whose pages was written a story.

Going with the idea that it was indeed a book, I let my imagination go free in hopes that the book would tell me its story, whatever it might be. Soon I was "reading" about the origin of a people, a story of a place, somewhere, told in signs and symbols that, though foreign to me, were somehow strangely familiar. The compelling figures stirred a deep, unconscious part of me. *It was then*

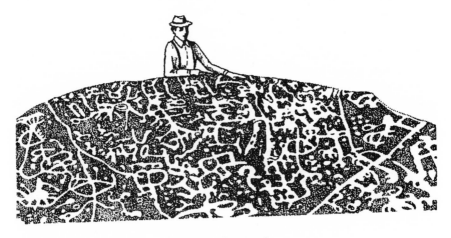

Judaculla Rock

that I knew I was viewing a map and that it was not one of any place on Earth. I was looking at a star map. This was a diagram of a part of the heavens! I knew it with an intuitive "knowing" that rose from the deepest part of me . . . from my soul. My vision left me with a profound sense of "certainty."

My conscious self then took charge of what I had felt, and I began to search the rock for any familiar symbols or patterns. I looked for wavy and straight lines, circles, arcs, possible Sun, Moon, and star designs, and figures that might bear resemblance to any constellations. I became increasingly curious about the straight lines, some of which were quite long and seemed to connect some of the symbols together. I also noticed what looked like the imprint of a human hand, an image I had seen on Hopi petroglyphs. I saw circles, some of which had "rays" coming out from them.

And, curiously, *all over* the rock's surface were deep, round "holes" or depressions that looked like someone had bored into the stone. Stars? An artist who got creative with circles? A map to point out, as a reminder for future generations, a planet or a star system from which the ancient carvers had come? It is not uncommon for

Petroglyphs

Native Americans to say they came from the stars! The story told by Judaculla Rock is a mystery, but there is no doubt that it tells a story of a people. To me, the rock tells about Sky Country and the stars.

So many circles in petroglyphs appear to represent the Sun. Because so many concentric circles are seen, they may have been meant to convey a "model" of the universe as a system of concentric layers or skins, like an onion. There are also often zig-zags, which may, like the wavy lines, be indicative of the risings and settings of the luminaries. Spirals are common to all rock art, as are the endless dots, diamonds, half circles, and straight lines. We can choose to rely on our intuition to determine what these symbols mean, what they imply about the ancient carvers and painters and what they may have known about the heavens.

Stars are also a common symbol found on rock canvasses worldwide. Most are simple designs made by intersecting lines. Their meaning is obvious. They appear so frequently that if they were the only symbols linking stone artists with the sky, they would do so conclusively. Single stones and slabs of rock are not the only

Petroglyphs

places where petroglpyhs have been discovered. They are on cave walls too, such as the famous Lascaux Cave in France. Another, the so-called *planetaria,* found on cave ceilings in the American Southwest will be discussed at length in the chapter on Native American star lore.

But, aside from figures and symbols carved and painted on rocks and caves, some of the most astounding prehistoric artworks are the massive figures that someone drew on Earth itself. On the coast of Peru, some 250 miles southeast of Lima, long lines are drawn on the ground, creating a colossal network of geometrical designs that have confounded archaeologists and other experts for years. Etched into a sublayer of the desert landscape, the patterns of the Nazca lines can only be detected from the air, giving rise to the speculation that they were drawn for or even by extraterrestrials who used them as landing strips for their spacecraft!

Careful mapping and research have revealed that of the 186 "directions" indicated by the lines, only 16 can be reasoned to be calculated alignments. Predictably, two involve the summer and winter solstices. (Hadingham, pp.173-175) Because the number is small, astronomers tend to chalk the few alignment lines up to coincidence. But can they be so easily dismissed? The Nazca markings portray giant images of animals, birds, spiders, a human, and a candelabra-type figure, all drawn on the yellow-sanded desert floor that is one of the oldest geological landscapes on Earth.

That human beings made the Nazca markings is relatively clear. But why did they do it? Did they trace out some unique terrestrial ley system? What value could the lines have possessed? What power could they have triggered or "drawn down" to the planet? What ritual was performed to "trigger" their power?

There are no obvious answers to these questions, but there are some clues. One is the climate. In every desert culture the major ceremonies have to do with rain. Assume for a moment that the giant figures were placed on the ground so they could be seen by the Sky Gods who would be appeased by or attracted to them. Then we could assume that the effigies were offered as "gifts" to the gods in return for sending life-giving rains to Earth.

Think about it. If this theory is correct, then the lines and figures were a sort of "insurance policy" that had to do with survival.

And it must have been the gods the people set out to signal since the full figures could be seen only from the air! In any case, to dismiss the effigies as a result of pure chance or from some human need to demonstrate artistic prowess is ridiculous. When we consider just one of the figures, the giant spider, it becomes even more unlikely that the lines and figures were without significant meaning.

In a PBS documentary, I learned that surveys to determine any possible alignments have shown that when one stands at the edge of the quadrangle, the constellation of Orion is perfectly framed in the spider. There's the quadrangle again! And Orion too! What's more, a line superimposed over the same figure pointed, in 350 B.C., directly to the star Rigel in that constellation. Now if that isn't convincing enough, additional Rigel alignment lines allowing for Earth's wobble, were deliberately drawn up to five hundred years after the first! Coincidence? You be the judge (but you may want to reserve final judgment until you learn the significance of the spider to other Native Americans, as presented later).

In that same documentary, I learned of another Nazca figure, the one called Owl Man, a male with one arm pointing to the sky and the other to Earth. I was immediately struck by the similarity between this image and the Magician card in the Tarot, which represents the age-old metaphysical adage, "as above, so below." I recalled how numerous cultures, both ancient and some not so ancient, believed that what occurs in the heavens is reflected in earthly events. Also, bird images appear at many prehistoric sites. Birds in general are considered by many Native Americans to be "messengers" from the spirits and, in some cases, the manifestation of the spirit itself. The owl, specifically, has long been heralded as the bird of wisdom.

The Nazca lines do indeed challenge us, both intellectually and intuitively, as to their true meanings. But I for one think that Maria Reiche, the primary researcher into what those meanings may have been, hit the nail on the head when she defined the Nazca lines as "the largest astronomy book in the world"! (Hadingham, p.174)

While on the subject of birds, I would like to propose a theory about their connection to Starwalking. The Nazca culture was known to use a type of peyote cactus whose tubular body, when sliced across, is shaped like a star. We know that the cactus was revered by the people of the Nazca Plains as its image is a recurring motif on pottery and other objects used in daily and ceremonial life. Its use gave a person the sensation of flying.

Were there Starwalkers among the Nazca shamans? If so, did they use peyote to "fly" into the sky where they were empowered with stellar energy, which they brought back to be used for both practical and sacred purposes? Since this kind of ritual is still done by Native Americans today, it seems likely that this was the case. So, does the presence of the bird motif identify the cultures who had Starwalkers among them? Again, I think so.

Let's turn our attention to Native Americans, their sacred sites, and the astronomy they reveal. We have seen that various monuments and sites worldwide contain numerous possible stellar and celestial alignments. This becomes even more clear when we realize that there are forty-six possible alignments for the Sun and Moon alone, all of which have remained unchanged since prehistoric times. These include the risings and settings of the solstice and equinox Sun and Moon.

But stars are different. We see an example of that difference in the Big Horn Medicine Wheel in north-central Wyoming. Some ninety feet in diameter, the wheel consists of a hollow central cairn from which radiate twenty-eight "spokes" terminating in a crude circle. Around the periphery are six smaller cairns, one of which is at the end of an extended spoke located outside the main orb.[7] Most astronomers seem to agree that the Wheel was built to serve as a calendar. (I will not dispute that conclusion. But I have been around enough Native people from various tribes to know that a medicine wheel would also have been a place for ceremony.)

In its service as a calendar the Big Horn Wheel marks the summer solstice Sun and certain stars that appear in the midsummer dawn: Aldebaran, Rigel, and Sirius.[8] This has been confirmed by astronomers. John Eddy, noted solar physicist and archaeoastronomer, pointed out that the twenty-eight spokes may have had some significance in that they represent the twenty-eight days in the lunar cycle. (Peterson, p.100) I also know that twenty-eight is an important number to the Plains peoples because the all-important buffalo has that number of ribs.

You will note immediately that these three stars have been mentioned as being of particular importance to the ancient Egyptians,

Babylonians, and the earliest Irish Celts. Now let's think about something here. These are three of the brightest stars seen from the Big Horn Mountains (and everywhere else in North America for that matter). More importantly, they were the only really bright stars that rose at dawn in the few months of the year when the Wheel was not accessible due to heavy snow. Were these stellar alignments for the purpose of "drawing down" or "receiving" energy from these stars?

It is also rather curious that the Big Horn Wheel was important to and most likely used by several tribes. Shoshone legends, for example, told of the construction of the medicine wheel by a race of "little people!" According to John Eddy, remains of a race of "tiny men" were found in that area of Wyoming and studied at Harvard, the American Museum of Natural History, and the Boston Museum. They were determined to be those of a full-grown, fourteen-inch-high, humanlike anthropoid! (Peterson, p.101) The legend reminded me of the "moon-eyed" people the Cherokee told about, also supposed to be very small. If a small race of people once lived in North America and other parts of the world, and they apparently did, how much more prehistory are we unaware of? I suspect the answer is: *a lot!*

Another medicine wheel, Moose Mountain in Saskatchewan, Canada, is similar in some ways to the Big Horn. And, the three stars to which Big Horn is aligned may the same as those aligned at Moose Mountain. All factors considered however, there are only five stars visible from Canada that are first magnitude (the brightest), and one of them is Capella. (Aveni, p.167) Capella is believed to have marked near north at Moose Mountain and, according to Aveni, who is an expert on Native American astronomy, it is aligned to two cairns at Moose Mountain, and maybe one at Big Horn as well. (Aveni, p.166) Aveni reports that surveys of twenty medicine wheel sites in the U.S. and Canada have shown specific alignments on the rising places of Sirius, Rigel, Betelgeuse, and Aldebaran. Aldebaran, he says, "seemed to be the most practical star marked at the Big Horn wheel, since during the late prehistoric and early historic periods it rose heliacally at summer solstice at the site." (Aveni, p.165) So why did the prehistoric Indians on our continent align their sacred calendric-ceremonial wheels to certain stars? Logically, they must have known the "power" inherent within those stars.

Remember John Michell's comment about Stonehenge being . . . "designed to attract and harmonize the forces of the cosmos . . ."? This is a revealing statement. It seems to suggest, and I believe correctly so, that sacred monuments, most especially those that were astronomically aligned, were built to serve as synthesizers of a terrestrial and celestial energy. Although I do not know the precise scientific knowledge or language to explain the working of such mechanisms, I feel that they may represent highly technological "instruments" that were triggered into operation by the specific heavenly bodies to which they were aligned, sort of like an alarm clock that goes off at the precise time it has been set to do so. These moments when the "activation" occurred would have conceivably resulted in the medicine wheel, mound, pyramid, or whatever to act as a generator or receiver—or both—of cosmic power. During these times, could the stargates have opened? Perhaps so. And there might have been other energies generated and/or received, energies not yet realized. I don't know. It is a theory worthy of consideration.

Finally, let's go to the Andes Mountains and take a look at one of the most celebrated sacred sites in the world, which gives us tremendous evidence that its builders were not only skywatchers par excellence, but Starwalkers too. Machu Picchu, part of the "Lost City" of the Inca, perches high atop a terraced rocky point. While the entire Machu Picchu complex is special, since it is undisturbed, a part of it called the Torreon is of particular interest. Krupp says that what appears to be an "altar" was cut and carved from the natural rock, and then enclosed by a semicircular wall, giving it the appearance of a ceremonial Sun temple. (Krupp, p.49) It may in fact have been a ceremonial temple.

Many of the standing stones in Peru, called gnomons, were damaged or destroyed. Spanish political authorities sought to do away with their religious significance. Gnomons are believed to have been used for measuring the Sun's shadow to determine the length of the year. Fortunately, the gnomon at Machu Picchu was found intact, but what it was really used for is not known.

Among the stars of importance to the Peruvians were the Pleiades and the tail in the constellation Scorpio, star groups located in opposite parts of the sky. On the Southern Hemisphere winter solstice in June, the Pleiades would have been framed in what is called the "solstice window." There are also other "windows" to be considered. In the southeastern window, the stars in the tail of Scorpio would be rising as the solstice Sun set. (Krupp, p.48) The details of Machu Picchu's Torreon are extremely complex, of course, but from the basics we get a clear notion that the Sun, the Pleiades, and some of the stars in Scorpio, at least, were of importance.

Furthermore, the physical site itself is not only sacred ground, it is *high ground*. This would have provided the ancient Peruvian sky shamans, the Starwalkers, with easy access to the heavens and afforded them a closer connection, literally, with the Sky Gods. I think of Machu Picchu as a "star temple" built to "receive" stellar energy from Scorpio and the Pleiades and the Sun at times when the sky door was open for the priests to draw down their specific power.

There are so many megalithic mysteries, so many stone circles and magnificent temple ruins to intrigue and baffle us. We tend to probe only with our intellect, asking why so many of the ancient cultures constructed such monumental structures. The ancestral peoples were not reluctant to use their intuition. Intuition was in fact their mental ally. They were keenly aware of the natural forces surrounding them, and they knew they were dependent upon those forces for survival. They sought to communicate with and to appease the forces. They made every effort to exist in harmony with both terrestrial and celestial elements in Nature.

We have clear evidence that our ancestors were endowed with profound spiritual awareness, which gave them sensitivity to inner personal and collective experiences of a transpersonal nature. Ultimately they were able to unite with those subtle energies that influenced them and their lives. Shamans, priests, and priestesses would have experienced a subjective reality that was denied the common folk (and is certainly denied to most of us today). The spiritual leaders made the will of the Creator known to the people and in doing so provided a valuable and incomparable service that was consistent the world over. The architects of Stonehenge, Newgrange, Machu Picchu, the Nazca effigies, Big Horn Medicine Wheel, and other megalithic sites knew something that we have either forgotten or chosen to ignore. Their worship and acknowledgment of cosmological and celestial influences such as stars, thunder, lightning, and wind, drew them into conscious contact with the same Nature that today we are mostly unconscious of.

One thing is certain: Wherever the stone circles, wheels, gnomons, and rock art are found, their builders placed great stock in the stars. What they had, we have lost. What, specifically, that loss constitutes for us, both individually and collectively, is one of the most important questions posed in this book.

CHAPTER NINE

SKIDI PAWNEE: STAR CULT OF THE GREAT PLAINS

To the Stars did Tirawa give powers to watch over the people.
If the people were evil, the Stars might send storms to destroy
them. But Tirawa himself is ever without anger. He is feared
by none. Tirawa is changeless.[1]

Saku:ru Ta'

Not all Native American astronomers were part of some unknown or prehistoric tribe. Quite the contrary. Among the most skilled skywatchers were the Skidi Pawnee, who once lived on the prairies of what are now Kansas and Nebraska. Though the Skidi no longer exist, artifacts, photographs, and a few reports and books written by anthropologists and researchers chronicle the cosmology and lifestyle of these exceptional and unique people.

From the moment I first learned of their existence and their remarkable relationship with the stars, I have sought out every possible bit of information about the Skidi Pawnee. No one knows where they came from, though it is generally thought that they migrated north from Mexico. They weren't like any of their neighbors, which included the Sioux, Omaha, Oto, Arapaho, and Cheyenne. In fact they were different from their contemporaries within the Pawnee Nation (the Skidi constituted one of the four South Bands).

It wasn't where they lived or being a South Band people that set them apart, however. It was their relationship with the stars. And it was that relationship that led solar physicist and archaeoastronomer John Eddy to make the following comment: "It is fair to say that the Pawnee were obsessed with the sky . . . particularly these of the Skidi band, who were, in a sense, the astronomers of the tribe."[2]

To the Skidi the sky was where they had come from and where they would someday return. They spent a great deal of time observing the Sun, the stars, and what went on in the day and night skies. What they saw formed the foundation of their religion and religious practices. They placed tremendous spiritual value, for example, on the Milky Way which they called the Spirit Path or "the Pathway of Departed Spirits."[3] They valued comets, meteors and meteorites, the Morning Star and the Evening Star, and the planets. They timed their lives by a celestial calendar, and arranged their twelve villages (the Federation) and individual homes in astronomical patterns that corresponded to what they saw overhead. In every way they were tied to the stars. While most American Indians call Earth "Mother" and the sky "Father," the Skidi went a step further by acknowledging the sky as "parent." Indeed, it was from the sky they and Earth had come, born of the stars. That made them unique among Indian peoples.[4]

Like all tribal people the Skidi possessed a large body of myths, the vast majority about the stars. In fact their creation myth reads like something right out of an astronomy textbook! The following capsule version is from anthropologist Gene Weltfish's *The Lost Universe: Pawnee Life and Culture*.[5] We owe a great debt of gratitude to Weltfish as it was she who pioneered much of the research,

Pawnee Star Symbol

and who did a great deal of the translating of James R. Murie's work, which was received first hand from the Skidi.

The universe that Heaven created was chaotic, so he decided to send out his thoughts to create celestial gods who would bring his thoughts into being. He made gods for each direction: the Evening Star for the west, with the Moon as her helper; the Morning Star for the east, with the Sun as his helper; the North Star for the north; and the star Canopus in the south. Heaven then placed four stars in the semi-cardinal directions: Black Star in the northwest; Yellow Star in the northeast to hold up the heavens for as long as the heavens last; White Star in the southwest; and Red Star in the southeast. To these stars Heaven gave numerous special powers, one of which was to create people. He told the stars to give the people the *sacred bundles.*

Then Heaven spoke to Evening Star, and gave her lightning, winds, clouds, and thunders. These would assume human bodies and appear as priests with gourd rattles in their right hands. This done, Heaven was ready to create the world. Storms carried out this command. One great thunderstorm created the lifeless form, the other gave it life. All this took a long time.

After five stages of creation, Heaven assigned the stars the task of creating human beings in their own image. But when Morning Star called all the stars into council, a conflict broke out between him and Evening Star. The only way to settle the conflict and bring light and life into the world was for Morning Star to conquer and mate with Evening Star. Alas, Evening Star did not make his task easy. To ward him off she placed animals in the semi-cardinal directions: wolf in the southeast had the power of the clouds; wildcat in the southwest with the power of the winds; mountain lion in the northwest with the power of the lightning; and bear in the northeast with the power of the thunder. To make matters worse, Evening Star equipped her vagina with sharp teeth. But Morning Star was smart! He broke the teeth with a meteor stone. Finally the mating occurred and from the union a girl was born—the first human being. She stood on a cloud and was carried to Earth by a funnel-shaped whirl-wind. Then the Sun and Moon mated and created a boy who also was carried to Earth.

Two more councils were held to make plans for the humans. At the second, Heaven told Evening Star to call her four priests to rattle and sing so that it would rain on the two earthly children. As the priests rattled and sang the lightning flashed and the thunder roared, and it rained. Then the girl was taught about the fruitfulness of Earth, how to build an earth lodge, how to talk, and all about the land. The boy was taught how to travel the world, how to hunt and fight, and how to procreate. The people then began to increase.

Although the entire myth is much more detailed, this abridged version provides us with a basic understanding about the intimate role stars played in the religious, spiritual, and physical aspects of Skidi life. Other Skidi myths concerned whatever was seen in the sky over long periods of time, their explanation for it, and how it influenced what they thought, how they felt, and who they were. The myths also embodied a great body of astronomical knowledge, which was passed on orally to the younger generations.

As is often the case when a culture vanishes, their myths vanished with them. We are left with often puzzling remnants that we can only attempt to piece together and try to interpret with some accuracy. Such is the work of anthropologists, historians, cultural archaeologists, and archaeoastronomers. Little or no room is provided for intuitives like myself to offer any credible interpretations of what remains of these peoples and their prehistoric counterparts worldwide. Even less room exists for intuitive attempts at filling in the gaps in knowledge and history. In time that may change. But for now many of the conclusions drawn in this writing are considered outside the realm of credibility.

I believe that wherever possible the first step toward understanding tribal peoples is coming to know about and evaluating their sacred rites. When we look at the Skidi from this perspective, we find that their ceremonial year began when the first thunder, the Voice of Heaven, was heard in the spring. The position of the stars was important in determining the timing of rituals. Stars were watched from dwellings called earth lodges, through the smokehole and the entranceway that opened to the east. Particular stars sighted were two small ones known as the "Swimming Ducks," in the northeastern sky near the Milky Way, and the Pleiades. When all the signs were in place, and the thunders had been heard, it was time to perform the Creation Rite.[6]

The first ceremonial act was to awaken Earth from the sleep of winter. During this ritual the twelve sacred bundles were opened, one for each of the villages that comprised the Federation. The same ceremony was done with each of the bundles so that the power inherent within them would be recharged. (More about the bundles later.) We can determine by these spring rites that the Skidi understood the cycles of Nature and that they took nothing for granted: The ceremony involved praying life back into Earth and all that lives.

The ceremonial year lasted from spring to autumn, and each ceremony was held at times heralded and/or fixed by specific natural, usually celestial, phenomena. As expected, the basis for the ceremonies was survival: hunting, planting, and harvest.[7] In addition to the major ones there were three special rites that were performed on an irregular basis, occurring only when it was deemed appropriate.

The New Fire Ceremony was a solar-oriented rite that petitioned the Sun to replenish life on Earth. The Chief's Ceremony had to do with the North Star, but details about its meaning are lost. The Morning Star Ceremony was done to reward the Great Star for fathering human beings.[8] The ceremonial year ended when the animals went into hibernation and the birds had flown south in October.

The Pawnee were buffalo hunters so they were nomadic during hunting season. Since their earth lodges weren't mobile and tipis were, the tipi was their dwelling as they moved about the vast plains. The earth lodge was a remarkable circular, dome-roofed structure somewhat reminiscent of the Navajo hogan. The roof was supported on the inside by four logs. Though the lodge was an earthly dwelling, it in fact had everything to do with the stars. Its entryway, built of eight poles and opened to the east, provided a view of the first light of the rising Sun. The lodge's features that symbolized heavenly powers began with the circular floor, representing Earth. The domed roof was the sky. The four posts that supported the roof symbolized the bodies the Skidi called the Four World Quarter Stars, which were central to Skidi stellar theology. An opening in the roof served to let smoke out, but was also a means by which the night sky could be observed, making the earth lodge a true observatory. It also let the stellar power stream in freely.

There was an altar in the west meant to coincide with the position of the Evening Star and the original circle of the gods in the sky. One of the sky gods, Paruksti, the Wonderful Being, gave the blueprint of the earth lodge to the people. (Chamberlain, pp.45,155-162,178-183)

Let me digress for a moment. It is well-documented that indigenous peoples had a close relationship with Earth, and that they and the planet benefited from that connection. The Pawnee earth lodge embodies a special dimension of that relationship by extending the relationship to the heavens. It was and is not uncommon for ancient and tribal peoples to view the sky as "home." The power inherent within the stars was, as a rule, tapped through rituals designed to reenact the drama of Creation and to connect the people with these powers. The earth lodge facilitated this link in a more personal and intimate way, one that influenced daily life, including the affairs that occurred within the home itself. Living in an earth lodge was to live in a duplicate of the heavens on Earth. This brought the stars down to Earth in a way that is reminiscent of "sympathetic magic," which is a reenactment or, in this case a duplication, of the state of place desired.

Skidi ceremonies and dwellings clearly reflected the special relationship the people had with the sky. But this only scratches the surface of Skidi star lore. They are the only people I have heard of who actually believed that the stars came down to Earth and became human beings. And it was a two-way passage. Chamberlain says: "The Skidi believed that the stars were either gods or people who had lived on earth and had been changed into stars at death." (Chamberlain, p.21) Like the ancient Egyptians, the Skidi had some definite views about death. They believed, for example, that when a person died the soul began a journey across the Milky Way, the ghostly star bridge that linked Earth and the sky, a belief common among Indian peoples. The soul was first received by a star in the north who sent it on the final leg of its journey. The journey ended when the soul reached the South Star, the Skidi "death star," which watched over and guarded the Spirit World. As to which star the South or Death Star was, the only real clue is that it "is not always seen," and " . . . at a certain time in the summer, just at dusk, it rises like fire for a moment, and then disappears." (Chamberlain, p.117) A number of stars are good candidates, but the great star Canopus seems most probable. It is the second brightest star in the sky, and surely ancestral cultures would have paid more attention to and placed greater stock in the brighter stars. Also, Canopus is seldom seen; and, Skidi chronicler James Murie said, "The South Star appears about 1 September and marks the beginning of the winter period." (Chamberlain, p.113)

Whatever the Death Star was, the Skidi view of death itself provides us with insight into what they thought about the deeper mysteries of life. "At death, the soul goes off the way a cloud comes up and disappears, or the way a wind blows up and dies down. The souls of people who have been seen by the Star of Disease and who have as a result died of illness are taken by the South Star to his home in the south. The disposition of all other souls is determined by the Morning Star, who decides whether they shall be restored to life, taken with him to the east, or sent to the south. And it is the Morning Star's importance in this matter that caused the Skidi to bury their dead with the head toward the east." (Chamberlain, pp.91-92)

While the above information sheds some light on the Skidi's view of death, it also raises some interesting questions. The first concerns the "Star of Disease," which astronomers think was probably the planet Saturn. (Chamberlain, pp.91-92) Since the ancestral peoples made no distinction between stars and planets, all would likely have been called stars. Another curious point is that it is clear that the deceased might be sent one of several places after dying. The "whether they shall be restored to life" passage strongly suggests that the Skidi believed in reincarnation. Becoming part of the Morning Star was a possibility, as was simply going into the spirit world in the south. What role the soul would play as a part of the Morning Star is a curious question to which I have no answer, nor have I encountered any answer in my studies and research. In any case the information regarding the soul's journey across the Spirit Bridge was apparently known only to the priests because the common people knew the Milky Way only as the dust of the Buffalo Spirit. (Chamberlain, p.21) So a priestcraft did indeed exist, and that is a matter worthy of pursuit here.

Several passages in *When Stars Came Down To Earth* offer
information about both the existence and function of the priests.
"The governing body of the Skidi was its society of chiefs, but the
highest [italics mine] authority rested with the priests, who acted as
mediators between the deities and the people and conducted ceremonies for the welfare of the people." (Chamberlain, p.48) And further, "the Evening Star bundle priest was the grand high priest of
the Skidi, and the keeper of the bundle was the chief of the Skidi."
(Chamberlain, p.55) It is also clear that the Skidi made a distinction
between "medicine men" and "priests." "The doctors, or medicine
men, sought assistance from animals and minor gods; this distin-
guished them from the priests, who ministered on behalf of the
major gods of the heavens." (Chamberlain, p.92)

I take special note of the mention of a "grand high priest," and
of the priests being defined as those who "ministered on behalf of
the major gods of heaven." It seems evident to me that the Skidi
priests were Starwalkers, that these astronomer-priests of the Great
Plains did not simply observe the sky, did not simply have a sky-
based mythology and cosmology, and did not simply perform
sacred rites to appease the gods. Their beliefs and sacred rites were
of a nature that permitted them *to go to the gods!* It is entirely likely
that the Skidi possessed the complete body of stellar knowledge
that came to Earth, and that was known to the ancient Egyptians
and others. All the more reason, don't you think, to carefully consider where the Ancients said it came from and how it came to our
planet.

The Death Star was not the only star that played a significant
role in Skidi religion and life. The Morning Star and Evening Star
identities present an equally interesting challenge. Like the Star of
Disease, it is possible, and even likely, that they were not stars but
planets.

The key may be that the Skidi called the Morning Star the Great
Red Star and the Evening Star the Great White Star. The former was
probably the planet Mars, the latter Venus. (Chamberlain, pp.72,74)
(Because of Venus' orbit there are times when it is the Morning Star
and times it is the Evening Star.) Although it can be difficult to determine a star or a planet's "color," Mars does have a distinct reddish
hue that is easily seen with a small telescope. A conjunction of the
Morning and Evening "stars" no doubt inspired the belief in the

"wedding" of the two, thus cementing Skidi celestial ancestry as told in their creation myth.

Just as interesting are the possible identities of the Four World Quarter Stars mentioned earlier. These were associated with the semi-cardinal directions, and each possessed a particular "power" bestowed by Heaven. They also gave the sacred bundles and ceremonies to the people. They were the pillars that held up the sky,— Yellow Star, White Star, Big Black Star, and Red Star. Chamberlain suggests *Capella* for the Yellow Star, *Antares* for the Red Star, *Sirius* for the White Star, and *Vega* for the Black Star. (Chamberlain, p.99) So, Sirius, Antares, Vega, and Capella, assuming these designations are right, become the most important of the Skidi stars.

This all "feels" right to me, but I must admit that I still have reservations about the Big Black Star's identity and I would like to single it out. All Indian tribes assign colors to the directions, including the semi-cardinal ones. And whatever else these four stars represented, they were definitely associated with the directions. But the thing that caught my attention was the use of the word "black." How or why would this word be used in relation to or defining a *star*, other than perhaps designating a direction? Why was the star described as big when none of the others were so defined? If it were literally a "black star," how could it be seen? And if it couldn't be seen how could it possibly be identified? What kind of star could be black?

The Big Black Star was associated with black clouds, thunder, storms, the night, the northeast, and flint. It was the brother of the Morning Star and because it was related to storms it would have also been associated with the process of creation. The Big Black Star was given credit for giving animals the power to communicate with humans. (Chamberlain, p.99) Its association with weather events and, even more interesting, its being the source of the traditional knowledge and the sacred bundles certainly attests that it was of great significance to the Skidi's deepest religious mysteries. Then I came across the information that it was also called the *Big Black Meteoric Star*. It wasn't a star at all! Let me explain.

The Skidi put great stock in other celestial objects and phenomena besides stars. These included meteors and meteorites, the latter being the most sacred of all objects. Skidi chroniclers confirm this fact as the following bits of conversation will attest. "[Dorsey] reported that the hot stones used in sweat lodges were full of the same power that is seen in shooting stars." . . . "a meteor is a star visiting". . . "Among the stars would be many signs. Meteors would fly through the sky." (Chamberlain, pp.143-144) In addition Skidi creation mythology says that Morning Star carried a ball of fire in his sacred bundle, and that he left the fire with the Evening Star who later gave it to the people. This was represented by the Evening Star Bundle, which was said to contain a fire drill that was no doubt related to fire. It is reasonable to conclude therefore that the fireball carried by Morning Star is symbolic of a meteor. (Chamberlain, pp.54-55)

Was the Big Black Star a meteorite? It was after all associated with black clouds and thunder, and a meteorite fall is often accompanied by a cloud of debris and a thunderous sound. But the black color of a meteorite is probably the most convincing clue of all.

Obviously, nothing related to the Skidi is more intriguing than the sacred bundles mentioned time and again throughout this chapter. Called the *chuharipiru,* the Skidi bundles were an interesting twist on the more common medicine bags and bundles used by other Native Americans. A common medicine bag carried by most Indian people contains various small sacred objects. So-called medicine bundles are used for wrapping the sacred pipe and smoking herbs, special feathers, and/or other ceremonial paraphernalia. The Skidi possessed numerous different bundles that were used for different purposes, each with its own significance. There were, for example, Federation bundles that belonged to all the people, village bundles that were sacred to a specific community, household bundles owned by a single family, and the personal bundles that held objects that were sacred to an individual. I imagine that all the Skidi bundles were decorated with symbols and images, as most sacred objects of the American Indians were and are. But the Skidi bundles and the ceremonies connected with them were unlike any others I have known about, so I cannot be sure.

The stars were the people's "teachers"; a relationship was maintained with them. From this powerful affiliation, instructions for the bundles were revealed by certain stars, probably through visions and dreams. With rare exceptions, each of the bundles was a "shrine" in honor of the patron stars of the villages. Two such bundles—the Skull Bundle and the North Star Bundle—actually federated the villages. The Skull Bundle was said to contain the skull of the first man on Earth and was related to special rites performed to acknowledge the sky gods and the blessings they gave to the people. (Chamberlain, p.35) The North Star Bundle on the other hand contained a spear with birds carved on it and was the property of the chiefs who believed it protected them. (Chamberlain, p.43)

Two others were the Morning Star Bundle and the Evening Star Bundle that embodied the power of the "stars" that parented humans. There were also the Leading Bundles that represented the four semi-cardinal directions. (Chamberlain, p.96) It seems to me that everything religious revolved around the bundles. So an understanding of them embodies Skidi cosmology as well as their religious beliefs and practices. As shown by the Big Black Meteorite Bundle, said to contain a meteorite, there is no doubt that meteorites were sacred objects. If a person was fortunate enough to find one, it was kept in his or her own special sacred bundle.

Comets were also important to the Skidi who called them "feather headdress stars." (Chamberlain, p.142) Their war bonnets were called "comet bonnets" and were of course worn into battle. The Skidi engaged in human sacrifice, although it was a rather rare event to appease the Great Star so that Earth would not be consumed by fire and so that life would be renewed. Sometimes the timing of the sacrifice ritual would come in a vision or dream. At other times it could be signaled by a comet. As far as I can tell from my research, the last time a human sacrifice occurred was in 1882, coinciding, interestingly, with the appearance of a great comet. (Chamberlain, p.60)

To the Skidi the sky had personality. It was populated with the Sky Gods, and stars and other celestial objects had great power. A star that held a prominent position in Skidi star lore was the "Star That Does Not Walk Around," the Pole Star. Also known as the Chief Star, Polaris watched over earthly chiefs. The Chief Star was related to the so-called Circle of Chiefs constellation as the star closest to the center. (Chamberlain, p.106) It possessed the power of longevity, and was the "overseer" who made sure the other stars didn't lose their way in their motions across the heavens. Recall the spear mentioned earlier that had birds carved on it. This spear was kept in the

North Star Bundle, and the Skidi believed it contained an actual piece of the North Star itself! Legend told of the bundle being given to the first chief, who in turn passed it down through successive generations.

I cannot resist making a few personal comments on the subject of the Chiefs' Circle. That it was the star group that ruled over earthly and human affairs seems to imply that the Skidi were aware of a heavenly hierarchy. When I first learned of the hierarchy's possible existence, I had a vivid vision that led me to an awareness of the relationship the Skidi Starwalkers had with the Chiefs' Circle constellation. I definitely feel that Starwalkers were among the ranks of the priests. Or better still, the grand priest was the one and only Starwalker, having inherited that special knowledge by and through his or her position within the priesthood.

In my vision I "saw" spirit Starwalkers traveling into the night sky and conversing with the Star Chiefs. I knew they were asking and receiving advice regarding earthly affairs. It wasn't just a matter of the star priests receiving information *telepathically* from the Star Council, or of simply respecting and honoring the existence of the Sky Gods through sacred rites. *The priests traveled to the Council!* This was not something mere starwatchers could do. It was not something star gazers, whom I identify as the "interpreters" of information and omens received, did either, for that would have simply involved ritual or "rank" within any medicine society that may have existed. The Skidi star cosmology was far more complex than that. If I am right, then the Skidi possessed knowledge and shamanic journeying practices that went beyond what has been proved or even imagined by Skidi chroniclers or archaeoastronomers.

In addition to Starwalker astronomer-priests, the Skidi had a sort of astrology, a system that helped guide them during their life on Earth. At birth a child was believed to come under the influence of a supernatural Star Being, predictably any star that was especially bright at that time. The Star Being served as a kind of protector and healer for the child as potentially negative events occurred in the course of daily life. Skidi youngsters were informed about the sky beings and the environment around them. The world and even the homes they lived in were copies of the greater male-female universe that had parented them.

A Skidi priest told James Murie about the North Star being the

Chief Star. "You [stars in general] are the chiefs. You [Polaris] represent the chief in the heavens himself and you have his name upon you. You represent his name on earth." (Chamberlain, p.106) This is similar to the Egyptian belief regarding Osiris as the "representative" of the stars, with every pharaoh in essence an incarnation of him. (After the death of a pharaoh a special ceremony called "Opening of the Mouth" was conducted for the purpose of resurrection—*as a star*—of the deceased. We know that the greatest Egyptian concern was immortality. The stars were immortal. By becoming a star the king's immortality was assured. The constellation Ursa Major, the Big Dipper, was the prime focus of the ceremony. The Big Dipper is a circumpolar constellation.[9]) Egyptian belief seems to imply two things: One, the Skidi were not the first to consider their earthly chiefs to be guided by stars; two, they were not the first to believe that upon death the chief returned to and/or became a star.

These two similarities had not been noted, or credited, until the publication of *The Mayan Prophecies* in 1995. Authors Gilbert and Cotterell point out the distinct similarities between the ancient Egyptians and the Indians of Mexico, from the Olmecs to the Mayans and Aztecs: "The Egyptians believed in a heavenly afterworld to which they hoped their souls would go after death. The Pyramid Texts, which are carved into the walls of certain of the later pyramids, provide abundant evidence that they conceived of this as being in the constellation Orion.". . . and, "Among many of the tribes of North America there is a belief that the Milky Way is a path through the sky along which the dead have to travel on their way to the higher heavens. Often it is conceived of as having a gate at both ends, where it crosses the ecliptic.". . . and, "It would also seem that the Maya, in common with the ancient Egyptians, believed that at least one of their afterlife kingdoms or heavens was near to the Milky Way."[10]

While Gilbert and Cotterell are relating this stellar theology of the earliest Egyptians primarily to the Maya, the same was true of the Skidi, including the information regarding the Milky Way sky bridge. I feel certain that these similarities attest that the star religion was widespread in the ancient world, and that it was essentially the same theology.

In conclusion it is important to bring another Skidi artifact to our attention. The Pawnee Star Chart is the most treasured relic that remains today in serene testimony to the knowledge of these mystical people of the Great Plains. On display since 1906 in the Chicago Field Museum, the chart had once been in the hands of Pawnee chronicler James Murie. It is made from an oval-shaped piece of buckskin that has turned a yellowish-brown-gray color from extensive use and age. The buckskin is covered with stars—four-pointed stars painted in four different sizes and arranged to form distinct patterns. Others were placed alone and apparently at random. Several of the star figures stand out because they are larger than the others. The entire chart is divided almost in half by a design of tiny dark dots, some of which are in clusters and obviously represent the Milky Way sky bridge. On one side of the bridge are the summer stars, on the other, the stars of winter. Traces of red and yellow pigments are on the chart, a band of yellow on one end, on the other a band of red and yellow. These are believed to represent dawn and sunset respectively. A dark green crescent-shaped figure on the chart is probably the Moon. The chart is estimated to be about three hundred years old. I feel it is much older, perhaps as much as 700 to 900 years. Some constellations—the Big Dipper, Corona Borealis, Coma Berenices, and the Hyades—are easily identified on the hide, as is possibly the star Polaris.

It is known that there was a special ceremony associated with the chart but little is known about it. At one time the bundle of the chart was said to contain a mysterious brass disk, but no one knows what it was, where it came from, or what happened to it. The bundle was used twice a year during the Great Washing Ceremony when the people ceremonially washed themselves and their houses before the buffalo hunt. (Chamberlain, pp.187-188)

For the most part, the Star Chart presents us with more questions than answers. Could it have been simply and only a map of the night sky, perhaps made in honor of the great Star Nation? Could it have "captured" the power of the stars and somehow preserved it for ceremonial use? That is precisely what I think, but in truth, no one can ever *prove* that it is so.

Speculation about the Skidi, what they believed and how it affected them and their lives, could go on endlessly.

Even when we can base what we know upon data and provable

facts we still come up short in terms of *why* they believed what they did. What, in other words, made them tick? Realizing how unique the Skidi were, even among their own people, a phrase like "the chosen" comes to mind.

No science can get into the soul of a people. For that there is but one tool: *intuition*. But from what is known about these unusual people it is apparent that the Skidi and their religion were unique in North America at least, not just compared to other Native Americans, but even to the other bands within their own tribe. A debt is owed to Von del Chamberlain for bringing together his own expertise on the stars with what is known about the Skidi. It seems appropriate to end this chapter with the words of the Skidi chronicler James Murie:

"The reader should always bear in mind that we are catching up the frayed-out ends of a vanishing fabric and that many times these come to us as but glimpses of what has passed into hopeless oblivion." (Chamberlain, p.207)

CHAPTER TEN

STARWATCHERS OF
THE DESERT SOUTHWEST

*We have to relate our lives to the stars and the sun, the ani-
mals, and to all of nature or else we will go crazy, or get
sick.*[1]

a Navajo girl

The Arizona desert swallows one in its vastness. The musky fra-
grance of hot earth saturates the air currents, the ever-present
ravens ride with acrobatic swoops and dives. The floor of the
ancient Colorado Plateau spreads in all directions, empty except for
the jagged sawtooth peaks and the flat top mesas that are the personality of the land. It is atop three of these timeworn mesas that
the Hopi live, a traditional people whose view of life rivals the
uniqueness of the world that surrounds them. Among the world's
most expert dry-land farmers, the Hopi honor the connection
between the Sun, the stars, and life on Earth.

Sometime during December, dependent upon the proper lunar
phase and its accordance with the setting Sun, a sixteen-day ceremony to celebrate the cycles of life embodied within the processes
of germination, growth, and harvest is reenacted as it has been for
centuries. This is *Soyal*, a rite to resurrect the Day Star on the winter solstice. And it is the stars that dictate the precise moment when
the rite preceding Soyal, *Wuwuchim* or "New Fire Ceremony," will
begin. Over the sixteen days that follow that beginning, the Sun will
be reborn and life will be renewed, clear proof that the Hopi take

neither for granted.[2]

Dug deep in the rocky soil of the Hopi villages are the *kivas.* Kivas are underground "temples," each a representative of *sipapuni,* the hole, the sacred opening where the ancient Hopi emerged from the Underworld into the Fourth World, the present day and time in which we are living. (Sipapuni corresponds to the opening or soft spot in the top of the head of a human being.) The opening allowed the ancestral Hopi to communicate freely with the Creator. Today the Hopi tell us that people's soft spots are almost closed due to humanity's departure from right living. (Waters, pp.126-131)

A wooden ladder is the vehicle of passage in and out of the kiva. Prior to Soyal, the medicine society descends into the kiva to wait for a particular stellar alignment to appear overhead in the kiva opening. Many other sacred rites are also held in the kivas as well.

My husband and I lived in Arizona for over ten years, in Sedona and in Flagstaff, a reasonably short drive from the Hopi Indian Reservation. Over the years we made many journeys there and became personally acquainted with several Hopi people, namely the Jackson family on First Mesa. Happily, we witnessed many sacred ceremonies throughout nine ceremonial seasons.

I know from personal experience that the kiva has special vibrations. Once, during the time of the night dances, my husband and I and two friends were invited to go into a kiva on Second Mesa for a ceremony, a privilege rarely presented to non-Indians. Once inside the kiva, I realized that I was inside the very body of Mother Earth. Never before or since have I felt so protected or more nourished by a sacred place or rite.

I also have fond memories of another visit to Hopi in mid-November 1982 during the time of the *Wuwuchim,* the symbolic ritual of rekindling the fire that represents the Sun's cosmic power. Sun Bear, the late Chippewa medicine man, and his two medicine helpers, Wabun and Shawnodese, were visiting us in Sedona at the time. Sun Bear had never been to Hopiland, but he had always wanted to go. So in a light snow shower we made our way through the alpine forests near Flagstaff and crossed the volcanic terrain of the high desert that leads to the reservation. We drove straight to Second Mesa, to the village of Shungopovi, just in time to see the Wuwuchim kachinas ascending out of the kiva. We watched while they formed a line and began to dance and sing, their voices and feet in perfect rhythm. The sights and sounds stirred shivers inside me, the kind that come with knowing that I am seeing something very powerful and very ancient. The ceremony filled me full of joy, inspired me, and touched a chord within me that had never been touched before. *Something inside me had awakened.* This I knew.

Stars govern most, if not all, the Hopi sacred rites, including the Wuwuchim. In *The Book of the Hopi,* Frank Waters relates an intriguing account of the Wuwuchim told to him over two decades ago by a Two Horn Society chief. What is revealed concerning the stars is of particular interest. Speaking about the importance of rain and the prayers that bring it, the chief told of seven sacred songs that are sung to seven specific stars. He called them *Choochokam,* which means the "Stars That Cling Together" or the "Harmonious Ones," and identified them as the Pleiades. (Waters, pp.146-153) At the song's completion, two additional stars, Castor and Pollux (in Gemini), are sighted by one of the elders. Called *Natupkom,* "The Two Brothers," these stars are followed by another, *Talawsohu,* that the Hopi call the "Star Before the Light." (Waters, pp.149-150) The appearance of Talawsohu, which is the star Procyon, marks the end of the ceremony.

It is another star however that plays the most prominent role, the "timekeeper" that signals the beginning of the ceremonials. The chief says, "We, the religious leaders, have always before us the celestial patterns which guide and control our rituals. The most important is the sun itself, and when the sun is down we conduct our ceremonies by the stars of night." (Waters, p.149) Watching through the opening in the kiva roof, the people wait patiently for the star called *Hotamkam,* the top star in the belt of Orion. First Hotamkam shows, then all three of the belt stars are seen lengthwise and the middle star is directly over the fireplace located in the center of the floor of the kiva. It is midnight. (Waters, p.149) At this point an important smoking ritual begins. This all has to do with seven aspects of life: *world preparation, germination, first plants, planting, growing, harvest,* and *rain.* (Waters, p.140)

Hopi star timing doesn't end with the smoking ritual. In the early dawn of the following morning, another star's appearance is awaited. Called *Ponochona,* "The One That Sucks From the Belly," this is the patron star of all animals. Ponochona is the star Sirius. Again, isn't it interesting that the stars involved in this all-important ceremonial are the same ones that were of such tremendous significance to the ancient Egyptians? (For whatever it is worth, I can't tell you how many times, while visiting Hopiland, I have commented on how similar the terrain, the smells, the houses, and the "vibes" are to so many of the places we visited in Egypt.) The belt stars in Orion are the most notable ones these two cultures have in common, cultures that are so widely separated by both time and distance.

As will be discussed in later chapters, the stars that are prominent with the Hopi are of equal or even greater importance to numerous other ancient and contemporary cultures worldwide aside from the Egyptians. Certainly the brightness of most of these stars is a large part of the reason why they rank so high among so many diverse cultures in so many eras. But I think there was and is more to it than brightness. I think it had to do with the specific power inherent within each star.

We can safely conclude that the Sun, Moon, and stars are Hopi ceremonial clocks that time rituals other than those discussed here. But the human participants in the rituals, all of whom represent spirit forces and entities in Nature, are equally intriguing in their obvious connection to the sky and its inhabitants.

One of these appears during another of the winter solstice ceremonies: *Mui'ingwa Kachina*, the god of germination, represents the cycle of life. The costume worn by Mui'ingwa's human representative includes a large star fastened to his head, indicative of how far his spirit had to travel to get to Earth. Made of white corn husks, the star is four-pointed and more than two feet long from tip to tip. In its center is a blue circle that represents the sky. White star symbols dot the rest of the kachina's body. *Mastop Kachina* also appears during Soyal. His body is painted black with white hands imprinted on it, and he wears a black mask to representing interstellar space. The three stars painted on each side of his head symbolize the stars in Orion's belt. (Waters, p.153)

I have made numerous references thus far to kachinas, or "cloud people," so it is time they were explained in greater detail. Numbering over two hundred, kachinas are manifestations of the invisible forces of life, tribal totems, and spirits. Many have a relationship with stars and other celestial bodies and phenomena. One is the *Ahola* or Chief Kachina who never appears at the sacred dances held in public. He is said to slow the Sun's passage. At specific times of the year, the Ahola goes out and bows to the Sun four times, asking for long life, health, and good crops. Another is the *Chasing Star Kachina* who is often related to a planet the Hopi do not identify for outsiders. He makes his appearance in February during the annual Bean Dance, carrying a yucca whip and a bell and wearing an enormous headdress made from a plume of eagle feathers. His entire face is painted with stars. Chasing Star's actual function has either been lost or is kept secret.

I have learned about *Sohu*, the Star Kachina, who wears a kilt of turkey feathers and never makes an appearance alone. There are also *Tawa*, the Sun Kachina, and *Ho'lolo,* the Moon Kachina. Ho'lolo's human representative has white crescents painted under his eyes. *Falling Star Kachina* is a god who appears only in the ceremonies on Second Mesa. His task is to bring a heavenly message to the people. (I think that both Mastop, the Death Fly Kachina, and the Falling Star Kachina are Starwalkers.) *The Meteor Kachina* is unknown outside the Hopi world, as are the *Summer* and *Winter Solstice* kachinas who are, curiously, found only on Third Mesa. Even more curiously, the *Soyal Kachina*, who represents the winter solstice, has not appeared in ceremonials on that Mesa in over seventy years! The Soyal Kachina is also called the *Returning Kachina.* His appearance, if and when he makes it, usually indicates the beginning of the sacred dances.[3]

We should keep in mind that any sacred information is usually based solely on second-hand reports and may not always represent actual facts. Such information oftentimes cannot either be validated or invalidated. The sheer number of supernatural beings associated with the sky establishes the close relationship the Hopi have with the sky and its cosmic powers. But of all those mentioned, none could be more beguiling than the so-called *Blue Star Kachina*. Let's take a look at who this entity represents.

The Blue Star Kachina is the subject of both a story and a prophecy. Both are surrounded by controversy due primarily to the fact that there is more than one version and interpretation. I have heard several versions, all of which came from non-Native sources, and not from the Hopi themselves. This kind of information is rarely reliable. I first learned of the Blue Star Kachina from Frank Waters' *The Book of the Hopi,* which foretells of dire catastrophes for Earth when the Blue Star Kachina appears in the plaza of a Pueblo during a sacred ceremony and removes his mask before uninitiated children. Waters goes on: "For a while there will be no more ceremonies, no more faith. Then Oraibi will be rejuvenated with its faith and ceremonies, marking the start of a new cycle of Hopi life." (Waters, p.333) He reports that the Blue Star Kachina has appeared before, in 1914 just prior to World War I; in 1940 before the United States entered World War II; and in 1961 before the U.S. involvement in Vietnam. The Hopi say that the time for the Blue Star to dance again is not far off!

And, yes, the Hopi do predict a Third World War, which they say will be started by those peoples "who first received the light [the divine wisdom or intelligence] in the other old countries [India, China, Egypt, Palestine, Africa]." (Waters, pp.333-334) (I have in fact heard rumors that the Blue Star has already danced and, according to when I heard it, that would have been around 1990 or 1991. To date I have found no one who knows of any such appearance and frankly I had doubts about the validity of the rumors when I first heard them. I would think that an occasion of such import would be extremely difficult to keep secret, especially in light of the numbers of people who are in close contact with the Hopi people on all the mesas, and the amount of interest in their prophecies.)

The people and the prophecies are now more mainstream than ever. I say with complete confidence that a new cycle of Hopi life is beginning, though it may not be of the magnitude that Waters or his sources intended to convey. But that we are living in changing times cannot be denied.

If and when a Third World War should occur, the Hopi say it will be a "spiritual conflict with material matters. Material matters will be destroyed by spiritual beings who will remain to create one world and one nation under one power, that of the Creator." (Waters, p.334) The fact, according to Waters at least, that the time when the Blue Star Kachina will dance in the plaza is not far off is of great concern, given the hot spots that exist all over the world today.

The following words are very revealing and, in essence, represent all that is known about the enigmatic Blue Star Kachina. It also connects "him" with the heavens. "He represents a blue star, far off and yet invisible, which will make its appearance soon." (Waters, p.334) We know that it is not uncommon for ancient peoples to refer to virtually anything in the night sky as a star, including planets and comets. *So what is the blue star? And is it a star? Could it be a planet? If it is a star, then which star? A planet? Which planet? And why the color "blue?"* We are told it is a "distant star" and that it is "yet invisible." All stars are distant of course, but the Hopi seem to be making a point about this particular star, which is "yet invisible." Does this mean it is invisible all the time or just invisible right now, to become visible in some future time? The latter seems more likely.

Any star that is now invisible but will become visible can only mean, astronomically, one of three things. One is that the Blue Star will be a supernova, which is the explosion of a big star. Novas can be seen sometimes even in the daytime; a supernova would appear as a bright "starlike" object where there had been no such object before. (Ancient Chinese observers used to refer to these as "guest" stars.) But the Hopi at the very least imply that the Blue Star has appeared before. Novas do not appear and disappear and reappear again!

It could be a star or even a planet whose orbit is so unusual that it would not be seen from Earth except at certain intervals of time. However, it would seem that we, with all the technological advances made in astronomy, might have detected such a "second sun" or an eccentric-orbit planet a long time ago. So neither of these theories really holds much water.

I cannot think of any sky object that would behave in the fashion the Hopi describe except for one: a comet. And a comet is precisely what I think the Blue Star Kachina represents. Ancient peoples the world over saw comets and made note of them, etched in stone, drawn on cave walls, painted them on rocks, tipis, and sacred lodges. As we have seen, comets have long had a notorious reputation, most often considered to be harbingers of doom! For the sake of argument, let's assume for the moment that the Blue Star is indeed a comet. This brings up a number of thoughts:

First, comets are not as rare as we might think. They are members of our solar system, meaning that they travel in orbits around the Sun like the planets do. Although we cannot always see them if they are too faint or their orbits don't bring them into view, comets are always out there. Some of them fit into the category called "periodicals": their elliptical orbits bring them into view from Earth time and time again. The particular period involved is different with each comet. (The famous Halley's comet comes around every seventy-five years, its latest appearance in 1986. Comet Hyakutake, the surprise visitor visible in the spring of 1996, hasn't come around for a visit in 10,000 to 20,000 years, and Hale-Bopp's last appearance is believed to have been some 4000 years ago.) As a rule both amateur and professional astronomers know far in advance when a comet will travel into our part of the solar system. Hyakutake broke the rule and sneaked up on us a few weeks in advance of its arrival.

Not all comets are periodicals. There are actually five possible tracks a comet can take through the solar system. One could be called a "suicidal comet," as its path leads to destruction when it crashes into the Sun. There are also the ellipse and circle, the parabolic and hyperbolic comets. Of these, the hyperbolic are one-time visitors that travel through the system and are never seen again. There is no point where such a comet reaches its greatest distance from the Sun, then begins its return.[4] But comets do come and many are visible. Of course, in the short span of a human life, we don't always see the same ones. I suppose it would also be feasible to say that any one of them might appear "blue," especially in areas like Hopiland where artificial light interference would be minimal.

Like us, the Hopi probably would not have paid special attention to faint ones or those that were low on the horizon. But when a big comet with a long trail streaked across the night sky, that was surely a different matter altogether. One just appeared, coming out of invisibility to light up the night. It was different from all the other "stars." Think about it. If something bad happened while the first comets were seen during the earliest times, they would have been considered prophets of terrible events. The Hopi Blue Star prophecy in essence forecasts war. Remember the Skidi Pawnee headdresses with long streamers of feathers that cascaded down the back to the ground. Researchers said they were called "comet bonnets." These were Pawnee *war bonnets*.

So when a major comet was seen it meant something important. Again, think about it. We are used to seeing the night sky in a certain way night after night (if we live in an area where we can still see it!). We know what to expect. Then we go out one night and there is a huge comet racing through the night, its bright dusty tail looking like a star-studded smoke trail. Of course we would stop to admire its beauty. Our technology would have told us when it would come, and exactly what it is, and every little detail about it. But could we really just look? Would there not be something way down inside asking what it could mean? I believe there is that much of an "ancestral gene" in every one of us. Comets are magnetic. They draw us to them, they lure us, they call to us from outer space, to a space deep inside us.

If the Blue Star is a comet, then the one the Hopi took note of would have been big and bright. Maybe Hale-Bopp is the Hopi Blue Star. Astronomers say it could be really bright and provide us with a great show. Right now, January 1997, Hale-Bopp is still invisible to the naked eye. But during February and March, the comet will go into the morning sky and be visible among the stars of Aquila, Vulpecula, and Cygnus. In March the comet will again move into the evening sky where it will remain until it is out of visibility in June due to its close proximity to the Sun. During this time, if the predictions are correct, the tail should put on a spectacular show as Hale-Bopp moves slowly northeast of the Milky Way. Obviously, the Hale-Bopp comet is known about long before our eyes can see it in the night sky. But, maybe a few comets like Hyakutake will slip up on us, and perhaps one of them will fulfill the Hopi prophecy. We can only wait and see.

The non-Native public does not, and perhaps cannot, know for sure what the Blue Star Kachina really represents. And many modern Hopi may not know either. But regardless of what the Blue Star may be, I think there is something far more important to keep in mind. The Hopi say that disasters like war happen because human beings don't live right. Our values for the most part don't include a respect for Nature and for Mother Earth, for the animals, or for each other. We can and must save ourselves from whatever turmoil the Blue Star heralds by taking steps now to reconnect ourselves with Mother Nature, to reassess and rebuild our values and priorities regarding our planet and all our relations. Time is short. We must begin now. This said, I will get to telling a story that relates to the Blue Star Kachina.

In 1993 I returned to Sedona on a working trip. For some time before going to Arizona I had been working on an article about the Blue Star Kachina. So I naturally wanted to go to Hopi to visit with friends there, and to see if I could find out any information about the rumors of the Kachina dancing. When my friend and I arrived on Second Mesa, we went directly to a shop to purchase a silver bracelet to replace one I had given to a friend. The shop was filled with several hundred kachina dolls. Although the primary purpose of the dolls is to teach Hopi children about the kachinas, they have also long been popular collector's items. For curiosity's sake I asked the clerk if there was a Blue Star Kachina doll among them. I knew that Blue Star dolls were rare; in fact, I had never seen one for sale anywhere.

The woman in the shop said she had no Blue Star doll for sale at that time, but that her cousin was carving one that would be available in a couple of weeks. That surprised me. I asked what the price would be. She quoted one that was out of my reach financially, but that *didn't* surprise me. Kachina dolls can be very expensive if they are done by well-known carvers and/or are of good quality.

During our conversation, she asked if we had attended the dances the night before. I told her I had not. She said, "Oh, you should have been there. It was great! There were all kinds of star dancers, blue stars, white stars, red stars, and yellow stars!" She said that she had not seen anything like it since she was a little girl. Then she was distracted by another customer and the conversation terminated at that point.

We left the shop and traveled on toward First Mesa. But my mind was reeling. Like me, my friend thought it was curious that we had encountered that information related so freely. Just past the Cultural Center, I noticed a small adobe-type store that had never been open during my previous trips. We stopped and entered the tiny shop. The plump young man behind the counter came up and greeted us happily. The inscription on his T-shirt read: Blue Star Singers. More synchronicity! I knew I was in the right place at the right time for whatever reason.

I asked him what the Blue Star singers were and he mumbled something about it being like a choir. I asked if he had a Blue Star Kachina doll for sale. He answered, smiling, "Right there," pointing to the wall. Several kachinas of various types had been made to hang on the wall instead of being the usual free-standing type. I wasn't sure which one he meant so he walked over and pointed out the specific one. It was painted gray and had a bluish-gray star on its forehead. The head had white feathers fashioned into a "spray" all around it. The rest of the figure was rather nondescript. I seriously considered buying it, but then declined. What can I say but that it just didn't feel right to own it?

Curiously, the young man also asked if we had attended the dances the night before. His eyes lit up when he began telling us what he had witnessed. "You should have seen them, they were everywhere . . . lots of them . . . blue ones, red ones . . . all colors." He then said something I didn't hear clearly . . . about the Kiva Chief calling in all the stars, or something like that. I began to question him. In a brief conversation he also said that he had never seen anything like it.

Then, out of the blue, the clerk referred back to the wall kachina and asked if I knew that the spray of white feathers represented meteors. Nothing else was said that was really relevant to the Blue Star or the dances of the night before. But his mention of meteorites stuck in my mind. At one point I specifically asked him if the Blue Star Kachina had danced the night before, but he was understandably more interested in making a sale. I did notice that my question seemed to puzzle him, as if he didn't know about the Blue Star Kachina dancing. I think that many Hopi simply do not know their traditions as written in the "old" language. We all know that sacred texts often do not lend themselves well to translation into nontraditional languages. Also, most of the younger generations seem to know less than the elders do, and I have not had the opportunity to date to speak to an elder specifically about the Blue Star.

On First Mesa, we visited for a time with my friends Ester and Maybelle. I told what we had been told by the shopkeepers. Much to my chagrin, they didn't seem to know anything much about it other than they had heard there were dances on Second Mesa the night before. I didn't get the feeling that the women were avoiding my inquiry, only that they didn't know much, if anything, about what I was asking.

By the time we left the mesas that day, my mind was full. I felt like I had been on a "mission," with implications I wasn't really sure about. But the purpose was clear. I had gone there to find out what I could about the Blue Star. No one told me that the Blue Star Kachina had danced in any plaza in any village. But from what I was told I was able to surmise that all the different-colored star dancers had possibly represented meteors. I wasn't sure what it meant or exactly how to piece it all together. But I left there believing that somehow the dances had either foretold or honored meteorite showers, and that those meteorite showers were of significance at the time, or would be in the future, to the Hopi and perhaps to all of us.

You will recall the importance of meteorites and meteor showers to the Skidi Pawnee of the Great Plains. A meteor shower would foretell the end of the world! I am not saying that the end of the world is near. I *am saying* that there is a good possibility that those bits of information I acquired that day point to an unusual occurrence on Second Mesa the night before my journey to Hopiland in April 1993. The starlike dancers, and the message they sought to convey or the reason for their appearance, were out of the ordinary.

The same desert sand and rugged mountain areas that are home to the Hopi are also inhabited by the Navajo. Formerly a nomadic tribe, the Navajo came up from the south and eventually settled in their present location in the high desert of the Four Corners area. They found the Hopi as an already existing, clan-oriented pueblo society, complete with their own agriculture, architecture, arts and crafts, and mythology. As might be expected the relocation brought some significant changes within many aspects of Navajo society, though they have retained their own distinction. Today the Navajo raise sheep and cattle, but before the arrival of the Spanish in New Mexico, they were hunters, gatherers, and seasonal farmers.

In remote areas of the huge reservation, Navajo dwellings are still largely traditional hogans built from logs cemented with mud. Each hogan is a replica of the original one known in mythology as the "Creation Hogan," built entirely of horizontal logs with a vertical one at each of the four direction points. Traditionally, the doorway opens to the east. These are known as the *female* hogans. The *male* hogan is a cone-like hut constructed of three forked poles covered with logs, brush, and mud.[5] These are now rare. All hogans, whether traditional or more modern, have smoke holes in the roof.

The sky has always played a major role in Navajo life. As with the Hopi, the heavens time their daily and ceremonial lives. Everything, including the stars, was in the Creation Hogan. I first learned of the legend that links the Navajo to the stars from Ray Williamson's *Living the Sky: The Cosmos of the American Indian.*[6] The story concerns a principal god in creation times known as *Black God*, or *Fire God*. His image (mask) represents the entire sky. Seven stars the Navajo call *Dilyehe* (the Pleiades) attached themselves to his ankles as he entered the Creation Hogan. Trying to rid himself of the pesky stars, Black God stomped his foot on the ground four times. But the stars just jumped up to his knees and shoulder before finally coming to rest on his left temple! Drawings of the Black God's mask show the stars clearly displayed as seven white dots.

According to Navajo mythology, it was Black God who arranged the stars in the sky and brought order to the heavens. The proto-stars were quartz crystals that Black God kept in a fawnskin pouch. One by one he placed them in the night sky, working in a clock-wise direction from east to north. With each he placed an "igniter," for the crystals had no light of their own. When the stars were in place, Black God scattered most of the remaining crystal dust across the sky, forming the smoky trail of the Milky Way.

While standing back to admire his work, Black God was approached by the Great Trickster, Coyote, who was irritated at not having been included in the star-placing business. Coyote proceed-ed to vent his displeasure by grabbing the pouch away from Black God. Peering inside, he found only one crystal remaining, which he took and placed in the southern part of the sky. Coyote named it *Monthless Star.* (Some astronomers believe that this may be the red giant Antares in the constellation Scorpio, others believe it is Sirius. The Navajo call it the "Coyote Star.") Angered that there were no more star rocks in the bag, Coyote slung the starry crystal dust at random into the night!

It is said that the stars placed by the Black God have names, but those tossed at random by Coyote do not. Notice that in this legend there are two occasions where the Milky Way is formed, first by Black God, again by Coyote. However, most of the versions I have read credit Coyote with the formation of the Sky Bridge, which has always played a significant role in Navajo astronomy and religion. (Williamson, pp.162-164.)

To the Navajo the rules to live by were dictated by the stars. The stars were "beings" who assisted in making life satisfying and prosperous. The Navajo grouped the stars in their own unique fashion, so they know a sky that is considerably different from ours. Navajo constellations have names like Horned Rattler, Thunder, the Bear, First Big One, the Hard Flint Boys, Revolving Male and Female, Doubtful Stars, and Rabbit Tracks. (Williamson, pp.162-163)

Of all the stars, the Pleiades were among the most significant. First and foremost they were a clock. We modern folks tend to forget the dilemma of keeping time faced by ancient peoples. Imagine having no calendars or clocks, both of which we take for granted. The rhythms and cycles of Nature had to be observed over a period of time before an unchanging, dependable, predictable order could be determined. So the art of timekeeping was born from a need that only the sky, relentless observations, skillful record-keeping, and myths could fill. For example, the rising and setting of the Pleiades served the Navajo as calendar markers, their appearance in the northeastern morning sky telling the people that planting time had passed. Their reappearance in the northeastern evening sky foretold the imminence of autumn's first frost. The famous stars also told the Navajo when it was time for the important Nightway and Mountainway ceremonials. But, as Williamson points out, the night sky was not the only means by which the American Indians kept time. Tracking the motion of the Sun and its "play of light and shadow across stationary objects" was also common. (Williamson, p.166)

Another of the Navajo religious practices involves creating *dry paintings*, often erroneously called sand paintings. Magnificent designs, which number in the thousands and are an important part of sacred ceremonies, are created using natural-colored desert sands mixed with pollen, powdered roots, crushed stone, and powdered pieces of bark. The paintings must be started, completed, and destroyed within a twelve-hour period because of their highly sensitive and spiritual nature. When the ceremonies are over, the medicine person gathers the painting's sacred ingredients in a cloth, then sprinkles them to the six directions: the four cardinal directions, up to the sky and down to Earth.

Williamson says: "Mother Earth and Father Sky are two of the best-known paintings because one or both are often reproduced in copies of sand paintings for sale to tourists. Together, they represent the entire physical universe. The black body of Father Sky is decorated with numerous stars in the shape of the major constellations; the sun, the moon, and the Milky Way are also generally included, the latter as a band of crosses on the chest or along the arms. The sun and moon are nearly always drawn with horns, a mark that they possess extraordinary powers." (Williamson, p.169)

Nowhere is there clearer, more thought-provoking evidence of Navajo stellar theology than on the high ceilings of shallow caves in magnificent Canyon de Chelly and other regions of northeastern Arizona and northwestern New Mexico. Called *planetaria*, these are sites where long ago someone painted cave roofs, some of which are nearly 300 feet high, with black, red, and gray stars. The designs range from simple crosses to more elaborate shapes. I have often wondered if the pigments reflect the actual colors of the stars they represent, or if they might represent the four directions since they were painted in colors.

Whatever they may mean, the existing star ceilings are sacred, but they probably are no longer being used or created. It is not known who drew them, but it is assumed to have been prehistoric Anasazi. The ceilings are so high that one of the deepest mysteries is how the painters managed to reach them to paint on them in the first place. In total there are between fifty and a hundred known planetaria. (Williamson, pp.174-176) The obvious questions are: What were they created for? For what and how were they used? I have always felt that the caves were ceremonial "chambers" where secret initiation-type rites took place and where elder astronomer priests trained Starwalker initiates. It seems to me that the actual locations of the planetaria would be known only to the initiates, that even if the general population had known where they were, they would not have dared to trespass the holiest of holies, the most sacred of all sacred places. I also feel that the initiations in the secret caves took place over many weeks of time.

The artists would have been star shamans too, and probably chose to paint on the ceilings for a number of reasons, one being that they intended to re-create the sky overhead. This would mean the cave itself served as the world-earth. I think they wanted and needed the privacy of the caves due, again, to the highly secretive nature of the ceremonials that took place there. The caves were "classrooms" if you will, where astronomer shamans taught the stellar secrets that comprised their religious beliefs and practices.

I seriously doubt that the Navajo had anything to do with creating the ceilings. They probably simply found the caves, and most likely took them over for ceremonial purposes, much in the same way the Druids took over Stonehenge. If this is the case, the *original* purpose and use for the star caves and the Navajo use of them were probably two different things. I have heard that Navajo medicine men still visit the planetaria sites as a part of some secret religious practice. If this is so, these practices and the significance of the ceilings today are highly guarded mysteries.

Since first learning of the star ceilings, I have been particularly curious whether any specific stellar patterns or individual stars are represented in the placement of the symbols. Williamson and other authors speak about the star panels, but suggest no concrete evidence for their intended use or of any evident patterns. Whenever I think about the star ceilings I often have visions of spirit beings, star spirits, being invoked by star shamans. It was these spirits who in turn taught and trained the Starwalkers. The only other place I have received an intuitive image quite similar was at the Great Pyramid, when I perceived part of the initiation rites for the star priestesses.

Whatever the star ceilings may have meant to the early Navajo, these people do believe that they have been instructed by star people or beings. In fact, the "Big Starway Chant," for one, was given to the Navajo by the star people and is a major part of their religion. (Williamson, p.168) Stars are believed to actually participate in the healing process the chant involves. The stars depicted in the sacred dry painting that accompanies the chant receive their powers from an unidentified bright star that shines through the smoke hole of the special hogan within which the painting is being designed. (Williamson, p.169) Although much of the magical star practice in Navajo religion is secret, we know enough to assign these people a definite place among the major sky cults of the world.

Few writers have inspired and educated me like Trudy Griffin-Pierce. Her *Earth Is My Mother, Sky Is My Father* takes readers on a journey through Navajo culture and religious practices, a journey whose final destination is the Great Star Nation. Through her work I was able to confirm that not everyone views the power inherent within the stars as being positive.

The Navajo fear no stars more than those known as the Great Black Star and the Great Blue Star though, according to Griffin-Pierce, they consider all stars as more or less evil.[7] It is to these two infamous ones that all sickness and misfortune are attributed, and to the Navajo this is the most negative way any star can be viewed. The Great Blue Star is associated with black magic and witchcraft, which are greatly feared. This information made me even more acutely aware that all things have positive and negative qualities, including the stars.

The Navajo divide "beings" into two types: earth people and sky people, the latter they call Holy People. The Holy People include the Sun, Moon, stars, lightning, thunder, wind, and virtually every form and force in Nature. Navajo chanter Mike Mitchell has explained: "All Holy People are powerful, and thus dangerous. The Holy People sometimes hurt us . . . the way we sometimes hurt little ants by accident." (Griffin-Pierce, p.198)

Navajo tradition says that when we get out of balance with the natural order, we get into trouble. The trouble manifests in the form of sickness and other kinds of misfortune. Most Navajo ceremonies are for the purpose of healing so that the imbalance, viewed as evil, can be transformed into balance, good.

It is our individual response to things, however, that determines what our personal experience will be. If the Navajo are right in their belief that illness and misfortune are the result of our being out of balance with Nature—and I believe they are—this explains why we are currently confronted with the severe violence, terrible diseases, and unprecedented social, political, and spiritual problems in our society. For example, is AIDS, which borders on being a plague, the result of our individual and collective disharmony with the stars? And is the current increase in social and spiritual apathy some more of the same?

Whatever the case, *balance with nature* is the obvious key.

Griffin-Pierce said it best: "The traditional Navajo awakens with the dawn and scatters pollen to the east outside the hogan, as Coyote taught in Blessingway. By beginning the day with prayers of protection and blessing, he or she summons not only the powers of the present but also those of the past. At night, the constellations, through the moral stories they index as well as through their repetitive, cyclic movements, serve as constant reminders of the right way to live one's life." (Griffin-Pierce, p.198)

As the Native peoples of North America evolved their lives grew more complex. Calendrical skills and astronomical knowledge increased steadily over time and at some point skywatching served both a practical and a religious-spiritual purpose. Diviners became revered chieftains who possessed great power. One source of that power has always been the stars. The Hopi still go down into their kivas and watch for certain stars to signal the beginning of the ceremonial times. Hopi Sun Priests still watch the Day Star in its movements across the sky. Navajo dry painters still draw their beautiful complex images upon the desert floor. And priests may still journey to the star ceilings, though we know not why. Few things on Earth remain unchangeable. But, if we are fortunate, the tribes of the Arizona and New Mexico deserts will continue their attention to the sky, connecting the Father with the Mother Earth.

CHAPTER ELEVEN

VISIONS OF THE COSMOS LAKOTA STYLE

Our minds are thus tuned or tunable to multiple dimensions, multiple realities. The freely associating mind is able to pass across time barriers, sensing the future and reappraising the past. Our minds are time machines, able to sense the flow of possibility waves from both the past and future. In my view there cannot be anything like existence without this higher form of quantum reality.[1]

Fred Alan Wolf

Thoughts of the Great Plains of North America bring to mind the great Sioux Nation, a group of tribes that once occupied more land than any other Native peoples within what is now the United States. Tall and imposing with high-bridged noses and broad cheekbones, these proud people, little more than a century ago, were accomplished horsemen, skilled buffalo hunters, and courageous warriors to whom war and conflict were no strangers. For over two hundred years they fought off enemies from other tribes and, for fifty years, did battle with the whites. No Native people were more aggressive and territorial, and at the same time more deeply spiritual.

The Sioux continue to live by strict religious and moral codes whose rules were reflected in intense sacred rituals designed to instill morality in the minds and hearts of the people. Indeed, the rituals held the people together. They still do.

The Lakota Sioux possessed one of the most elaborate stellar theologies ever known, one that may in the end be as complex as that of the neighboring Skidi. As a definitive written record, Ronald Goodman's *Lakota Star Knowledge: Studies In Lakota Stellar*

Theology provides a simple, yet incredibly profound account of the Lakota's religious view of the stars. But before we can in any way understand a people's astronomical and religious beliefs we have to know something about the people themselves.

Occupying the vast expanses between the Rocky Mountains in the west and the Great Lakes in the east, and from the Canadian Shield to the Republican River in what is now Nebraska, the early Sioux were nomads. When they got horses they became expert horsemen and buffalo hunters. By the time they consolidated their bands in the Dakotas they had become virtually undefeatable. Within the Sioux Nation there are numerous bands: Tetons, Lakota/Dakota, Yankton, Brules, Hunkpapas, Miniconjous, Oglalas, Two Kettles, Sans Arcs, and Blackfeet. Today most Sioux live on eleven reservations in the Dakotas, although there are some in Wisconsin, Nebraska, South Carolina, and along the Gulf Coast.

This chapter primarily concerns the early Sioux who were the ancestors of the Lakota, a religious people whose primary aim was to have their life on Earth mirror the good life that existed in the realm of the stars. The global esoteric tradition contained within the age-old statement "as above, so below," is at the core of Lakota religion. Lakota elders say that for almost three thousand years they have acted out their belief that what takes place in the stars happens *simultaneously* on Earth. During the past few years several Lakota elders and medicine people have spoken candidly about their religious beliefs and ceremonials and in doing so have revealed a powerful tradition. The meanings inherent within their rituals, many of which I have witnessed, reflect a profound and heart-felt and passionately held belief system that may be unsurpassed among American Indians.

When I investigated Lakota star knowledge, I immediately realized that these people felt and experienced "a vivid relationship between the macrocosm, the star world, and their microcosmic world on the plains."[2] One piece of evidence of particular significance involves certain "maps." Unknown by researchers until 1985, the maps in question are of at least two different types. One depicts Earth, complete with mountains, rivers and streams, hills, and valleys; the other shows the heavens and singles out individual stars and constellations. (Goodman, p.18) These maps are different from the Skidi Star Chart (mentioned in chapter 9) in that there are two of them and one is of the land. The fact that this second map exists points to a direct relationship between Earth and the sky in a way that we shall see is even more complex than that of the Skidi. To be more precise, it suggests a relationship between the heavens and *certain places* on the land. When we learn what these certain places were, pieces of the puzzle begin to come together. In short, investigation of Lakota sacred sites on Earth is the key to our gaining any real insight into these particular people. But let's consider first how the Lakota viewed the stars and the role they played in earthly life.

In order to gain some understanding of how the Lakota viewed the stars, Goodman used the term "mirroring" (Goodman, p.15): What is above—and we can assume that means everything above—mirrors or reflects what is below and vice versa. Nothing happens on Earth that isn't mirrored in the sky. And nothing happens in the sky without being reflected in earthly events. We can ask, Do our actions affect the heavens? Or is it that what happens in the heavens actually causes earthly events? Which comes first, the chicken or the egg? I suspect the truth lies within both perspectives. Whatever the answer, there is no doubt that the Lakota knew, and lived their lives accordingly. And an integral part of that life was ceremony.

I think most people envision ritual as a carefully orchestrated performance of dance, sacred words being chanted or sung, and special prayers and incantations being made, all for the purpose of honoring and/or invoking the power of deity or the forces of Nature. The Lakota certainly engaged in various sacred rites. But when it came to the stars, the rituals involved were both complex and unique. One, known as the Spring Journey, was an annual journey occurring during the three months between the spring equinox and the summer solstice. The journey was designed to follow the path of the Sun through the sky. The Sun's path was literally mirrored by a group of people as it passed over certain sacred sites. By Goodman's account, the sacred sites involved were the Black Hills, Harney Peak, *Pe Sla* (the center of the Black Hills that is called Reynolds Prairie), and *Mata Tipila*, or Devil's Tower in present-day Wyoming. As the pilgrims synchronized their arrival at these sites with the Sun's entrance into specific constellations, which they knew by the season, they were reenacting its journey across the sky. At each point along the way, ceremonies were done, culminating in the Sun Dance at Devil's Tower at the summer solstice. (Goodman, p.11)

Not only is this ritual journey fascinating evidence of the intimate relationship between the people and the stars, it may be the only such journey that any culture anywhere has ever done. I am not sure whether it is still being done today, though I have been led to believe that it is, at least in part.

Unlike the Skidi Pawnee who drew simple crosslike stars on dwellings and various personal and ceremonial objects, the Lakota portrayed the stars as "cones," rendering them unrecognizable to the uninitiated or non-Lakota. The cone symbolized a vortex of light, suggesting that a star is a three-dimensional body filled with vital life force, a living spirit or god if you will. (Goodman, p.18) In addition to the maps mentioned earlier, there also exists a single chart that Goodman alleges depicts the telltale cones painted red and blue. The fact that they were painted made them different from those on the more common charts. That particular map serves as both Earth and star chart in one, and is symbolized by two connected cones, like an hourglass, a further, more precise indication of the Earth-star connection. The red cones represent rivers, valleys, hills, and mountains on Earth, while the blue ones represent stars. (Goodman, p.19) Whether or not the Lakota star cones were also painted on garments or ceremonial objects I am not sure. But the design did play an important role in Lakota daily life.

Like all American Indians the early Lakota were avid skywatchers. The most practical reward of skywatching was the order it provided to life on Earth, and its revelation of the cyclic nature of the entire physical world. The Lakota knew and understood both. But they also discovered sacred order. To the Lakota the stars were the "holy breath of the Great Spirit" and the movement of the stars provided spiritual instructions! (Goodman, p.1)

When viewed from the perspective of Jungian psychology this implies that the stars and constellations were responsible for the most deeply ingrained and profoundly influential archetypes in Lakota consciousness. (And I daresay that these archetypes still reside in Lakota consciousness.) Even if the star journey and other stellar-oriented ceremonies are no longer practiced, the Lakota star stories exist. The stories serve to keep the archetypes alive. Stories comprise the foundation of a people's place in the world and in the universe. In that way tribal legends determine a people's identity.

Jung also said that archetypes can be dormant. If and when specific ones "awaken" into activity, they can have profound effects on the individual or, in this case, the collective people. I believe the Lakota will experience just such an awakening in this time leading up to and on into the next millennium. Such an awakening will surely empower them in any number of ways.

Spiritually the empowerment will most likely effect an appreciation for and value of the old spirituality, the Tradition if you will, in its entirety. This in turn will ultimately reinstate the Tradition and its practice far beyond what it is today, and assure its survival. I feel that the birth of Miracle, the white buffalo calf, a few years ago, was an omen of Lakota resurrection. Other signs, such as the Star Knowledge Conference, are appearing all the time.

However, speculation regarding the future must not cause us to lose sight of the all-important and revealing point made earlier: The movement of the stars, heaven's activity if you will, provided *instructions* to the people on Earth. This belief carries the meaning of what goes on in the sky beyond timekeeping purposes, beyond a simple belief in the "livingness" of the stars. Stars were the teachers. They were the Divine Authority. The knowledge they provided gave them input in virtually every aspect of Lakota life.

Our question then is: What were the people taught? The nature of the heavens? The existence of life forms in other star systems? Prophecies concerning the future of Earth and its inhabitants? The technique of Starwalking? The location of stargates and other secrets regarding the vast starscape, or even the universe as a whole? My guess is all of the above.

An intimation of Lakota star lore both profound and subtle is found in the construction of the most common of the early Sioux dwellings, the tipi. Shaped like a cone, *and thus a star,* the tipi was built around poles erected to form a triangle. Seven more poles were added to represent the four directions, up, down, and center. Another two symbolized the twelve months in a year. (Goodman, p.1) Legend says that the first twelve tipi poles represent the Morning and Evening stars, the seven stars in the Big Dipper, and the three belt stars in Orion: twelve stars, twelve months, twelve poles. (Goodman, pp.16-18) The tipi symbolizes the true inner shape of Earth, which, like that of a star, is a vortex of light. The seven poles added to the basic structure not only stabilized the "world," but also provided order to space, time, and movement, an order that was first established by the Sons of the Wind. The last two poles controlled the flow of air in the dwelling, air being the vehicle of the spirits. (Goodman, p.17) The magic in this is that when all the poles are in place the tipi becomes a *living, breathing entity* that can communicate with the higher powers of the universe.

The building of the tipi was a rebuilding of the primal star, the reestablishment of the directions and the reaffirmation of the cosmic laws that express Divine Will. Living inside a tipi was to experience the equivalent of living inside the Earth Mother, and within a star! When the structures were complete the tipis were covered with buffalo hides, yet another indication of the Lakota's connection with the stars. The buffalo is believed to embody the power of the Sun. (Goodman, p.17)

It would be fair to say that there are different levels of Lakota stellar theology. As is usually the case the uninitiated knew only a certain amount. The deeper spiritual knowledge was known only to an initiated few. The knowledge was passed on orally, making the keepers of the Tradition, the Wisdomkeepers, the most important members of the tribe.

At the core of the knowledge are the stories of a stellar deity known as Fallen Star. It is safe to assume that the entire stellar tradition is concealed within the words, the story, and implications of the Fallen Star mythology. Born of a terrestrial mother and a stellar father, Fallen Star was a tall male sky god from whom brilliant light shone. He was "the protector, the bringer of light and higher consciousness, [who] travels from one Lakota band to another, and everywhere he is recognized, expected, and reverenced." (Goodman, p.18)

It almost sounds as if this star being was physical, a human rather than a spirit. I would not be surprised if that were the case, that an actual human being, a male, was the Teacher at a time long ago, and then became a mythical figure. It is the evolved "light nature" of Fallen Star to which all humans aspire and which they must ultimately achieve in order to become enlightened beings. But a deeper spiritual truth concerning existence is contained within the entity that is Fallen Star. He was a sort of "messiah" figure who provided an example for the people. We know the Lakota believed in life after death as evidenced by the mention of the soul's return to its home in the stars. (Goodman, p.13) Here again, these are a people who believe their ultimate home is in the heavens.

The reenactment of the Sun's journey and the sacred rites that were performed at each sacred site along the way assured the renewal of life on this planet, and that renewal was never taken for granted. The people had to participate in bringing it about, they had to do their part. The rites also assured abundance, a good hunt and food for another year. It was the ritual journey that depicted the exemplary life of Fallen Star, and that maintained the tradition for the entire tribe. (Goodman, p.21)

The ritual journey began when the Sun moved into Dried Willow (Aries and Triangulum constellations) in the spring, and ended at Devil's Tower, which the Lakota called the Bear's Lodge (eight stars in Gemini), on the summer solstice. There one of the most intense and powerful of all Lakota rituals, the Sun Dance, took place. (Goodman, p.12) The entire journey involved what the Lakota simply called the Sacred Hoop, which was comprised, collectively, of Orion, the Pleiades, and the stars Capella, Sirius, Procyon, Castor, Pollux, and Auriga B.

For the ceremony, a symbolic tipi embodying the power of the Sun was created and in doing so the cosmic cycle was reaffirmed. Only through this incredible ritual act of suffering (the Sun Dancers' flesh was pierced by an eagle's talon, wood splinter, or some other sharp object which was then tied to a heavy buffalo skull or some other object the dancers could pull on until their flesh was actually torn) could a sense of complete freedom be known and joy reign throughout the world. The entire spring journey and the sacred Black Hills were encircled by the corresponding stars overhead. From the journey the people once again received spiritual guidance, renewal, and power from the Sky Gods. (The Sun Dance still is celebrated by many western tribes. It is the time when all major tribal decisions are made; a time when flesh and blood are voluntarily given by the participants so that the world might be re-created and all life renewed. It is an *act of giving back to the Spirits what has been given to the people*.)

The Lakota, like the Hopi and others, knew when the solstices and equinoxes occurred by watching the stars. Starwatching in fact timed every major event in Lakota life, including the buffalo hunt and major ceremonies. The Spring Journey made a loop that must surely have corresponded with what Black Elk, the Oglala holy man, called the Sacred Hoop of Life, which is the unity of all things that exist. When the Sun's journey along the ecliptic carried it into the constellation called Dried Willow, the people were in their winter camps in what is now Nebraska and western South Dakota. At this official beginning of the symbolic trek, the sacred pipe ceremony took place in order to assure the renewal of life.

The travelers next moved on to Harney Peak, arriving there as the Sun moved into the Seven Little Girls (the Pleiades) star group. Goodman's sources described the ceremony that occurred as "a spiritual power which manifested itself through thunder and lightning," and as "a life-giving and life-destroying power that fights against evil." (Goodman, p.12)

The next leg of the journey carried the people from Harney Peak to the center of the sacred Black Hills. The Sun had now entered "Race Track" or the "Sacred Hoop" constellation. Here, a ceremony was performed for welcoming back all life in peace from winter. By May, a ritual to welcome back the birds, animals, and plants was performed at what is now called Reynolds Prairie. (An interesting sidenote of that ceremony is that prayers were made for a white buffalo to come during the year! We could think of Miracle, the rare white buffalo calf, as a "gift" from the stars. This is the way it works, is it not? Prayers get answered all the time. But sometimes the prayer is a petition for a "sign" that is important to a people and their nation. With Miracle's birth, the Sioux got their sign . . . and it is a good sign indeed. Aho!)

Finally, when the Sun moved into the Bear's Lodge area of the heavens, the people arrived at Devil's Tower. Then the Sun Dance took place, a dance the travelers had been preparing for by fasting, purification, and silence. (Goodman, p.12)

The constellations, as we know them, involved in the Sun's passage in spring are Aries, Triangulum, the Pleiades, Gemini, Canis Minor, Orion, Canis Major, and Auriga. In some constellations only certain stars were significant to the Lakota and those stars were part of Lakota-defined stellar groups. These individual stars were Sirius, Castor and Pollux, Rigel, Betelgeuse, the three belt stars in Orion, Procyon, Capella, and the Beta star in Auriga. (Goodman, p.12) Notice that these stars were of importance to virtually all ancient cultures so far discussed in this book.

Certain of the constellations and single stars that mapped out the ceremonial pilgrimage are worthy of a more detailed mention. A case in point is the Big Dipper, composed of seven stars (as seen from Earth). The Lakota sort of "divided" the constellation into parts. The four stars in the handle helped the spirits of the dead to enter the celestial realms and guided them in how to live in Sky Country. (Goodman, p.44) It is easy to see why they thought of them as a bridge when the handle stars are viewed this way. They really do look like an arched roadway. They were called "the mourners," a further indication of the constellation's connection to death and to the human soul's return to the stars. Within the ladle part of the Dipper a sacred coal was kept by the Spirits to light the fire of the original sacred pipe. (Goodman, p.22) Curiously, there is a Lakota legend about a star that was once in the center of the Dipper's cup. Where the star was there is now a hole through which the dead may pass into the spirit world.

This concept of a "hole" in the cup of the Big Dipper really gave me some interesting food for thought: Are there such "features" in other parts of the Star Nation? If so where? How did the Lakota know about this odd feature? Were they Starwalkers? How else would they have known so intimate a detail as the "hole?" Obviously answers to these questions would reveal an even greater depth and complexity to Lakota stellar cosmology and probably other star cults. I have long felt that star shamans or Starwalkers would have had intimate knowledge of our neighborhood in the galaxy, going beyond simply knowing the nature of the power inherent in the stars. Unusual sky features would include "portals" or stargates, star "ladders," and stellar arcs like those created by the belt stars in Orion and the handle of the Big Dipper.

I personally know they exist because I have encountered and experienced them in my own Starwalking and stellar-oriented ceremonies. By "portals" I mean that there are many openings or entryways in interstellar space, thus portals or stargates into other dimensions of time/space. Going through a portal of this sort allows a Starwalker to go into another dimension or level of space, into the "subconscious" of space if you will. In this dimension Starwalkers come into contact with interdimensional beings, for lack of a better term, Star Spirits, galactic beings, many of those entities who "work" with humans as sources of channeled information, and Innerplane Teachers. These are precisely the types of beings that the Lakota and the Skidi spoke about as Fallen Star and Pahokatawa.

Entering these portals facilitates what I would call *interdimensional travel* or *time travel*. Starwalkers who know where to enter these openings (because they were taught or they intuited where they are) can travel into the depths of space; can enter into the network of space, so literally into a parallel universe. The starwalking experience is more than just a journey into the Star Nation. It is also a time-travel experience the likes of which only an altered state of consciousness can deal with and understand.

Let's pursue this further. Throughout my studies of astronomy and physics I have had a particular interest in quantum mechanics, oftentimes referred to as the "new physics." Discovered earlier in this century, born from Einstein's theory of Special Relativity, the theory of the existence of parallel universes has been on the cutting edge of physics for some time now. Fred Alan Wolf answers the question: What is a parallel universe in this way. "Like an everyday universe it is a region of space and time containing matter, galaxies, stars, planets, and living beings. In other words, a parallel universe is similar and possibly even a duplicate of our own universe. Not only in a parallel universe must there be other human beings, but these may be human beings who are exact duplicates of ourselves and who are connected to ourselves through mechanisms explainable only by using quantum physics concepts." (Wolf, p.22) He also explains how Einstein's theory predicted the existence of black holes, that the black hole isn't really a "hole" at all, but a "tube" that bridges possible parallel universes! (Wolf, p.22) This tube has been referred to as the Einstein-Rosen Bridge.

While I do not believe Starwalkers travel through black holes to get into other dimensions, I do feel that these constitute "gateways" into other universes. Time travel and black holes and the "physics" of it all are matters certainly far more complex than what has been stated here or than I personally understand. The fact remains that modern physicists are delving into theories that carry them and us toward an idea of reality that is a far cry from ordinary Newtonian mechanics.

Throughout his book Wolf takes the all-important element of mind, which I believe is the real key, into careful consideration: "Our minds are thus tuned or are tunable to multiple dimensions, multiple realities. The freely associating mind is able to pass across time barriers, sensing the future and reappraising the past. Our minds are *time machines*, [italics mine] able to sense the flow of possibility waves from both the past and the future. In my view there cannot be anything like existence without this higher form of quantum reality." (Wolf, p.151)

Mind . . . understanding it and working fearlessly with it . . . that is indeed the key. When it comes to what we know about the human mind and the nature of the universe, it is not enough for anyone to simply say that the "stargate" or "portal" entryways into parallel universes do not exist. As we investigate the star myths, what we find there may surprise us. I am certainly not saying that Starwalkers traveled into deep space physically. The mind was their spacecraft.

Stargates were known to many of the ancestral peoples, including the Lakota. I feel that the "hole" in the ladle of the Big Dipper, a constellation of tremendous significance to virtually all cultures who place stock in the stars, is a mythical indication of just such a portal. It is interesting to note that Comet Hyakutake appeared in the spring of 1996 in the precise area where the "hole" was reputed to be. The huge comet was an unexpected visitor that slipped into our solar system, unseen a couple of weeks prior to its being clearly visible to the naked eye. This suggests that it might have been an interdimensional traveler! If the Lakota "knew" there was a hole or portal in that area, chances are it still is there.

Before leaving the Big Dipper let us note its connection to what may be the most powerful object the Indians possess: *chanupa*, the Sacred Pipe. While the pipe is of importance to virtually all Native peoples, it is particularly so to the Lakota. Chanupa was a gift to the people from White Buffalo Calf Woman, which explains why the white buffalo is at the heart of Lakota religious symbolism. The people viewed the Dipper as the heavenly counterpart of the wooden spoon used to carry the contents of the pipe. For the Lakota, if there is a pipe ceremony going on on Earth, there is one going on in the heavens. (You will recall the significance of mirroring, surely made very clear in the Big Dipper's role in the sacred pipe ceremony at the beginning of the Spring Journey.) Goodman poses the obvious questions when he asks, "What is the live coal? What is the pipe?" (Goodman, p.310) He says the Sun is the hot coal, and the Pipe is the Dried Willow constellation. He also points out that dried willow is a main ingredient of the smoking mixture for the chanupa.

For the Lakota to perceive the pipe ceremony taking place in the sky is nothing less than remarkable. It certainly makes crystal clear that the stars are the teachers who provide spiritual instructions to the people. When I first learned about the "pipe in the sky," I was reminded again how bland our non-Native view of the stars really is. How much we are shown when we have the eyes to see!

In addition to the Big Dipper, the Lakota paid attention to the five stars in the constellation we know as Leo, which they called "The Fireplace." These stars correspond closely to the firepit inside the lodge where the Sweat, a purification rite common to many Native Americans, takes place. The constellation known as "The Hand" is related to a story of a chief who lost his arm because of his selfish behavior and his unwillingness to give of himself. (Goodman, p.27) In this story divine intervention came in the form of the Thunderers who took the chief's arm against his will. It is regeneration of the arm, therefore life and fertility and harmony on Earth, that the people seek by doing the Sun Dance. The Hand constellation includes the stars in Orion's belt, Orion's sword, the star Rigel, and the star Beta Eridani in Eridanus. (Goodman, pp.26-27)

The Lakota also took special notice of the Milky Way, called the "Road of the Spirits," which leads to the spirit world somewhere in southwestern Sky Country. (Goodman, p.23) There is amazing consistency in how many peoples the world over thought of the Milky Way as a "road" or "bridge" that led into the sky. Most of the references imply that it is a road used by the deceased. The concept of a celestial road is intriguing to me because I think the Ancients saw roads all over the sky. And star shamans, knowing of the heavenly byways, have long made use of them through transcendental means and experience. It seems obvious to me that the major road would have been the Milky Way. Because of the way it appears in the night sky, it is easy to see how it became the major visible link between Earth and sky, making it the logical and easy jumping off point for any journey into the Star Nation. In a later chapter I propose the existence of what I call *celestial leys*, invisible "roadways" in the sky that form the celestial or cosmic grid, and that link stars to other stars in a fashion reminiscent of the terrestrial leys that criss-cross Earth, further evidence of mirroring. As above, so below.

So, what are we left with here? The Lakotas' long stellar tradition stands out. Why was this tradition unique to this one band of people within the great Sioux nation? (Just as their Skidi neighbors, also a small band within a larger nation, knew things that apparently the rest of the Pawnee did not.) It is my belief that the uniqueness of each is due in part to their having Starwalkers, not just sky-watchers or stargazers, but Starwalkers. Such bands or tribes would have had access to the entire body of ancient star wisdom. Starwalkers had access to the stars and their power. They knew the heavens inside and out, so to speak.

All the ceremonials performed by the Lakota took place within the Black Hills because for them no place on Earth held greater power or more power. Being in a sacred place, if we know it to be sacred, and doing ceremony can enliven and inspire the mind and propel us into experiences we might never have otherwise. Goodman states that "[T]he ceremony, on earth and in heaven, sends a voice that, with the four relations, we may live well in the manner suited to the way the Power of the World lives and moves to do its work, that we may all walk with our generations in a dancing manner on the good red road." (Goodman, p.12)

That among the Lakota there were specially trained individuals whose task it was to "keep" the Moon and the stars, including the Sun, is beyond doubt. Were these "keepers" Starwalkers? Yes, I say. We know it was imperative to the Lakota to be doing on Earth what the stars were doing in the sky, that this was the absolute rule by which life must be lived. And right living could only take place under the watchful eye of the Sky Gods. We also know that certain stars were lauded and given special attributes. How long have the

Lakota known what they know about the stars? How long have they been taught by the Star Spirits?

Based upon precise calculations of Lakota constellations when the Sun was moving through say Dried Willow in the spring and taking precession into account, it becomes apparent that this knowledge has been a part of the Lakota stellar tradition for 2000 to 3000 years! (Goodman, p.35) This puts the early Lakota in roughly the timeframe of the ancient Egyptians, Babylonians, Maya, Aztecs, Olmecs, and others. It looks like around that time there was an "awakening" of sorts. People on Earth were "given" or became aware somehow of a tremendous body of stellar knowledge that formed the foundation of star-based religions throughout the world.

Admittedly, it is difficult to believe that so sophisticated a star cult could be totally gone from the lives of those who once lifted their minds and souls from the hold of the Earth Mother to stroll in ecstasy and peace among the stars. What would our world be like today if we, the people, were still conscious of the spiritual link between heaven and Earth? By regaining that sacred link we could once again look to the stars to help us learn of our place in the cosmos. Today, the Lakota and other Indian peoples are experiencing a renewed interest in their spiritual tradition. We can only hope that a revitalization of the Lakota star theology will come to pass and that this sacred knowledge will someday be open for us all to know and understand. Aho!

CHAPTER TWELVE

STAR PEOPLES OF MESOAMERICA AND SOUTH AMERICA

It is only now, as their alarm-clock is about to ring, that we are at last able to see what it was that drove them [the Maya]. We are beginning to understand that they had knowledge vital not only for their own time but for the very survival of the human race in our own.[1]

Adrian Gilbert

There is an old saying that goes, "It is all in how you look at it." During my study of the astronomy of the ancient peoples it has become clear to me that different cultures had their own way of looking at the world, at life, and at the sky. The views of each culture set it apart from all others. Sometimes a perspective is so unique that it assures them a place in time long after the people themselves have disappeared. The ancient Maya were such a culture.

The ancient Maya lived in present-day Central America. They were pyramid builders and architects of great cities, and their art continues to rank among the world's greatest. If their civilization was primitive by today's standards, they "were richly endowed in other respects. Recent researches show that they developed their psychic faculties in ways that we have not even suspected are possible. Like the Aborigines of Australia they made active use of dreaming as a way of foretelling the future and of understanding the present. They also followed the planets and stars with uncanny accuracy even though they had no telescopes or modern instruments. Above all, they were deeply religious, believing, like many medieval Christians, in the need for mortification of the flesh and

191

self-sacrifice if they were to gain entry into heaven." (Gilbert, p.2) To place undue attention on the violence of human-sacrifice and self-sacrifice would be to do these Mesoamerican star people an injustice, and almost certainly lead to a misunderstanding of them and their religion.

We find that Mayan concern with "the endless progress of time" is the supreme mystery upon which their religion was based. According to Mayan scholar Eric Thompson, this concern in fact "pervaded Mayan thought to an extent without parallel in the history of mankind."[2] Although the Mayan view of the cosmos had their particular imprint on it, it was not unique. Their universe was centered around a tiered pyramid that rested on a crocodilian in the middle of a cosmic ocean. They divided Earth into quarters and associated each with a color; the center of Earth created a fifth dimension. Heaven was a two-headed dragon whose body was composed of a parade of sky beings held up by four divine spirits. Heaven arched over Venus, the Sun God, and the Moon Goddess.

The Maya also believed that Venus and the Sun were made of the bodies of the Hero Twins who won over the Lords of Death in a series of ball games.[3] As unlikely as it may seem, the games may also provide a major key to our understanding of the Mayan star mysteries. While the Sun and Moon were significant, the Maya singled out Venus and followed that planet's movements closely. It was Venus that formed "the basis of a complex calendrical system that stretched over thousands of years."[4] Their calendar has been subject to various interpretations and speculation on how the Maya arrived at the particular dates they did. The calendar's mechanics have been deciphered, but Mayan reasons for such a complex system for counting time have remained a mystery.

The significance of the planet Venus was multifaceted, evidenced by the fact that it was known by several names. The names may simply have been descriptive, or they may have signified particular powers the planet possessed. In *Beyond the Blue Horizon*, E.C. Krupp provides a list of names by which Venus was known: "great star," "red star," "bright star," "he that awakens the Earth" [herald of the dawn], and "wasp star." (Krupp, p.201) I was immediately struck with its being called "red star," curiously reminiscent of the Great Red Star of the Skidi, who may have counted the Maya among their ancestors. Krupp suggests that this name most likely has to do with Venus being "a morning star in the east" (Krupp, p.201) because assigning colors to the four directions is a common practice among Native peoples. There is no evidence that the Skidi related the Great Red Star to the east, but I instinctively sense that there is more to it than that, I just don't know what.

The Maya had a 584-day ritual calendar founded upon an idealized cycle of Venus. After being the Morning Star for 236 days, the planet disappears for 90 days before reappearing in the west as the Evening Star for 250 days, and 8 days when it is invisible due to its two conjunctions with the Sun. The intricacies of the Venusian cycle were well-documented; five of its 584-day cycles are equivalent to eight of the Sun's tropical years. (Krupp, p.202) (The Maya were not the only ones who paid special attention to Venus transits as the Morning and Evening stars. The Apaches of the American Southwest also have a ceremony that takes place during the time when Venus is changing from the Evening Star back into the Morning Star. A special sacred dance is held to honor the event.)

Well-known astronomer and expert on the Mesoamerican cultures Anthony Aveni stated that "pre-Columbian astronomy was strongly wedded to astrology and religion."[5] This point applies to virtually all ancient cultures and their present-day descendants, so insight into Mayan belief can help us understand these others. For example, Mayan priests saw the universe as having thirteen layers. On each layer there was a planet, a star, a constellation, and a moon. The nine layers below Earth layer constituted the Underworld. Above Earth were the Sun, Moon, and Venus, which made up the so-called "Fire Sticks," a constellation that Aveni suggests may have been the stars in Orion's belt and sword. (Aveni, p.33) A layered universe may have marked time as much or more than it designated "station." The layers culminated at the thirteenth where male and female "creator gods" resided; Earth was closer to the middle. Humans were not gods; neither were they demons. Humans did not live in heaven, or the upper worlds, but neither were they in the lower worlds of darkness.

The Mayan Prophecies is the most compelling book to date about the Mesoamerican cultures and their star-based religion. British authors Adrian Gilbert and Maurice M. Cotterell discuss the significance of the Mayan calendar, particularly its role as the key to realizing just how sophisticated was their knowledge of the heavens. Because I am not particularly mathematically inclined, I find the math difficult. But the basics are clear enough.

Actually, the Maya had two calendars. One was based on the length of Earth's revolution around the Sun; the other was derived from the Moon's cycles and eclipses. They also kept track of the cycles of Mercury, Mars, Jupiter, Saturn, and Venus as noted.[6] This was accomplished with astonishing accuracy and yielded a unique system of counting by twenties instead of tens. (Argüelles, p.19) We mostly think of a calendar as simply a means of counting time. The solar calendar, and the numerical system contained within and reflected by it, is the key to why the Maya approached the subject of timekeeping with such interest; the Venus calendar was used to time rituals. It seems apparent that the calendar was a "code" concealing astronomical knowledge that, by any measure, was nothing short of amazing.

What then did the Maya know about the heavens? Some answers are found in the layout of their cities, and the inscriptions found on temples, statues, and other artifacts. We know that the risings and settings of particular stars, the movement of the setting of particular stars, the movement of the Pleiades constellation and the aforementioned planets, as well as the activities of the Sun and Moon (which led to the ability to predict eclipses) tell us what celestial bodies and phenomena were at the root of their stellar wisdom. Great cities that included temples, huge stepped-pyramids, and ceremonial centers were at the center of their everyday life, religion, and culture. The gods lived in the heavens, humans on Earth. The temples and the rituals that took place within them connected the earthly realm with the "unattainable divine."

Defying the climate, the topography of the land, and numerous other factors, Mesoamerican architects and astronomers laid out grids of huge cities such as Palenque and Teotihuacan in grand and precise orientations aligned with specific astronomical events. An example is seen at Teotihuacan where the heliacal rising of the Pleiades signaling a change of seasons is the model for the city's curious orientation. The great ceremonial center was built in such a way as to mark the rising and setting of the Sun and certain stars and the movements of the Pleiades and certain of the planets. The incredible feats of construction coupled with a sophisticated knowledge of astronomy allowed these ancient people to build cities that continue to baffle archaeoastronomers. The great grids are testimony to the fact that nothing was more important in the lives of the astronomer-priests of Mesoamerica than what went on in the heavens.

But as incredible as Mayan astronomy was, and as marvelous the civilization they constructed, it didn't last.

Why did they abandon their temples and cities? What caused their civilization to collapse? What drove them to retreat south into the hills, or to the plains of the Yucatan Penisula to the north? (Gilbert/Cotterell, p.3) Were they invaded? Or was it something more catastrophic? Something celestial? If the Gilbert and Cotterell theories are right, it was indeed something celestial, something that concerned the Sun. And, that something affected not only the Maya but the other well-known cultures of the area, including the Aztecs.

The warriorlike Aztecs arrived in the Valley of Mexico northwest of the Yucatan during the thirteenth century A.D., led from the north by a prophet named Tenoch. Once there they settled on a snake-infested island situated in the middle of a huge lake, and soon became the dominant tribe. It is thought that the Aztecs adopted religious beliefs and practices including human sacrifice from the five other tribes in the region. The Toltecs in particular believed that a human heart appeased the Sun and assured its remaining in the sky. (Gilbert/Cotterell, p.5) Like their contemporaries, and the Maya before them, the Aztecs were avid skywatchers.

Similar to the Maya, the Aztecs divided time into ages. Each age was ruled by a particular deity, and each was destroyed by a cata-clysm. (This is quite similar to the Four Worlds of the Hopi, the first three of which also ended because of natural disasters brought about by the people's wrongful living.) The ages were called "Suns," and the four previous to the present fifth one consisted of varying timespans that ended by flood, wind, fire, and what was described as a "rain of blood and fire." (Gilbert/Cotterell, p.72) Whether it is "World" or "Sun," the end was the same: *natural disasters of catas-trophic proportions!* Surely the prevalence of these prehistoric myths extended far beyond mere coincidence. We shall see that this could very well indicate events with dire consequences for our future.

Like the ancient Egyptians, both Maya and Aztecs were pyramid builders. Of these structures, the most celebrated were the impressive Sun and Moon pyramids built by the Maya at Teotihuacan outside Mexico City, and the complex at Tenochtitlan, the Aztec capital. Also, like the Egyptians, both Maya and Aztecs placed great importance on the Milky Way, viewing it as the bridge over which the dead traveled into the heaven world. But it was a particular feature of the Mesoamerican Milky Way that caught my attention: It had a "gate" on each end! One lies between the constellations Gemini and Taurus, the other between Scorpio and Sagittarius. (Argüelles, pp.155-156)

The earliest civilizations in the Americas were the Olmec, and somewhat later, the Zapotecs. These peoples perhaps were the originators of what the Maya and Aztec knew. True or not, where did the Olmecs get their knowledge? Gilbert and Cotterell fly in the face of orthodoxy when they propose this answer: the Atlanteans! (Gilbert/Cotterell, p.165) This is not surprising for, when we are tracing an-cient esoteric and exoteric knowledge, the path often seems to end up with Atlantis and its priestcraft. (In fact we can only go back so far in any area of human history before running into the probable existence of that advanced ancient culture, brought to the world's attention by the philosopher Plato. *The Mayan Prophecies* offers a sensible and credible argument for the existence of Atlantis, suggesting that stellar knowledge came from sources more ancient than the early Egyptians, Maya, Aztecs, American Indians, or any historical others.) Regardless of its origin the astronomy of the early peoples of Mexico was the factor that shaped their mysterious, intriguing civilizations more than any other.

Another Western Hemisphere people, the Inca, had a special relationship with the stars, especially with the Sun. They watched the heavens carefully. Unlike their contemporaries and predecessors, the Inca were not known for their astronomy as much as for their architecture. However, placement of many of their structures was based upon the movements of celestial bodies. Temples enclosed by massive stone walls were built throughout western South America and comprised an integral part of the entire Incan empire.[7] Of these, the Temple of the Sun at Cuzco reveals the most about how the Inca viewed the world.

Located at the center of the great Incan empire, the temple was divided into great halls that were dedicated to the celestial bodies of primary importance to the Incas. Aveni quotes the sixteenth-century chronicler Garcilasco: "Another hall, next to that of the Moon, was dedicated to the planet Venus, the Seven Kids, and all the other stars. The star Venus they called Chasca, meaning 'having long curly hair.' They honored it saying that it was the Sun's page, standing closest to him and sometimes preceding and sometimes following him. The Seven Kids they respected for their peculiar position and equality in size. They thought the stars were servants of the Moon and therefore gave them a hall next to that of their mistress, so they would be on hand to serve her. They said that the stars accompanied the Moon in the sky, and not the Sun, because they are to be seen by night and not by day." (Aveni, p.295) These comments shed a lot of light on Incan astronomy.

I do not remember ever before coming across any text like this. I found the Moon's relationship with the stars exclusive of the Sun especially interesting. The reference to the seven lunar attendants probably represents a constellation, most likely the Pleiades or the Big Dipper. Venus as the Sun's attendant was also of particular importance as both Morning Star and Evening Star. The temple was oriented to the summer solstice sunrise and the winter solstice sunset, as was the complex of main streets. (Aveni, p.246)

The Pleiades played an important role in Incan religion. Curiously, the star group is sometimes portrayed as being comprised of *thirteen* stars, which Aveni points out would not be an unusual number that could be seen in the thin Andean air. It is also shown as the familiar seven, representing the seven eyes of Viracocha, the Incan god of thunder. If it was the Pleiades depicted two different ways, each has its own meaning. What those meanings might have been however, I don't know.

The identities of other stars and constellations that played a part in Incan astronomy are in dispute. For example, some astronomers think that a particular configuration of stars represents the Southern Cross constellation, while others suggest that it may be the three belt stars in Orion, with the brilliant *Betelgeuse* and *Rigel* forming the top and bottom of the cross. (Aveni, p.33) According to Aveni, "an unmistakable depiction of Orion appears on the temple at Coricancha, where the region of its Great Nebula is circled in the exact place where it exists." (Aveni, p.33) Again, this is most interesting and another first as I have not seen any other reference to a nebula as part of the astronomy of any other ancient culture. It certainly bears taking a close look at the Great Nebula in question.

A nebula is a gas cloud where protostars, or newly-formed stars, are continuously condensing out of the nebula material. The Great Nebula in Orion is a stellar nursery. Whether we view a star "birth" from a purely astronomical perspective or an esoteric one, it is an event that generates tremendous energy. On a clear night like those common in the high altitude Andes, the Orion Nebula can be seen with the naked eye, making it entirely possible for Incan astronomers to know of its existence. I have seen it many times, without the aid of a telescope or binoculars, in the clear skies over the Southwestern deserts.

Why was the Great Nebula of significance? One possibility has to do with direction since the general vicinity of its rising is east. Directions were particularly important to the Indians of the Americas. Another possibility is that the nebula might have been considered a rich source of incoming stellar power, power that Incan shamans could have employed for healing, prophecy, or divination. It might also be the location of a stargate. Of course this is only speculation. The Inca, in any case, surely had a special relationship with and connection to the sky and the gods who reside there.

The Mesoamerican's concept of time is a point worth further consideration. Whether it is the Mayan "Long Count," a complex system of counting time, or the sun god, Tonatuih, upon whom everything in the Aztec world depended and without whom time would end, (Krupp, p.24) nothing was more important than time. This concern led the Maya to develop one of the most unique and sophisticated calendars ever. The Gregorian calendar used today bases dates upon the birth of Christ, which was not known to the Maya. The "event" the Mayan calendar was based upon was a celestial one: *the "birth" or first rising of the planet Venus.*

That the Long Count was complex is an understatement. Comprehending it is somewhat easier now due to the work of Mayan expert Joseph T. Goodman, who was able to correlate Mayan dates with our own Gregorian calendar. Goodman's efforts enabled scholars to arrive at a full chronology of the Mayan civilization. This was an incredible revelation! The most significant aspect concerns the end of the last "Sun," or Great Cycle, on August 13 in the year 3114 B.C. Because the end of one cycle is also the beginning of another, this date gives us a structure to predict future calendrical events. Counting forward we find that "the end of the present age will come on . . . 22 December 2012. There is not long to go, for we are living in the closing years of the present cycle." (Argüelles, p.37)

The significance of this date is twofold. First is precisely what it indicates: the end of an age. But then we realize that Mayan history says that all the previous ages ended in catastrophe! A clear understanding of the implications the year 2012 could have for us today is presented in *The Mayan Prophecies*. Cotterell explains the one factor that enabled the Maya to identify the events at the close of each age. Before entering into a study of Mayan astronomy, he had developed his own system of astrology which he called *astrogenetics*. Cotterell came to the conclusion that *"the root of astrology lay in solar influence and the variations of the solar year."* [italics mine] (Gilbert/Cotterell, p.43) Solar variations therefore were what he kept coming back to in his attempts to break the Mayan calendar code. Focusing thus on the Sun eventually led him to the key: sunspots.

Sunspots are relatively cool patches that appear as dark spots on the Sun's surface. Astronomers believe that they are related to the magnetic field, caused by events occurring deep within our Sun's core. There is a rhythm in the phenomena, over a period of some 11.1 years, but the rhythm is not dependable. The spots appear first at the poles, but gradually move to the area of the solar equator. Sunspots can vary not only in appearance, but also in intensity.

In addition to sunspots, Cotterell also investigated the Sun's magnetic field and found that when a sunspot cycle ended, the magnetic field reversed, and this reversal was the "mechanism behind the collapse of one age and the start of another." (Gilbert/Cotterell, p.58) The Maya knew of this sunspot cycle. And they knew that when an age came to an end their world would collapse.

Cotterell and Gilbert say that "As we approach the doomsday year of 2012 which the ancient Mayans prophesied would be the end of the last age, one can only feel apprehension for the future of our Earth." (Gilbert/Cotterell, p.211) I must admit that I share their apprehension. A.D. 2012 is not far off. That the Maya knew such intricate details about the Sun and its behavioral cycles is astonishing, but predictable perhaps when we realize that their astronomer-priests focused practically their undivided attention on a given celestial body. When we study relentlessly, we learn.

Sacred rites were an important aspect of the religious beliefs and practices of the Aztecs too. In my studies I encountered information about the timing of an Aztec feast day that I found particularly interesting and that warrants some discussion. It concerns an event that seems curiously similar to the cosmology of the Hopi. (Keep in mind that it is thought that the Pueblo peoples may be the descendants of the Mesoamericans.) In a discussion of the Pleiades' relation to the timing of the Aztecs' most important feast day, which took place every 52 years, Aveni pointed out that the feast was timed to begin when the Pleiades was overhead at midnight about mid-November. "When the time approached, the priests ascended the Hill of the Star to watch the movement of the Pleiades with great anxiety. And when they saw that they had now passed the zenith, they knew that the movements of the heavens had not ceased and that the end of the world was not then, but that they would have another fifty-two years, assured that the world would not come to an end." (Aveni, p.33)

I remembered the Hopi watching for the belt stars in Orion to be straight overhead at midnight, also during mid-November. That is the time the Hopi Wuwuchim ceremony begins and precisely how it is timed. The stars involved with the Hopi ceremony differ from those of the Aztecs, but the practice is the same. Aveni's reference to the Aztec "Hill of the Star" brought to mind a theory I proposed years ago concerning what I call beacon vortexes. I will discuss the theory in detail in chapter 14. Suffice it to say that the star hill mention leads me to believe that the Aztecs, and possibly the other Mesoamerican peoples, had Starwalkers among their astronomer-priests.

One has to wonder why a civilization would pick out a certain star or planet or constellation to base its religious beliefs upon. I found a statement by Krupp about Mayan timekeeping extremely insightful. He writes: "These intricate calculations were not performed as part of a scientific investigation of the motion of Venus. Instead they were intended to help Maya prognosticators interpret omens based upon their calendar and the behavior of Venus. They installed their kings, sacrificed prisoners, and went to war by those omens. *They were not watching a planet—but a god.*" (Krupp, p.202) (italics mine)

Planets and stars were gods. And that is precisely the point! While the "science" of the Maya and others shows in their intricate astronomical knowledge, that may not be the most revealing factor in understanding what motivated these enigmatic people. The gods were the driving force behind these civilizations. The planets and stars were alive.

Any culture, or any person for that matter, has views about the world . . . the stars . . . each other . . . everything. When some future commentator reports on those views purely from the perspective of what was being viewed instead of why and *what it meant*, how much insight does that provide? What does it reveal about a person or a people? Precious little. This is why we cannot rely on science alone to tell us about a given civilization. Eric Thompson hit the proverbial nail on the head when he said: "Maya astronomy is too important to be left to the astronomers." (Aveni, p.3) In order to develop a relationship with the sky we must be willing to go beyond where science leads us. We must allow the stars and planets to come alive.

Mesoamericans and South Americans were deeply interested in the movements in the sky. They were great astronomers, and their astronomy was in no way "primitive." The Sun and Moon, stars, and planets helped them deal with the sometimes harsh and unrelenting realities of life. Celestial bodies and phenomena helped them cope with often hostile environments, provided order, defined time, and predicted the future. Sky Gods presided over sacred rituals that honored and celebrated both the real and the perceived relationship between heaven and Earth, as well as the one between humans and those supernatural beings who influenced their lives.

Should we envy what these Ancients had and what they believed? Were they simply enslaved by "imaginary" celestial forces whom they feared? Were they hopelessly superstitious? I think not. Let us envy only the simplicity of the ancient mind, for all their sophisticated calculations were made for one purpose: *so they could understand and be at one with the Sky Gods.* Let us celebrate the innocence of this purpose. At the same time let us continue the search deep within ourselves for the archetypal imprints of those same Sky Gods. By their very existence, they have made an indelible impression upon the individual and collective human consciousness.

CHAPTER THIRTEEN

STAR KNOWLEDGE
OF THE DOGON

*When I first read the article, which is entitled 'A Sudanese
Sirius System' I could hardly believe what I saw. For here was
an anthropological report of four tribes, the Dogon and three
related ones, who held as their most secret religious tradition
a body of knowledge concerning the system of the star Sirius,
including specific information about that star system which it
should be impossible for any primitive tribe to know.*[1]

Robert K.G. Temple

Have you ever picked up a book and, by the time you finished
reading it, you knew that you would never think of or see
the world in quite the same way? That was how I felt when
I read Robert Temple's *The Sirius Mystery*. Temple poses a question:
"Was Earth visited by intelligent beings from a planet in the system
of the star Sirius?" (Temple, p.2) His research carries the reader on
an incredible journey into the heart of one of the most mysterious
tribes on Earth: the Dogon of Mali in northwestern Africa. These
people possess a remarkable body of astronomical knowledge.
What they know is baffling enough. *How* they know it is the real
mystery.

Dogon religion revolves around just one star, Sirius, the brightest star that can be seen from Earth, and its invisible companion
they call *po tolo. Tolo* is the Dogon word for star; *po* is a particular
grain that grows in West Africa. The name was chosen, according to
the Dogon, because the po seed is the tiniest thing known to them.

Reading Temple's book, my mind often went back to the Skidi
Pawnee of the North American Great Plains. They, like the Dogon,
were unlike the tribes around them. They too stood out from their

peers like gems. With each it wasn't their culture, lifestyle, or where they lived that made them different; it was their cosmology and the unique religions born from it. Though the Skidi star cult of the Great Plains no longer exists, the Dogon do. And with them the star tradition survives. Like the Skidi, it is what the Dogon know that makes them such a unique people.

As a long-time student of astronomy I have a pretty good grasp on the general nature of the universe. So when I learned what the Dogon know about the stars, I appreciated it from two perspectives and had two reactions. I was first overwhelmed by the spiritual and esoteric implications of their astronomy. Then I was baffled that they know it, for from a purely physical *and* scientific perspective, they cannot. *But they do!* No matter how unbelievable the Dogon and their astronomy may be, the fact is they know what they know . . . period.

It is from this factual basis that we all, scientists and laypersons alike, must proceed if we are to learn about and, in the end, gain some understanding of the knowledge itself and of the Dogon who possess it. This knowledge sets them apart from all other human beings. The only answers about their knowledge and where it came from are those the Dogon give us. Should those answers prove to be accepted, they will undoubtedly make the most profound impression upon the collective human psyche of *any answers* to *any questions* ever posed by humanity.

Now let's stop right here! We have come to the first impasse. The Dogon *know* that Sirius is not a single star spinning alone in space. They know that it has a companion, and they are right. But . . . that fact cannot be known by the unaided eye! You must have a telescope. This information regarding Sirius (astronomers call it Sirius A, and its companion Sirius B) is just the tip of the iceberg of what the Dogon know. For them to know that a distant body like Sirius is not a single star but a *star system* is nothing short of remarkable.

There is more. The Dogon say that Sirius actually has *two* companions, the other being the star they call *emme ya.* What's more, they tell us that emme ya has a planet that orbits around it! Emme ya, the "Star of Women," (Temple, p.26) is purported to be larger, yet it weighs about one fourth of po. More incredibly, each star revolves around Sirius A once every fifty years! Both po and emme ya are invisible! (Temple, p.21)

So, Sirius is not one star, but a star system. One of its companions, po, is the smallest and heaviest and revolves around Sirius every 50 years. What's more, the material that po is made of, which the Dogon call *sagala*, is not found on Earth! The other companion, emme ya, is bigger than po but weighs one fourth as much; it also has a 50-year orbital period. Both companions are invisible. The Dogon know the emme ya orbit takes it along "a greater trajectory in the same direction and in the same time as po . . . 50 years. (Temple, p.26) How could they know . . . or even guess . . . about these things?

And it doesn't end there. Dogon astronomer-priests say they know that Saturn has rings . . . a "permanent halo" (Temple, p.28) . . . and that Jupiter has four moons (only four can be seen, and then only with a telescope). They know that planets revolve around the Sun, not in circles mind you, but in elliptical orbits! They have even likened planetary and stellar orbits to the circulation of the blood in the human body. Blood circulation was first traced (by scientific methods) by William Harvey in the 1600s. (Temple, p.29) The Dogon used the analogy long before that. They know that Earth revolves on its own axis, and that this is what makes the sky appear to turn overhead. (Temple, p.30)

Amazingly, they define the Milky Way in terms like "worlds of spiraling stars . . . [the Milky Way] sums up the stellar world of which the Earth is a part, and which spins in a spiral . . . [and there are] spiraling worlds that fill the universe—infinite and yet measurable." (Temple, p.30) This information regarding the Milky Way is quite accurate when we remember that our galaxy is a spiral galaxy that contains so many stars that it is easy to think their numbers are infinite. It is also clear that the Dogon know that Earth is a part of a greater galactic community.

To say that what the Dogon know is astounding is an understatement. Knowing about blood circulation is one thing (and that is only one thing they know about human blood), but knowing that planets revolve around stars, in elliptical orbits no less, that po is invisible and the smallest and heaviest kind of star, and that emme ya is invisible, larger, and weighs four times less, is downright mind-boggling! An even greater appreciation for Dogon astronomy comes when we investigate it from a purely scientific perspective. Keep in mind that the following information is general, and that much of it has only been known as a result of the technological advances of recent times.

Canis Majoris or Sirius, the Dog Star, lies at a distance of nine light-years from Earth. (A light-year is how far light, moving at the speed of 186,000 miles per second, travels in a year.) The star's diameter is twice that of our Sun. Sirius' companion, known to us as Sirius B, is a white dwarf star whose density is more than 90,000 times that of Sirius A; it revolves around Sirius A once every 50 years.[2] (A white dwarf is one whose matter is extremely compressed due to the star's stage of evolution and the relentless law of gravity.) To date, emme ya, the planet companion, has not been found. With the aid of telescopes and, more recently, sophisticated space photography, we know about Saturn's rings and Jupiter's moons. We know that Earth turns on its own axis and revolves around the Sun, and that it is part of a spiral galaxy.

Obviously the Dogon are armed with intricate astronomical facts, facts that are impossible for a "primitive" tribe to know. It cannot be said that they only claim to know these things, or that the knowledge is mythical and cannot be proven, or that it has no basis in scientific fact. Quite the contrary. That knowledge has been proven, dear reader. We know it is so.

To simply dismiss Dogon astronomy is sheer folly. That leaves but one choice: We have to take the Dogon at their word and accept what they know at face value. The willingness to be open-minded brings us to the next step in our journey to gain understanding of these perplexing people: What pray tell is the source of their knowledge? Asking *what* yields us no answers. But when we ask *who*, the Dogon themselves tell us precisely what we want to know.

Long a secret society, the Dogon first came to the world's attention in an article written in the late 1950s by Marcel Griaule and Germaine Dieterlen, two French anthropologists who lived among them for a time and gained their trust. The article, "A Sudanese Sirius System," reveals their unique cosmology and provides insight into their religion and ceremonial practices. The knowledge shared with Griaule and Dieterlen by four Dogon astronomer-priests represents the collective wisdom of four Sudanese tribes: "the Dogon, the Bambara and the Bozo in Segou, and the Minianka in Koutialia." (Temple, p.35)

Their religion centers around the chief god, *Amma*, who is the creator and the monitor of the cosmos. (Temple, p.30) It was Amma who made the stars. Griaule and Dieterlen were told about the existence of other planetary worlds that the Dogon say have creatures living on them, an obvious testament to their belief that we are not alone in the universe. Griaule and Dieterlen report: "The worlds of spiraling stars were populated universes, for as he created things, Amma gave the world its shape and its movement and created living creatures. There are creatures living on other 'Earths' as well as our own; this proliferation of life is illustrated by an explanation of the myth in which it is said: man is on the 4th earth, but on the 3rd there are 'men with horns', *inneu gammurugu*, on the 5th, 'men with tails', *inneu dullogo*, on the 6th, 'men with wings' *inneu bummo*, etc. This emphasizes the ignorance of what life is on the other worlds but also the certainty that it exists." (Temple, p.30)

(In light of this I cannot help but reflect on the recent discovery of a planet revolving around a star located just above the Big Dipper constellation. Astronomers say the planet is very similar to Earth, and is a good candidate for life to have developed. One wonders what kind of life it might be. We tend to be set in thinking that life means the kinds that live on Earth, but of course that is but one possibility. Lifeforms evolve in different planetary environments so their physical makeup and appearance can and probably do differ. The discovery of this planet is a true milestone for it is the only planet known, to date, to exist outside our solar system.)

A group of intelligent beings from the Sirius star system are credited by the Dogon as the source of their astronomical knowledge. These collective beings they call the *Nommo*. It was Nommo or Nommos who founded civilization on Earth. Their home, called *Nommo's placenta*, is different from Earth and the other planets in our solar system which reside in a separate placenta called *Ogo*. (Temple, p.32) The day the Nommo came to Earth is remembered as the "day of the fish," an obvious reference to the description of the Nommo provided by the Dogon: amphibious creatures strikingly similar to the half-man, half-fish god *Oannes* of the ancient

Sumerians/Babylonians. (Interestingly, it is Oannes who is credited
with bringing writing and *astronomy* to our planet.) (Temple, p.269)

Can we accept what the Dogon know as fact (except for emme
ya) because we know it is without at least giving serious consideration to the validity of their source? Some astronomers have voiced
their skepticism or even disbelief regarding the Sirian connection,
yet no one has offered any alternative explanation that credibly
explains how the Dogon came by this knowledge. Krupp proposes
that "it seems more likely that their astronomical *ideas* [italics mine]
are either a collection of good and bad guesses or a garbled record
of old and recent astronomical knowledge which somehow con-
taminated older Dogon beliefs"[3]

Astronomers seem to want it both ways. Most purport to believe
that, in light of the sheer number of stars that exist and the probability that some at least have planets revolving around them, it
would be chauvinistic to think that we are alone in the cosmos. But
attributing Dogon astronomy to "a collection of good and bad
guesses" seems equally as preposterous as believing in fish-men
from Sirius! Whether we choose to believe it or not, the fact remains
that they know things that they cannot know when measured by
today's scientific standards. This alone makes me willing to consider the source the Dogon credit with their knowledge. I am willing
to view the universe from their perspective.

Consideration of the origin of Dogon astronomy leads us to
question what we really know about the universe: Could what we
now regard as science fiction in reality be scientific fact? Temple
anticipates our question when he states: "But in considering the
very origins of the elements of what we call human civilization on
this planet, we should now take fully into account the possibility
that primitive Stone Age men were handed civilization on a platter
by visiting extraterrestrial beings, who left traces behind them for us
to decipher. These traces concerned detailed information about the
system of the star Sirius which is only intelligible to a society as
technologically advanced as ours today. Today was the time when
we were meant to discover these coded facts, I feel sure. Today is
the time we should prepare ourselves to face the inevitable reality
that extraterrestrial civilizations exist, and are in all probability far
more advanced in culture than we ourselves, not to mention in tech-

nology which could enable them to travel between the stars"! (Temple, p.200)

Like Temple, I am coming to believe that Earth has been visited by beings from other star systems, but I personally find the probability of life beyond Earth both disturbing and exciting. Temple says: " . . . intelligent beings from elsewhere in the galaxy have already visited Earth, already know of our existence, may possibly be monitoring us at this moment with a robot probe somewhere in our solar system, and may have the intention of returning in person some day to see how the civilization they established is really getting on." (Temple, p.36) Until they are proven wrong I choose to put stock in the probability of their being right. The Dogon and other indigenous peoples down through time have known something that we have abandoned today as mere superstition.

Like all tribal cultures the Dogon have a ritual around which their entire ceremonial life revolves. Called *Sigui*, the rite takes place only once every sixty years! Diederlen and Griaule report that the purpose of the Sigui rite is the "renovation of the world."(Temple, p.36) The Dogon priests told their French friends about a rock located in the village of Yougo Dogorou. The rock has what sounds like a large fault that is said to light up with a red glow sometime during the year before the time for Sigui to occur. It is also supposed to contain "altars," which house the busts of a race of little people who once lived in the rocks, and a rock painting they call *amma bara*.

The glowing rock is only one omen that heralds the time for Sigui. Another is the prolific growth of an elongated type of gourd at a particular site outside the village. After all the signs have appeared and the necessary astronomical calculations have been made, one of the most mysterious and rare sacred ceremonies currently known to humanity begins. (Temple, p.36) The ceremony is closed to outsiders, which is most likely the reason it has survived in its pure, original form for so long.

While the details of Dogon astronomy are vast and far-reaching in their implications, there are selected parts of it that I feel are of particular significance. The first concerns a symbol I find most intriguing. Known as the *Kanaga*, it is written] — [. The glyph seems strongly reminiscent of the astrological glyph) - (for Pisces.

When I saw it I remembered that the Dogon refer to the day the
Nommo landed on Earth as the "day of the fish." Curiously, the symbol for Pisces is two fishes tied together swimming in opposite
directions! Could there be a connection between Pisces and the
Nommo? Perhaps a "time" is somehow involved? It was after all during the current Age of Pisces that the Dogon first revealed the nature
and source of their secret tradition to the outside world. And perhaps the most provocative point of all, the chief Dogon god Amma
and the Babylonian/Sumerian god Oannes are both depicted as fish-
men!

My second comment concerns the third star the Dogon say is
part of the Sirius system, emme ya. While its existence has not yet
been confirmed, I think it's safe to assume that it does exist since
the Dogon are right about all the other astronomical information. If
the star is there, the Hubble telescope will find it sooner or later.
Learning how the Dogon view this particular star and the planet
they say revolves around it triggered some intuitive thoughts that
bear mention here. That they call emme ya the "star of women" is
what interests me most. The phrase triggered a vision of a planet
populated by a race whose inhabitants include a highly evolved
order of priestesses, skilled in shamanic knowledge and practices.
They appeared to me as amazon-like women, strong and vigorous
both physically and spiritually. I think they are Starwalkers, that they
possess the same body of ancient stellar knowledge that somehow
came to Earth. In light of the tremendous amount of information
coming through various channelers and teachers during the past
several years concerning the Goddess, feminine-based spirituality,
and feminine issues that gave birth to the women's movement, it
makes me wonder if there is *incoming energy* from the Sirius star
system that is influencing women on Earth.

The belief that stars (and planets) exert an influence upon our
lives on Earth is not new. That these influences are "periodical,"
meaning that they are emanated and transmitted to our planet at
strategic times in order to trigger specific energies for specific reasons and results, is an integral part of the Wisdom Teachings, such
as are found in the work of H.P. Blavatsky, Alice Bailey and others.
Are the Sirius/emme ya women of this distant planet the spiritual
ancestors of the women of Earth? Are they sending energy to Earth
women that has triggered an awakening of the Great Goddess with-

in us individually and/or collectively? Are the Sirius women a bio-physical or a genetic prototype of Earth women? Or are they representative of, or the actual manifestation of, the *female archetype* that resides within the collective unconscious of the human psyche? Is the stellar energy from emme ya guiding and influencing the evolution of *all* feminine lifeforms on our planet? I find the Dogon "star of women" most fascinating.

Dogon prophecy says that "a certain 'star' in the sky will appear once more and will be the 'testament' to the Nommos resurrection!" (Temple, p.32) A couple of things stand out in this prediction: A certain star will appear once more, and *it has been visible before.* Which star? It is hard not to notice the similarity in wording to the Hopi Blue Star Kachina prophecy discussed earlier. Each refers to a star, makes it clear that it is referring to a specific and particular star, but neither tells which star.

As pointed out, it was not uncommon for ancient people to refer to just about any celestial body as a "star." This gives us a wider range of candidates to consider. The obvious clue, and most likely the real and only key to deciphering, is found in the words "will appear once more." Both prophecies suggest that the "star" has been seen before. Again, stars do not appear, disappear, and reappear. The one celestial body that fits this description is a comet, which seems to appear out of nowhere, and then it is gone.

But a comet may not be the only candidate for the Dogon or Hopi star prophecies. When I thought about portents that involve celestial events or objects, it came to mind that it could also be a meteor. Most meteors are small and create a less-than-spectacular event. But they do call attention to themselves, particularly if they are large enough to be accompanied by a sonic boom and/or a lighted smoke trail. There have of course been those of significant size as evidenced by Meteor Crater in Arizona, but thankfully these are rare. A meteor might be what the Dogon are referring to as the "return" of the Nommo, because it seems they are talking about an actual object, and a meteorite would be the physical object that falls.

Genesis 1:14 reads: "And God said, 'Let there be lights in the firmament of the heavens to divide day from the night; and let them be for *signs* [italics mine], and for seasons, and for days, and years.'" Whether we today believe in or take celestial signs seriously, we can be sure that many cultures have done so over many centuries.

To return to American Indians for a moment, the Skidi took celestial signs seriously. The Skidi prophecy that tells of the "return" of the prophet Pahokatawa, who claimed to be a meteorite incarnate, is related to the appearance of a "savior" not unlike the Nommo of the Dogon. In any case, the "return" event of both peoples is undoubtedly a celestial one.

In his definitive work on the Skidi Pawnee, *When Stars Came Down To Earth,* astronomer Von del Chamberlain relates a story about what could be called the "latter times," one that has all the elements of a prophecy in its own right. "When the time comes for things to end our people will turn into small stars and will fly to the South Star, where they belong. When the time comes for the ending of the world the stars will again fall to Earth. They will mix among the people, for it will be a message to the people to get ready to be turned into stars."[4]

There are several things that are particularly interesting about this prophecy. Note the suggestion that the people . . . obviously the Skidi . . . will "turn into small stars." Why use the adjective "small?" Why didn't the prophet simply say "turn into stars" . . . period? With my mind still turning over with the Dogon's "smallest star," po, the word "small" seems like it should mean something important. But what? Once the people have turned into small stars they will "fly to the South Star," the Skidi Death Star. The South Star is *"where they belong"* . . . where they came from. . . . Is that their home?

Chamberlain says: "The original South Star may have been Sirius, which rises heliacally in mid-August and would have easily been visible in the sky as a signal to the Pawnee hunters to return home for the harvest." (Chamberlain, p.113) If Sirius was the Skidi South Star it would have been one of the most, maybe *the most,* important stars to the Skidi star cult, comparable to the value the Dogon place on it. The prophecy of the people "flying" to the South Star "where they belong" then would suggest that the Skidi believed they either came from Sirius or that Sirius played some "genetic-spiritual" role in their existence.

The last sentence of the Skidi prophecy is also quite intriguing.

In the "end times" the people who have already "turned into small stars" will return to Earth and mix with the people. Now let's look at this closely. The wording clearly says that stars, who are really "people," will return to Earth, highly reminiscent of the "return of the Nommo" predicted by the Dogon.

Returning to the all-important Dogon ceremony of Sigui: As best I can figure from Temple's information, the time for the next Sigui is around the year A.D. 2023. Perhaps by then we will know a lot more about these people than we do now. Maybe emme ya will have been found. Maybe we will be more willing to take a longer look at what the Dogon know and how they know it. Maybe we will have learned to value the truths hidden within ancient myths and cosmologies enough to investigate them with open minds and hearts. Better still, maybe we will have grown beyond the need for "proof." Hopefully, we will also have come to value and rely upon intuited information with the same respect we now have for scientific theory and evaluation. Only time will tell.

The Dogon are phenomenal people. That is obvious. Their knowledge, regardless of its origins, throws the proverbial monkey wrench into our sophisticated worldview and our version of human history and evolution. They have garnered the attention of astronomers. Surely the research into these people will continue.

My final comment and question concerning the Dogon must be: Are they Starwalkers? I think so. It seems highly unlikely that the Nommo would have given these people such a vast body of astronomical knowledge but not have taught them how to "journey" into the great Star Nation. I suspect that the secret purpose, at least in part, of the Sigui ritual is for Dogon Starwalkers to go to the Sirius star system. To bring back Sirius power to Earth? To be with the Nommo to maintain the memory of them within their collective psyche? I can only speculate. But, their knowledge doesn't bind them to Earth. It binds them to the stars.

What they know is there for us to learn. They await the fulfillment of the return of their "saviors," the Nommo. Have we any choice but to wait with them?

CHAPTER FOURTEEN

BEACON VORTEXES: STAIRWAYS TO THE STARS

*Gratitude to the Great Sky who holds billions of stars -
and goes yet beyond that -
beyond all powers, and thoughts and yet is within us -
Grandfather Space.
The Mind is his Wife.*

so be it.[1]

Gary Snyder (AFTER A MOHAWK PRAYER)

In 1989 while doing research for my book *Terravision: A Traveler's Guide to the Living Planet Earth*,[2] I was having difficulty obtaining information about the location of Native American sacred sites in the southeastern part of the United States. I decided to get in touch with my friend, the Cherokee medicine man, Harley Swiftdeer. As it turned out I already knew about the sites he mentioned, but talking to him turned out to be fortunate in another way because it led me to understand some channeled information I had been given by my Spirit Teacher, Albion, a few years before. Let me explain.

In 1980 my work as a teacher changed directions. I had moved to Arizona and become extremely interested in Native American spirituality. I met the Chippewa medicine man, Sun Bear, and along with the knowledge and Native American connections I gained from my association with him, I came to look at the planet and all that lives on her through different eyes. I became aware that Earth is alive, a living, breathing, evolving entity. With that awareness came an acute interest in the environment and in what has been called *sacred ecology*. I learned about the dire ecological conditions we now face that threaten the very survival of Earth Mother and her children. The more I learned the more I was influenced by the intimate relationship the Native Americans have with the planet and the other kingdoms of life. I realized just how precious this connection is and, like our relationship with Father Sky, how much of it we have lost. I now believe that loss is the root of every environmental crisis we now face.

In the early 1980s I engaged in the study of *geomancy*, the name given to the science of selecting the proper sites for temples and churches. Though this is the "technical" definition, the subject has become much broader over time. It now addresses the existence and nature of natural Earth energy, the flow of that energy through the landscape, and the location and quality of energy at sacred sites worldwide.

My first book, *The Earth Changes Survival Handbook*, is about power spots, which I call vortexes, and sacred sites all over the world. I believe that Earth has a life force and we can develop the ability to sense that natural power; we can "read" the planet's energy and know how that energy affects us physically, emotionally, mentally, and spiritually. Vortexes function as acupuncture points in Earth's body, points where her energy is emitted more strongly than at other places. We can draw upon that energy and use it in constructive ways.

Ancient peoples all over the world knew the locations of these power places because of their close relationship with the planet. In these places they built their stone circles, temples, pyramids, and other ceremonial structures in order to tap into Earth's natural power. Some vortexes are human-created over a period of time by either positive or negative *human events* like ceremonials (positive) and battles (negative). In my mind the existence of vortexes proves that Earth is alive and that her life force can and does affect all that lives here. I have adopted geomancy principles to encompass my own perspective of the way nature works, and to develop techniques by which we can better detect and understand power spots, sacred sites, ley lines, and the planetary aura.

The ancient peoples could sense and work with Earth energy. They knew of vortexes and their power. They knew that at vortex sites, human consciousness can slip more easily into the altered state necessary for attunement to and communication with Nature's subtle forces and the realm of spirits. They were aware of the effects Earth's living energy had upon them and their lives, and how to align themselves with and make use of the energy present at sacred sites. Over time, as ceremonial structures were built at sacred sites worldwide, the connection between Earth and humans intensified. Earth religions sprang up, based on the link between humans, Earth, and the sky.

Archaeoastronomers surmise that ancient sacred sites such as Machu Picchu in Peru, the Big Horn Medicine Wheel in Wyoming, and Stonehenge in England served *dual* purposes: They were both ceremonial centers and astronomical observatories. Gerald Hawkins' 1965 book, *Stonehenge Decoded*, supported the astronomical alignments at that famous site. That book opened the door for speculation about other sites. Many were simple stone circles, or had circular features built into them. Structures that contain circular features include the great Sun Kiva at Mesa Verde in Colorado and the Caracol in the Yucatan. All of these, particularly the deliberately placed stone circles, probably marked natural vortexes that were known to the builders. Natural vortexes can be mountains and hills, springs (particularly those that possess healing power), rivers, waterfalls, active volcanoes, and even an entire valley or canyon. Almost always vortexes have some outstanding or unusual feature. Examples of natural vortexes are the Grand Canyon, Mt. Shasta, the Glastonbury Tor, and numerous sacred wells located throughout the world.

In the early 1980s during a channeling session with Albion, I received some information that added significantly to my perspective of Earth and the ancient people. The communique concerned a particular type of vortex identified for its uniqueness, and also for the role it plays in connecting Earth with the other planets in the solar system and with the stars. Albion called these vortexes beacons. Beacons are located all over the planet, and are connected to one another by terrestrial leys. Furthermore, beacons possess an exclusive feature that the Teacher called *celestial leys*. These serve as "connectors" that link Earth with other celestial bodies. Albion explained how some celestial leys are conduction lines through which planetary, stellar, and cosmic energy comes to Earth. Others are lines through which Earth energy is sent or emitted into systemic, galactic, and interstellar space. This constant reciprocal and cyclic activity joins Earth not only with the other planets, stars, and galaxies, but with the entire universe. In short, celestial leys form a sort of cosmic network that links all celestial bodies together.

The Teacher identified the locations of a few beacons, including Bell Rock in Sedona, Arizona; Stone Mountain in Georgia; Ayers Rock in Australia; and Silbury Hill near Avebury in Wiltshire, England. Beacons continued to intrigue me. I felt like I had a lot of pieces to a puzzle, but I just wasn't sure how those pieces fit together. Then Harley Swiftdeer made the pieces fall into place.

I had asked Swiftdeer, an Oklahoma Cherokee, if he knew the location of any sacred sites of Eastern Band Cherokee. The conversation turned to the fact that so many ceremonial sites have been desecrated. One in particular was mentioned because it has been "altered" with the likenesses of several non-Native Civil War generals carved into its rock face. This, of course, is Stone Mountain outside Atlanta, one of the largest natural mounds of granite in the world. When Harley told me that Stone Mountain was sacred to the Indians of the area and I asked why, his reply floored me! He said, "That was the place where my people went to gain access into the Great Star Nation!"

In a flash it all came together in my mind! *Stone Mountain is a beacon vortex!* I knew instantly what beacon vortexes were and why and how the ancient peoples used them. Beacon vortexes, both natural and human-made, are places where the ancient and tribal peoples went to perform star ceremonies, to gain access to the power of the Great Star Nation and connect with the Sky Gods.

Since that time I have learned the location of numerous beacons. Many are natural hills, tors, and mountains, but others are constructed mounds and earthworks like the mounds in North America, the Babylonian ziggurats, the Egyptian pyramids, and Silbury Hill. Beacons are closer to the sky both literally and symbolically. Standing atop one, a shaman would have both a physical and a psychological advantage. He or she would have been elevated! More importantly, the shaman would be closer to Sky Country. Beacons are the vortexes and sacred sites where Starwalkers walked into the heavens.

The natural beacons are intact, but many of the created ones have been destroyed or worn down by time. Of those I know about, many are natural features in the landscape that were terraced or otherwise altered by humans. Unlike the defacing of Stone Mountain, however, most of these have been altered so that they lend themselves to precessions and other ceremonial uses.

A prime example is the mysterious Glastonbury Tor in Somerset, England, the site of ancient Avalon. A natural beacon, the Tor's terrain was changed when "terraces" were carved into the hill's slopes. A popular theory attributes them to Druid initiates who carved terraces around the 518-foot conical hill to form a backtracking septenary or seven-layered spiral that is still visible today. The assumption is that the Tor was a ceremonial site or a natural temple that was once part of a Druid college complex. The same type of design shows up in Crete, Ireland, and various sites in North America.

I find it hard to believe that anyone could see or experience the Tor and its energy and not know that it was a sacred place. Various authors and teachers who have studied the Tor and its history for many years offer some valuable insights. One of these is long-time Glastonbury resident and expert on megalithic sites, Nick Mann. He has written, "Given the interest of the ancient British peoples in astronomical-calendrical alignments, as for example at Stonehenge, the chambered mounds of Ireland, or the local long-barrows, whatever the Tor was, it might have been perceived as becoming operative when its axis aligned with certain astronomical events."[3] Bingo! I know Nick Mann and I know his work. I trust his conclusions about the sacred sites. Now, he didn't say aligned with any star or constellation; he said that it is aligned with "astronomical events," which could be eclipses, solstices or equinoxes, or the Full Moon. What is really important is that the Tor might have been *activated* when its axis aligned with one or more of those events.

Let's assume that Mann is right. The "activation" would occur at specific times due to particular astronomical events involving the movement of one or more celestial bodies. This could account for the numerous stone circles and other monuments all over the world being oriented as they were, most commonly to the Sun and Moon. Of course the activation was easily predicted, allowing for advance preparation for the sacred rites during the time the site was at full power. These might, in fact, have been the only times some sites were used for ceremony. During all other times, some may have been like giant celestial "clocks" and served simple calendric purposes. Others may have served as astronomical observatories.

Mann's suggestion is compatible with my opinion that beacons are connected to the stars (including the Sun) and to the solar system's planetary bodies (including the Moon and quite possibly the satellites of the other planets) by celestial leys. The incoming planetary and/or stellar forces transported through the leys provide the energy that empowers both the ritual and the participants. In other words the leys are the means through which the incoming celestial energy activates a given site. They are also the means by which a star shaman transmits energy into space. For Starwalkers celestial leys provide invisible lines of force or "waves" that can be "ridden" into Sky Country.

Although my theory of beacon vortexes is difficult if not impossible to prove, through my study of archaeoastronomy I have discovered that a similar concept was once widespread, though it concerned only one site: the world axis. Many cultures believed the axis was a mountain rooted deep in Earth. The mountain supported the sky, clearly an indication of the Earth-sky relationship imprinted in the minds of the earliest humans. Some cultures . . . the ancient Israelis, the Greeks, and some Native Americans . . . singled out particular mountains, real or mythical, as the axis site—for example Mt. Sinai of the Israelis and Mt. Olympus of the Greeks. The Chumash Indians of Southern California believed that Mt. Pinos was the center of the universe.[4] This made "axis sites" the major vortexes to the cultures within which they were found. These vortexes always had to do with the sky and facilitated the Earth-sky connection. However, natural or mythical mountains are by no means the only types of beacons.

Central Java is home to Borobudur, a massive human-built "mountain" that is the largest ancient structure in the southern hemisphere. Its builders went to a great deal of trouble, over eleven hundred years ago, to construct the monument, which is 105 feet high and 403 feet long. It contains some two million cubic feet of stone upon which scenes of the life and teachings of the Buddha and other religious matters have been carved. Three miles of turns and

stairs lead to the top, which is open to the sky. (Krupp, p.291) The
colossal structure obviously served both religious and spiritual purposes. Borobudur was somewhat like a temple or church and was
a pilgrimage site. I feel that spiritually it is an energy generator that
empowered the priests, and perhaps all the people, somewhat reminiscent of the famed Ark of the Covenant.

But was there more? Was the great stupa really another type of
stairway to the stars? Was it a human-made beacon vortex?
Throughout the world there are sacred mountains where the faithful make annual pilgrimages for spiritual renewal, to commune with
the gods, and/or to symbolize reaching Enlightenment. Were artificial mountains like Borobudur, Silbury Hill, the stepped-pyramids in
the Yucatan, created for the same purpose? Both Borobudur and the
Great Pyramid have huge bases that perhaps pull natural Earth force
to the top where a celestial ley shoots it to the stars. One thing is
certain: Being on top of a mountain, a mound, a pyramid, or any
other type of summit, one is closer to the sky and the stars.

While on the subject of mountains let me digress to explore
some mysterious ones that were believed to exist but that were not
terrestrial. *These were in the sky.* Numerous cultures believe that Sky
Country is a duplicate of Earth, complete with trees, rivers, valleys,
mountains, and other familiar terrestrial features. The Paiute, for
example, believe the sky is an inverted world whose mountain
peaks point toward Earth. Similar concepts are found in China and
India. (Krupp, p.291-292) Whenever I go ritually into Sky Country
to work with individual stars I often perceive them with Earthlike
landscapes. The mind seems to have a natural tendency to "human-
ize" alien landscapes and sky beings.

Recently some fuel was added to the fire of my concept of
Starwalking and how it was achieved when I was gifted with an
exceptionally interesting book by Belinda Gore of the Cuyamungue
Institute in Santa Fe. The book concerns specific body postures and
positions assumed by the human figures that appear in the art and
artifacts of numerous cultures, many of which were widely separated by time and distance. Gore explains that the postures, some of
which are highly unusual, were assumed for the purpose of helping
a person get into a trance state. This in turn transported that individual into an altered state of consciousness, giving her or him

access to worlds or dimensions, entities, and powers that would otherwise be inaccessible.

In the book, renowned anthropologist Felicitas Goodman reported her first revelation regarding images drawn upon the walls of a cave near Montignac, France. The drawings, believed to date back to 15,000 B.C., show a male stick figure in ritual posture lying at a 37-degree angle in front of an auroch. Interpreting this posture as one that triggered a ritual journey is a credit to Goodman's skill of observation. She noticed that the man's body was not lying flat and was therefore not meant to show a hunter who had been killed by his prey. In Goodman's estimation this was no ordinary hunter. He was a shaman. Gore says, "[T]his very precise angle was a hallmark of spirit-journey postures performed by hunters, especially for journeying to the Sky World."[5]

She also reports on a workshop participant who was instructed to assume the same body posture as the figure on the cave wall. After her meditation-posture experience the woman told of soaring into the sky world. "I saw a huge snowy-topped mountain encircled with stars like the Paramount Pictures logo—except we were the stars and were dancing in a circle around the peak; we joined hands and flew out into the stars to bring back gifts for our friends." (Gore, p. 174) Goodman and Gore are definitely on to something, surely a long-lost Starwalking technique!

I recently decided to do some research on human-made mound sites wherever they are found, beginning with the moundbuilders of North America. Most of the mounds are located east of the Mississippi River, spread out over some 20 present-day states and in two Canadian provinces. They were built by pre-Columbian architects whose true identity evades us to this day. Mound-expert Richard Balthazar says that "Everywhere a trade link was established, mound building spread, and societies began to take root, including among numerous others, Crystal River in Florida, Marksville in Louisiana, the Copena on the Tennessee River, the Kansas City Hopewell on the Missouri, the Havana Hopewell on the Illinois, and the Effigy Mound peoples of Iowa and Wisconsin."[6] I soon came to believe that most if not all mound, pyramid, and ziggurat builders were societies that possessed the body of ancient star lore in its entirety. *They were Starwalkers.* Of all the sites I have studied, none interests me more than Poverty Point in northeastern Louisiana.

The Poverty Point inhabitants set for themselves an incredible task when they decided, for whatever reasons, to build a complex array of earthen mounds overlooking the Mississippi River floodplain. The end result of the builders' labors was a fascinating construction consisting of six concentric ridges, which at one time were five to ten feet high! Believed to have been built around 1500 B.C. and to have taken as much as five million work hours to construct, the entire complex covers about 400 acres, making it unmatched among North American archaeological sites. Some of the tools they used were imported from the Ohio and Tennessee valleys. Soapstone for vessels had come from the Appalachian foothills of northern Georgia and Alabama, clear evidence of a far-reaching trade network that was a remarkable feat in and of itself.

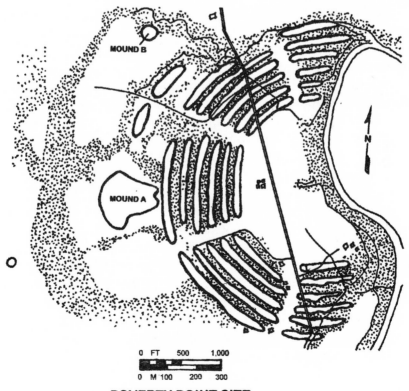

POVERTY POINT SITE

Poverty Point is thought to have been a very large ceremonial complex of earthworks and dwellings surrounding a 37-acre plaza. The four aisles and five sections of the ridges are suggestive of an octagon, although most archaeologists don't think they ever formed that shape completely. The site was occupied for over a thousand years and was most likely home to several thousand people. (Balthazar, p.2) Of all the splendor of Poverty Point, the striking Bird Mound stands out as testimony to the most glorious time in the builders' history. Though eroded from its original height, the mound once rose 70 feet toward the sky. An avenue leading up to it was the focal point around which the village was uniquely arranged.

My first question was why the village was built in concentric semicircles, not likely for purely aesthetic reasons. Further study convinced me that the people of Poverty Point were much more than ancient architects with an eye for design. They were sophisticated skywatchers whose shamans were most likely Starwalkers!

Poverty Point's astronomical features seem to include solar and lunar alignments (solstice and equinox), the risings and settings of a number of stars, constellations, and star groups (open and closed clusters), and planets. These occur in the orientation of streets, houses, and other buildings and are quite like those at other sites worldwide. Astronomers have long had a keen interest in the site. The following was written by the esteemed British astronomer Sir Joseph Norman Lockyer. "It seems natural to assume that standing at the center of the earthwork and viewing along the broad avenues could have provided a well-defined means of marking the setting position of some astronomically interesting object or objects."[7]

As with other sites like Stonehenge and the North American medicine wheels, Poverty Point's northwest and southwest avenues, at the time they were constructed, are in keeping with the summer and winter solstice sunset. This is no accident. Neither is the fact that Canopus, the second brightest star in the sky, sets on a line pointing along the southernmost avenue. Other possible stellar and celestial alignments Lockyer suggests include the setting of the midsummer and midwinter Full Moons, the stars in the belt of Orion, the stars Castor and Pollux, Sirius, and Arcturus. (Lockyer)

I find it particularly interesting that the midsummer and midwinter Full Moons are included in his list of possibilities. This suggests that the Poverty Point people were a *lunar-oriented* society, possibly a matriarchal fertility cult. This might have been the case with many moundbuilders. I also took special note of the mention of the belt stars in Orion, for I am beginning to think that they and Sirius were the most important stars to humans down through time, both calendrically and spiritually.

Most mound sites contain numerous interesting glyphs and figures. These include huge effigies like the Bird Mound at Poverty Point and the famous Serpent Mound in Locust Grove, Ohio. Stone tablets, pendants, pottery, effigy pipes, and shells with glyphs and symbols etched on them have been found at the various sites. Others display pictographs like the so-called *piasa* bird that was carved in the limestone bluffs in Madison County, Illinois. (Balthazar, p.82) Though the figures and glyphs are numerous and vary in style, bird designs are among the most common. It is natural for birds to be associated with the sky and thus the Sky Gods. The bird motifs and effigies found in Wisconsin particularly caught my eye, as some of them almost look more like humans with long winglike arms than they do birds.

A bird is one of the enigmatic effigies found among the Nazca lines in Peru, as is the spider, which is also found etched on a shell at a mound site in Illinois. (Balthazar, p.80) While I cannot say what the spider may have meant to the moundbuilder societies, I do know that it is the symbol of Grandmother Spider, the Creator for the Hopi. The Sioux also tell of a spirit called *Iktomi*, the Spider Man, whose task it is to build cobweb-type ladders to the sky so that the children of the heavens can come to Earth and vice versa.

Bird Motif

The obvious bird-type designs are plentiful and often appear numerous times at a given site. The Wisconsin site also has animal effigies that are simple in design and could be interpreted as being bears, buffalo, wolves, or any number of other animals. (Balthazar, p.34) Whether the bird and animal motifs can be considered symbolic of tribal totems, or whether they represented the Sky Gods themselves, I cannot say. But the thought has crossed my mind that they might represent constellations to which the moundbuilders were especially drawn. They might have also symbolized and/or represented the characters in sacred myths.

The fact that the animal, bird, and reptile figures at many of the sites were mixed with huge human figures is also a curiosity. To me some of the human figures found on the artifacts from mounds in Tennessee, Georgia, and Illinois are highly reminiscent of the Aztec, Incan, and Mayan motifs shown in the art and on temples and artifacts. Could this mean that there is some connection with these Central Americans? Were they the ancestors of the moundbuilders? Did the human figures represent Starwalkers? Priests? Sky Gods in human form? Do the bird figures add to the possibility that the moundbuilders were star cults? We can only ask the questions.

I think that the mounds that were not built or used for burial or generic ceremonial purposes were constructed specifically for use by star shamans in ceremonies that propelled them into the sky. Using this theory as a guideline it becomes relatively simple to determine which moundbuilding societies had Starwalkers and thus possessed the entire body of ancient stellar tradition. A case in point is Bird Mound at Poverty Point. There is no question in my mind that the huge mound was where these unique shamans worked, like their counterparts at places like the Glastonbury Tor, Stone Mountain, Silbury Hill, and Ayers Rock. Clearly, not all moundbuilders had the complete body of knowledge, and their ceremonials surely varied and were performed for varying purposes. So while not all mounds were beacon vortexes, many of them were. Of that I am certain.

The pursuit of mound sites inevitably leads to the famous Cahokia Group in Madison County, Illinois, the largest known group built during the so-called Mississippi period. Numerous mounds and earthworks exist at the site, of which Monk's Mound is the largest. Rising almost 100 feet high, Monk's Mound is "the largest earthwork by volume in the world." (Balthazar, p.52) It is believed that at one time the site may have contained over a hundred mounds. Although many of them are now gone, enough remain to make it one of the most important sites in the world, evidenced by its having been designated a United Nations World Heritage Site. Other big complexes existed across the river where present-day St. Louis is now located. (Balthazar, p.52)

Because of Cahokia's importance, many archaeoastronomers have a special interest in the astronomy of the site. Krupp says that the entire site, including most of the mounds, was oriented to the four cardinal directions. Though the mounds were used for burials, it is still obvious that the builders were concerned with the order in the sky, and that the "city" was constructed by what Krupp calls "a deliberate cosmological plan." (Krupp, p.117) We get a feel for the incredible size and significance of the place when Krupp says that "in its day, Cahokia politically dominated the broad alluvial valley where the Missouri and Illinois rivers meet the Mississippi and influenced more than a million square miles of North America. Perhaps 40,000 people lived there at its height." (Krupp, p.116)

Monk's Mound is not the only Cahokia structure that may shed some light on the people who constructed this magnificent prehistoric city. Uncovered during excavations in 1961, the so-called Sun Circle seems to have originally been a giant circle with as many as 47 significant "points," three of which marked important astronomical events: winter solstice sunrise, summer solstice sunrise, and the sunrises at the equinoxes. Krupp advises that the astronomical alignments may not be precise enough to really count, but he speculates that "[T]he Sun Circle may not have been a device for measuring the movement of the sun, but perhaps it was the place where the sun's actual travels were ritually observed."(Krupp, p.32) If so, this would have been analogous to the annual spring ritual journey of the Lakota.

I feel that Cahokia's builders were a solar-oriented society, and in that way were similar to the solar-oriented inhabitants of Poverty Point. The Bird Mound at Poverty Point and Monk's Mound at the Cahokia site probably served exactly same purpose: They were places where Starwalkers "walked" into the sky.

Arguably, no site in the U.S. is more mystifying than the Great Serpent Mound in Locust Grove, Ohio. While I do not consider it to be a beacon vortex, it is an intense power spot that is extremely important and its builders were closely connected to the stars.

A couple of years ago I led a group to view that giant effigy; it also provided me with an opportunity to do a channeling to see what Albion might say about its energy. When opening to the mound's energy, I immediately sensed that it was not a beacon, but was closely connected to the Sun and to the constellation Draco. When Albion spoke he said that once during a full solar eclipse, night replaced day. In the moments while the eclipse was taking place, a large meteor blazed across the dusky sky, leaving a serpent-like trail in its wake! To the people this meant that a snake had swallowed the Sun! The meteor's unexpected appearance intensified what was already a terrifying experience, and foretold a terrible time of bad weather and famine to come. There are scholars who support the theory that the oval-shaped object that is in the serpent's mouth may depict the Sun being swallowed or regurgitated. Personally, I think the object represents the meteor.

Before leaving the subject of mounds and moundbuilders, I would like to mention an old book about the mounds by E.G. Squier and E.H. Davis.[8] I have thumbed through the book's numerous diagrams to see if any showed mounds arranged to correspond to the belt stars, or any other familiar star patterns. I came across a couple that seem curiously similar.

The first is a site located near Chillicothe in Ross County, Ohio, where the mounds are arranged in the manner shown in the illustration on the facing page.

Another shows the three mounds at O'Byam's Fort in Hickman County, Kentucky, where the mounds were part of a village complex that contained a number of dwellings. Both sites show a striking similarity to the Orion belt stars. Another site located at Rice Lake in Barron County, Wisconsin, looks very similar to the constellation Scorpio. I found others that appear to be shaped like the Corona Borealis constellation, the stars the Skidi called the Council of the Chiefs.

Of course I cannot be sure that the principle involved with the placement of the pyramids in the Egyptian desert was intended by

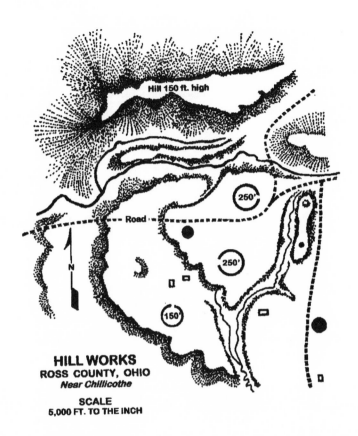

HILL WORKS
ROSS COUNTY, OHIO
Near Chillicothe
SCALE
5,000 FT. TO THE INCH

the moundbuilders in North America. But it seems likely that what one society of Starwalkers knew, and the practices they engaged in, would have been known worldwide.

In the beautiful Linville Gorge in the Blue Ridge Mountains, I came upon a feature in the landscape that greatly enhanced my appetite for beacon vortexes. Amazingly, I discovered that the gorge is the site of two (vortexes are seldom in pairs) extremely rare and powerful beacon vortexes: Table Rock and Hawksbill Mountain.

Table Rock, so named because of its flat top, is a strong beacon that has a potent electrical charge. Perceiving it astrally, I "saw" the mountain, surrounded by a clear blue mist or haze, emitting a darker blue ray from its summit. I realized that the mountain possessed powerful celestial leys that connect it to all the other planets in the solar system! Nowhere else had I encountered a beacon connected to all the systemic bodies. Because Table Rock has an electrical charge, its celestial leys transmit natural Earth energy to each of the planets in our solar family.

I also perceived the presence of the Spirit of the mountain who told me telepathically that the energy of Table Rock vortex is extremely intense, and should be approached with some degree of caution as it can burn or tear the human astral body. Such a high degree of electricity can result in mental and/or emotional stress, disorientation, and mild sensory deprivation or nervous tension that could last for several hours in a healthy person. An unhealthy person would suffer the same consequences, but they might be more damaging and longer-lasting. Because of its planetary connections Table Rock's energy is conducive to conscious astral travel and out-of-body experiences such as those employed in Starwalking.

Hawksbill on the other hand is an impressive magnetic-type beacon whose physical contours resemble the bill of a giant hawk. Like those of Table Rock, Hawksbill's celestial leys are connected to each of the planets in our solar system, but they serve as leys through which the planetary energies come to Earth. I perceived the mountain as having an indigo-colored aura that gives it an other-worldly and mysterious air.

As I sat looking out over the magnificent gorge with the two beacons side by side on its floor, my eyes drank in the beauty and serenity. My mind began drifting slowly as if at the whim of the soft, gentle breeze that was rustling through the trees and bushes on the gorge's rim. After a few moments of quiet daydreaming I slipped into an altered state. Then, Hawksbill suddenly became transformed right before my eyes, providing me with a compelling vision of its indwelling Spirit. The summit became the head of a huge hawk with reddish-bronze feathers and piercing black diamond-like eyes. In a second the vision changed into a silver-colored bird whose dark eyes were flashing silver rays. Although I realize that when I am in an altered state time is of no consequence, the vision seemed to last for several minutes. Afterward, I was left with the distinct feeling that I had bonded with the mountain and the Spirit within it, who embodies its tremendous power. As my vision faded, not entirely to my surprise, red-tailed hawks appeared in the sky, seven of them gliding and circling over Hawksbill's summit. It was both a wonderful and an intense experience.

Together, Table Rock and Hawksbill form a cooperative pair of natural beacon vortexes in a partnership of sending and receiving planetary energies that both vitalize and send out Earth's life force. This site may be unequaled on the planet. It is a wonderful place to go for doing ceremony to honor our Earth Mother, for prayer and meditation, for aligning the body human with our planet's natural rhythm, and for connecting with the other planets in the solar system. It is also a place where the ancient art of Starwalking can be more easily achieved, as is true with all beacon vortex sites.

At this point I would like to return to a beacon vortex discussed earlier, the Glastonbury Tor. I want to take a closer look so as to offer more insight into beacons in general, and to provide a proper mind-set for a more in-depth discussion of what may be the most baffling astronomically related site on the planet.

Once called *Ynis-Witrin*, the Glassy Isle, the Tor is thought to have housed a Druid college where priestesses of the Great Mother were trained. It is also believed to be a point of entry into the Otherworld of the ancient Celts. Legends say that the Tor is hollow, and that its inner region is home to Gwynn-ap-Nudd, the legendary King of the Faeries.[9] Numerous tales tell of tunnels and subterranean waterways that crisscross the landscape directly beneath and for distances around the site, adding to its mystique. I have had several psychic experiences with the Tor. Frankly, while I find its energy to be mostly positive, at times I find it to be a bit uncanny, even eerie.

Terraces lead to the top of the 518-foot natural cone, where stands a lone bell tower, all that remains of a centuries-old church dedicated to Saint Michael. Erecting Christian churches and monasteries on pagan sites was a common practice throughout the British Isles. It was the Christians' way of dominating pagans and thinking they were changing evil into good. Geomancers reveal that the Tor lies on the most famous terrestrial ley line in England. The powerful St. Michael's ley links the Tor with many other powerful sites such as Stonehenge and Salisbury Cathedral. Personally, I perceive the Tor's celestial leys to extend out from its summit, connecting with the Big Dipper and the Moon. Because the Big Dipper is a circumpolar constellation, the Tor is receiving star power from it all the time. The site's natural magnetic-type energy is particularly strong when the Moon is full, and during lunar eclipses. (In keeping with Nick Mann's concept, I suspect that it is these lunar events that activate its power.)

In 1935, while sitting atop the Tor, British sculptor Katherine Maltwood noticed something odd in the landscape. Shaped by the natural contours and features in the terrain below, an earthly counterpart of the celestial zodiac unfolded before her eyes! Carved into the soil of Mother Earth was a human-created zodiac about which it was later written, "so accurately indeed does it mirror the heavenly pattern that the stars of the zodiac fit over its terrestrial effigies when the planisphere is scaled to the map of Avalon."[10] *Maltwood had found a Temple of the Stars!*

Legends and literary commentators aside, the fact that this astonishing artifact had been "hidden" and forgotten for so long may have been partially due to its size. Like the Nazca lines in Peru, it is simply too big to be seen in total except from the air. The thirteen giant figures, *one of them measuring five miles across,* lie over a great circular area that is ten miles in diameter! The Tor is the zodiac's northern sighting point. The colossal effigies that compose the zodiac are formed by natural and artificial waterways, hills, contours, ancient field boundaries, earthworks, roads, and footpaths. All the twelve signs are clearly represented in proper order. A thirteenth effigy, called the Great Dog of Langport, lies to the southwest just outside the great circle. The dog guards the sacred Annun, the Otherworld. Most of the constellations/signs are depicted in familiar fashion. Exceptions are: Aquarius is a phoenix instead of a human waterbearer; Libra is a dove; and Cancer is a boat. Cancer and Libra are also located slightly to the west of their usual positions. In addition, the sign of Pisces is represented by three fish instead of two, the third depicting another constellation, Cetus the Whale. Cetus is close to Pisces but lies slightly outside the actual zodiacal belt or ecliptic.

Carving these giant figures out of the landscape would have been a superhuman task requiring thousands upon thousands of work hours. To do so, some tribe or prehistoric race must have had a special link with the heavens physically, psychologically, religiously, and spiritually. This was a people who wanted to bring the stars to themselves, maybe Starwalkers who wanted to walk in a sky world on Earth. Maybe they performed sacred ceremonies at each effigy at certain times of the year. Maybe they, like the Lakota, were Sun worshippers who followed the Day Star's path through the sky.

At any rate they created a place of worship that is possibly the largest human-made circle on the planet. Perhaps they made it to attract the attention of and to appease the Sky Gods. Does Glastonbury hold the key to the star lore of the ages? Were the zodiac builders among the original Starwalkers? And did those Starwalkers climb the Tor to be closer to the Sky Gods? Of course we cannot know for sure, but these questions are consistent with theories concerning other sacred astronomical sites discussed.

Not far from Glastonbury lies Avebury, the largest megalithic circle in Europe. Its importance in Stone Age times is apparent to anyone who has walked among the great weathered stones. The complete set of rings was designed in a series of arcs and all the stones stand within a circular ditch with entrances that open generally to each of the four directions.[11] Today the circles are broken and some of the stones are missing. But the power of the place is still very much in evidence. Personally, I never feel that I am walking among "ruins" when I am there. It has an air like no other, a place filled with ancient voices and the essence of so many lives, so many ceremonies, so much time . . . so much Earth power and human power and star power preserved.

Some fifteen hundred yards south of the great circles of Avebury stands Silbury Hill, a huge mound that is both mysterious and enchanting. Its outer appearance hides an interior that contains a central primary mound that is 120 feet in diameter, built of layers of clay, chalk, flints, dirt, and gravel. The great outer mound was constructed around the interior one. English author and megalithic expert John Michell describes how Silbury might have looked: "It had the form of a seven-stepped pyramid and was glistening white. Earth was then piled onto its terraces, and the whole structure was buried and grassed over."(Michell, pp.93-94) I feel that the interior mound was a ceremonial chamber not unlike a Hopi kiva. Some 4500 years after its construction, the great mound continues to mystify pilgrims who journey there.

Aside from my personal assessment of Silbury being a human-built beacon vortex, and the possibility that it provided ancient shamans with a stage from which they had a clear view of the heavens and access to the stars, there is something else. Like most beacons, Silbury Hill was also an astronomical observatory. It is my sense that Silbury is linked by celestial leys to the star Antares in Scorpio, to the Moon, and to the constellation Draco. There is no question that the real celestial scenario that has replayed itself for centuries involves an intimate dance between the great mound and the Sun and the Moon. The power of that dance not only captured and portrayed the energy contained within the structure itself, but the great mound may very well be one of the few places in the world where this kind of feat was actually accomplished. Let me explain.

In his book *The Silbury Treasure* Michael Dames offers more insights into the fascinating monument than anyone else to date. Dames claims that the key to understanding the Hill is knowing that it was built during the Neolithic Age. "[T]he Great Goddess is the mystery of the hill (the image of her body permeated all the Late Neolithic Avebury monuments), and her account is truly extraordinary."[12] Throughout, Dames makes his case for the role of the Goddess in Neolithic Britain. The people worshipped not a female deity, but *the* female deity, the great universal Mother, a fact that indeed ties the enigmatic hill to the Moon. The Goddess both symbolized and embodied the power of fertility. As a celestial deity she could be called the Great Regulator, for it was she who controlled the movement of the celestial bodies, the seasons, and all the cycles in Nature, including the cycle of life and death.

Clearly, the Silbury builders were a matriarchal/goddess-oriented society, based upon found artifacts. Furthermore, Dames boldly states: "The Silbury monument is the Great Goddess in her pregnant state. Her womb is the Hill, 520 feet in diameter, and 150 feet high." (Dames, p.54) This is amazing! So revered was she that her body, pregnant with the very life force that assured the necessary fertility power for all that lives, was actually built on Earth! Within the overall plan of Avebury therefore, the cosmic scheme of things was defined in human form and shape. (I first thought that this must be unique in the world. It isn't. This sort of structure has in fact been found in Malta, West Africa, Orkney, and other parts of Britain for certain. (Dames, p. 54) Many more probably remain unknown.)

Every year in early August the faithful gathered at Silbury Hill to celebrate Lammas, the beginning of the harvest season and the cycle of birth. This was the time the Full Moon cast shadows that produced the drama of birth being enacted, to assure life, growth, fertility, and abundance. The birth process was represented by and through the specially designed landscape. Silbury is also a rare sort of solar-lunar beacon—the Sun casts the shadows, the Moon uses them to reveal a mystery of life. Dames says "The Neolithic Silbury synthesis depended upon drawing up power (water) from the underworld, and drawing down power (light) from the sky. (Dames, pp.54-55) At Silbury the Sun and Moon were locked in a celestial dance, a duality that embodied the power of continuity, pure and simple.

Whether or not my feeling that there is an Antares-Draco connection at Silbury is valid I do not know at this point. There is much more to be learned about this incredible monument and time always tells. We do know for certain that the earliest inhabitants of Britain were tuned into celestial bodies and events that influenced and dominated their lives. They left signs that tell us precisely that.

It is imperative to understand that in ancient Britain a breed of astronomer-priests were the mediators between the people and the Sky Gods. The people depended upon the priests for everything necessary to keep their lives prosperous, healthy, and in harmony with the Great Heavenly Powers. They were stargazers. The elite among them were Starwalkers. Looked at in this way makes it relatively easy to understand why earth-based monuments such as Silbury Hill, Stonehenge, the Great Pyramid, and others were built in the precise way they were and for precise astronomical-religious purposes.

An ocean away from England on the plains of northern Wyoming stands the awesome Devil's Tower, *Mata Tipila*, the Bear Lodge, a 1267-foot beacon vortex sacred to the Sioux, and the site of their annual Sun Dance. I feel that this giant beacon is connected to the Sun and to the stars in the constellations Ursa Major and Ursa Minor, the bears in the sky. We know that when we look closely at the legends connected with a place we can usually discover a great deal about the power of that place, a power that the indigenous people intuited and sought to explain through story. The main legend connected with Devil's Tower is most revealing when viewed from this perspective.

The legend tells of people being chased by a big bear around

Mata Tipila. While running to escape the bear they find themselves being elevated by the giant rock that lifts them up to the sky! The really interesting end to the story is that the spirits of those who are saved are transformed into stars or star groups! (Michell, pp.95-96) If this doesn't indicate that the immense rock tower was associated with the stars I can't imagine what would. I label the tower a beacon with complete confidence.

The fact that the bear is associated with this site brings another thought to mind. Numerous Native American tribes related the bear to the sky. (So did the ancient Celts. King Arthur himself was related to the bear and, if Arthur did indeed live, his Romanized name would have been Arturios, the Bear.) But while many Indian peoples have held the stars in the Big Dipper (Ursa Major) sacred, that fact may have had little or nothing to do with the bear. The animal itself was sacred even if not related to any particular stars. It was often the three stars in the handle of the Big Dipper they paid close attention to. You will recall that special attention many peoples paid to the three belt stars in Orion. I think the *arrangement* of these stars was the reason for their being considered sacred. It leads me to think that reaching the sky on a chain or ladder of stars was a common Starwalking practice.

The aboriginal peoples of Australia also have a rich star lore that indicates their connection to the sky. The climbing-into-heaven practice appears in an aboriginal myth that tells about two specific stellar energies in the southern hemisphere: the Southern Cross constellation and the nearby star Centaurus. Centaurus, the father of a human family, became a star when he died. The shamans were able to reach him in the sky by climbing his long beard that served as a rope.

This "climbing" seems to be a shamanic step-by-step mental process that was employed by Starwalkers, facilitated by a ladder of stars. Star chains are located in virtually every area of the night sky. (I wonder about the origin of the well-known children's story of Jack and the Beanstalk? Could it be a Starwalker legend? Just a thought.)

Australia is the location of Ayer's Rock, another extremely powerful beacon vortex. Located in the geographical center of the continent, the massive 1100-foot-high natural red sandstone mound is

estimated to be over 230 million years old. Since the earliest times
it has been sacred to the Aborigines who call it *Uluru*. The rock is
said to be the home of a variety of mythical beings, birds, reptiles,
and all sorts of animals.[13] Aboriginal shamans accessed beings
through their ancient and unique practice of the *Dreamtime*. That is
also how they communicated with the stars and the Sky Gods.

It seems obvious that Ayer's Rock is connected by celestial leys
to the star Centaurus and the Southern Cross constellation. Aboriginal Starwalkers most likely reached these stellar locations by
traversing the Milky Way star bridge, which they think of as a river
in the sky, complete with lagoons. (Mountford, pp.258-271) There
is also mythic evidence that the Aborigines know how to draw upon
stellar power: a girl who had supernatural powers given to her by
the stars; an Aboriginal tradition that the Sun and Moon were married, and when they made love there was an eclipse of the Sun.
(Mountford, p.164)

Another legend gives evidence of the importance of the Pleiades
and the belt and sword stars in Orion. Interestingly, like the Inca at
the Temple of the Sun in Cuzco, some aboriginal tribes depict the
Pleiades with thirteen stars. The stars are shown on a particular bark
painting as thirteen women gathered in a grass hut-like shelter,
while their husbands are shown below them as three fishermen in
a canoe. The belt stars are the husbands and the sword stars their
campfire and fish. (Mountford, pp.242-247) There are also stories
that refer to star men, *Dreamtime* people who take their meals in
the Milky Way. (Mountford, p.66)

Of all the Australian myths I have come across I find the one
about *Antares Woman*, "Purupriki" the most interesting. Not only is
it a good story, but it also points out the importance, albeit mythical, of a particular star. The story tells of a human woman who was
carried into the sky by a pack of flying foxes. Astounded by this, the
men gathered to sing her a farewell song. As the woman looked
down on them she was transformed into the star Antares (the bright
red giant in the constellation Scorpio), and the flying foxes turned
into the Milky Way. (Mountford, p.32)

While these legends do not represent the entire body of aboriginal star mythology, they do serve to show the intricate role the stars
play in their cultural, religious, and ceremonial life. They also point
out, in part at least, which constellations and single stars are of sig-

nificance to a culture that is among the few who still practice their ancient sky ceremonials.

Why did various cultures worldwide hold certain stars and constellations sacred? These were the stars upon which they founded their religions, that were the homes of their deities. There certainly were plenty of stars to choose from, but they consistently chose only certain ones. What answer could there be other than that they knew, *intuitively*, of the specific "power" inherent within specific stars? Naturally they would want to honor and draw upon the stellar force they considered the most morally and practically useful. Naturally they would focus their attention on those stars whose energy they knew would empower them. Evidently, the ancient peoples knew how to "capture" star power through magic and ceremony, and how to use that energy for practical and spiritual purposes.

Standing silently, on a desert floor an ocean away from its counterpart in Australia, is another red sandstone natural monument, the impressive Bell Rock in Sedona, Arizona. There are numerous Yavapai Apache legends about the bell-shaped stone tower. One says that it is the home of the eagle who embodies the power of the Great Spirit or Creator.

Bell Rock is extremely popular with tourists and residents alike. It is a site where spiritual seekers go to do all kinds of ceremonies. The rock has been the site of numerous alleged UFO sightings over the past several decades. This is not an uncommon occurrence at many beacon sites throughout the world, especially in North America. I feel that Bell Rock is connected by celestial leys to the Sun, Moon, and the planet Pluto. Doing ceremony there provides the seeker access to these celestial bodies and to the energy inherent within them, essentially the powers of vitality and change.

Another site in the American Southwest, Chaco Canyon, is of importance in relation to natural beacon vortexes. At the southern entrance of the canyon stands a 400-foot rock outcrop known as Fajada Butte. The now-extinct Anasazi Indians who once occupied the area accomplished something unusual there, something that had to do with sky watching and sacred solar rites. In fact, Fajada Butte may be one of the few sites that proves the reality of the existence of beacon vortexes. Atop the butte there is an unusual configuration of rock slabs put there in ancient times by a people who used them as a calendar for detecting the solstices and equinoxes, a task the huge rocks fulfilled with great accuracy.[14] The cycles of the Moon would have been observed by the same calendar stones. The stones were either put there deliberately, hauled 400 feet up the butte, or the people rearranged boulders that were already there.

Did these Ancients build a solar observatory atop their sacred mountain so they could be closer to the sky and the Sky Gods?

Far south and west of Chaco Canyon there is a ruined city in Mexico that is the site of two huge pyramids estimated to be over 2500 years old. These are the Sun Temple and Moon Temple in Teotihuacan. The largest of the two, the Pyramid of the Sun, is so situated that its corners point exactly in the four cardinal directions. It is thought to have been the main ceremonial structure of the ancient Maya. The city was aligned to coincide with the predawn setting of the Pleiades on the morning of the midsummer solstice. The Maya were in the habit, so it seems, of orienting their cities to sacred astronomical views, obviously for both calendrical and ceremonial purposes. Symbols of the Sun, Moon, and Venus were frequently engraved on the walls and above the doorways of Mayan temples.

Another pyramid, at Uxmal, was called the House of the Magician and was aligned to Venus. Others are located at Palenque, Tikal, Chichen Itza, Copan, and Montagua. (Hadingham, p.190)

I think all of the solar and lunar pyramids were human-built beacons that were used as ceremonial "stairways" to lead ancient Mayan Starwalker astronomer-priests upward toward the sky. Whenever I see a film or a photograph of any of the impressive pyramids of Mexico and Central America, particularly those in the Yucatan, a vision always comes to me of a procession of special priests, decked out in feathered kilts and wearing sprays of brightly colored feathered headdresses, ascending the steps of these monuments. When they reach the top I know they will do a ritual. I believe that these are images of Starwalkers or a special order of astronomer-priests.

I believe that another particular place in Mexico, the Temple of Kukulcan at Chichen Itza, is also a beacon vortex. It displays a curious illusion at sunset at both the spring and autumn equinoxes. It is not known if the stepped-pyramid was purposely oriented so that the image of a serpent can be seen descending the north steps, or if this is simply a shadow cast by the temple's northwest corner. Whichever the answer, it is an eerie phenomenon. A clue may be found in a Mayan prophecy that tells of the "return" of Quetzalcoatl, the "Feathered Serpent." (Kukulcan is another name for Quetzalcoatl.) It has been suggested that the light phenomenon is the return of the god, and that the prophecy was never meant to imply an actual being. I feel strongly that this beacon is connected by celestial leys to Draco and to the Sun and Moon.

Now to recap a bit. Since the original channeling in which Albion revealed the existence of beacon vortexes and those he identified at that time, I have identified several others. Some are natural rock formations, mountains, and hills, most of which were sacred to the indigenous peoples of the area. Some of the natural ones that have not been discussed in detail in this writing include Bear Butte in South Dakota, Mount Babaquavari in southern Arizona, and the so-called Building J at Monte Alban near Oaxaca City in Mexico.

Other human-created ones include the stepped-pyramid of Zoser in Egypt, the Aztec Hill of the Star, the sacred mound at Heliopolis in Egypt, the ziggurats in present-day Iraq, and the Nakawsi Mound and Peachtree Village in western North Carolina. Of course neither of these lists are complete, but they do give a good cross-section of both natural and artificial beacons.

Ancient Starwalkers had a need to be literally close to the stars. For this reason they went to great lengths to erect observational and ceremonial structures ranging from simple mounds and stone circles to the more elaborate temples and the colossal pyramids in Egypt, Mexico, and Central America. They are all both puzzling and revealing. Wherever the human-made vortexes are and no matter who their builders were, they all have a story to tell. Wherever the natural beacons exist, they were climbed by priests and priestesses who were on a journey, a journey to the stars. The beacons lifted them up to the heavens, and at the same time kept them safely and securely bound to Earth. In that way the Starwalkers had it all.

CHAPTER FIFTEEN

STAR MYTHS: OUR CELESTIAL LEGACY

American Indian folklore and mythology are rich in tales of the natural world and how humans relate to it. Sky stories play an especially important part in these accounts of the world. Many of them tell about the Beginning Time, when animals could speak and people could change into animal shapes and back with ease. At that time, the earth was young and pliable, and monsters often roamed at will. Human beings were lifted into the sky, and sky beings came to earth.[1]

Jean Guard Monroe and Ray A. Williamson

*S*tar myths are ancient stories. They tell about what goes on in the heavens. They personify celestial bodies and cosmic forces, making them into either gods or demons, depending upon the specific influences they are believed to exert upon Earth and human life. Of the myths passed down through time, we are probably more familiar with those of the Greeks and Romans because most of us studied them in school. But those that came from our African, Asian, Polynesian, and Native American ancestors are no less fascinating and revealing. All kinds of myths have their roots in the earliest cultures, but those that concern the heavens are among the oldest.

No individual in our time has impressed upon us more vividly the value of myth and the role it plays in society and in the individual and collective human psyche than Joseph Campbell. During his celebrated interviews for the Public Broadcasting System with Bill Moyers, Campbell revealed the very core of the power of myth: "[T]hese bits of information from ancient times, which have to do with the themes that have supported human life, built civilizations, and informed religions over the millennia, have to do with deep inner problems, inner mysteries, inner thresholds of passage, and if you don't know what the guide signs are along the way, you have to work it out yourself."[2] Later, Bill Moyers made an equally provocative statement: ". . . what human beings have in common is revealed in myths. Myths are stories of our search through the ages for truth, for meaning, for significance." (Moyers, p.5)

In her marvelous book *The Fruitful Darkness*, author and anthropologist Joan Halifax says that "storytelling is the most ancient form of education. It is about the remembering, making, and sharing of images that bind together time, nature, and a people." She goes on, "tellings also confirm the ancestral continuity."[3] Our stories have been around for a very long time.

Myths are woven from the cosmic threads of Nature into culturally diverse fabrics that have survived over the course of thousands of years. They reflect the desires and fears of specific peoples. They bestow the right to life to us and the stewardship of the planet on us. The Oxford dictionary defines a myth as "a traditional story containing ideas and beliefs about ancient times and about natural events." This means that stories serve two extremely important purposes. First, they provide insight into the head (mind) and heart (soul) of the people who tell them. Second, they tell us what various peoples down through time have known and understood about Nature. Both of these "services" are pertinent to us today as a legacy that links us with the past, our own past, and with our ancestors and the world they knew. It is upon this foundation that we grow and our world is built.

Our very early ancestors were closer to Nature than we are today. That closeness involved not only their earthly environment, but also the sky and the celestial bodies. Awareness and understanding of the sky were absolutely essential to their existence and survival. Ancient as well as present-day tribal cultures have relied upon myths for meaning in their lives. To them myths contained social and spiritual values, and in many cases established both their identity and their role within the universe. It was through stories that the people explained their existence, and their relationship with all else.

We have seen throughout this book how stars were the calendar and clock of the ancestral peoples. In order to "read" the heavenly clock, the earliest humans watched the skies by day and by night. They grouped the stars together into "readable maps" so that their regular movements could be read with greater ease and accuracy. The very act of observing the sky linked them with it. Their sky maps were filled with images of all sorts: bears, birds, human figures, serpents, a dipper, and a chalice (cup), to name a few. These images are the constellations—eighty-eight sky figures that arrange the sky into neat, recognizable, familiar patterns. The sky figures that comprise the constellations helped to define the daily and yearly cycles, as well as the religious beliefs of our ancestors.

American Indian star lore tells about the natural world, a world that is oftentimes a far cry from the world we know and live in today. The quote at the beginning of this chapter said it was a world young and still changing, when monsters roamed about at will. Humans were lifted into the sky, and Sky Beings came to Earth. Today's tribal storytellers are the recipients of legends passed down by their elders. Their myths were told around campfires on cold winter nights under the canopy of stars on the Great Plains, or in the warm confines of a tipi or earth lodge. They were told in the summer, spring, and autumn too, while the stars danced overhead.

In this chapter we will explore some Native American star myths in hopes of gaining insight into the tribes from which they originate, as well as the nature of the universe within which they lived and which we have inherited. Although every culture has their star myths, I have chosen to focus mainly on Native American stories because they are the ones with which I am most familiar. Other cultures discussed will include the Maya, Aztec, ancient Egyptian, Babylonian, and the Dogon of Africa.

Anyone who has spent a night in the vast, empty, and beautiful desert terrain that is home to the Navajo can attest to the brilliance of the stars in that rarefied atmosphere. The Navajo call the sky the Dark Upper. (Monroe/Williamson, p.5) They see the stars as guides who influence human behavior. They have watched the sky for centuries, and in doing so have developed a stellar calendar that is not only highly accurate, but that also serves to connect them with the star deities. Navajo children are taught games designed to inform them of the existence and work of the Black God and other celestial divinities.

The Black God star myth (see chapter 10) tells us some impor-

tant things: One is that order is no accident. There was always
meant to be a plan to the sky, representing universal order, divinely ordained. It was the way things should be on Earth. But things
are not that way, are they? We experience unpredictable change,
wars, famine, violence . . . all sorts of "disorderly" events and circumstances, all because Coyote threw the stars at random and
messed up the order. Our task as humans is therefore to search for
balance between the disorderly world we live in and the orderly
and predictable world created by the Black God, Ambassador of the
Creator. I once heard a very wise teacher say that the problems we
encounter in life are but grist for the mill of evolution. So Coyote
has his place. His actions provide us with the "grist." His actions
explain why we humans have to struggle to find the balance that
was a gift we rejected, balance that is Enlightenment, which aligns
us with the genuine order of things."4

Another star myth comes to us from the Skidi Pawnee of the
North American Great Plains, a people whose complex stellar theology is unequaled on this continent. (see chapter 9) To them the
stars were Spirits who brought wisdom, prosperity, and good fortune of all sorts to humans on Earth. We learn from this story about
the value placed on dreams by the Skidi, and I daresay all the early
peoples. We are also made aware of the prophetic nature of some
dreams. More importantly we see clearly that the Skidi knew that
the stars have indwelling "spirits," spirits that can and do make personal contact and do communicate with human beings.

Of the celestial bodies none have held a greater attraction and
mystique for the earliest people, including the American Indians,
than the Pleiades. The following story originated with the Luiseno
Indians who once lived north of what is now San Diego.

Seven young sisters lived during a time when humans went into
the sky to escape death. Climbing on a rope that had been let down
for them, the girls were followed by Coyote. Being the pesky sort
that he was, Coyote told the girls that he would become their husband, an idea the sisters didn't exactly take kindly to. As the sisters
continued to climb, they thought how they could get out of their
horrible predicament. Finally, the eldest girl came up with a plan
which she kept to herself. So the girls kept climbing, and Coyote
kept following. Upon reaching the sky, the eldest girl cut the sky-
rope, with Coyote on it, with a flint knife she carried with her.

Coyote fell away and became the star Aldebaran (in the constellation Taurus), the bright star that follows the seven sisters in the sky.

This story tells us some significant things. The key is the "sky-rope." Clearly, most if not all ancestral peoples believed that humans could go into the sky, and that Sky Beings came to Earth. There were no barriers separating the two. Now in reality of course there is a physical separation of Earth and sky, so there must have been ways to overcome the barrier and allow such journeys to occur. These included dreams and visions, sacred songs and chants and dances, rituals, hallucinogenic plants and the mental freedom they induce, sacred art and architecture, myths, and perhaps others that we know nothing about. The story also tells us that once in the sky, meaning when we are in a state of balance and order, humans can meet and overcome the challenges and disorder that Coyote represents.

However, going into the sky or being in the sky did not simply imply a Starwalk, a ritual journey into the heavens. It also implied a *state of mind* in which the individual medicine society or even the entire tribe, depending upon the ceremonial occasion and the particular "design" of the ritual involved, entered into a state of perfect balance on all levels, physically, emotionally, mentally, and spiritually. When true balance was experienced, the person or group was in harmony with all things, all beings. This balance and harmony are so difficult to achieve as human beings on Earth, but shamans are able to experience it by "going into the sky," *which is the same as entering into a state of ecstasy.*

An interesting feature of many myth stories is that they take place in the Beginning Times. Animals and plants could talk, giants roamed the Earth, and gods walked among humans. Many things about "the way things are" were decided, the rules and regulations and ultimately the ethics of living on Earth were put in place. They were times when the "barriers" between the heavens and Earth were nonexistent, when humans could fly and birds could talk, truly magical times.

But something happened to change all that magic. In virtually every story, human beings got out of balance with Nature and with their relations in the other kingdoms. As a result there was war, disease, famine, death, and all sorts of turmoil and pestilence. There was separation: humans were separated from the plants and animals and from each other and, most significantly, the sky and Earth were separated too. This brought the "struggle" to reinstate balance and harmony that continues to this day.

Most myths tell of events that occurred at the Beginning Time, but not all do. Some predict the future and could be called "prophecy myths." This type of story often sprang up during times of crisis, and usually faded from importance once the crisis had passed. Examples of this type of legend are related to the stars or some other celestial body or phenomena.

The first I heard told was said to come from the Wichitas of Kansas. The tale involves a star called "Moving Star." It seems that the voice of the Sun told a hunter that three deer would jump out of the water, and that he was to kill only the last one. The first deer was white, the second black, and the third black and white. The black and white deer represented the natural cycle of darkness and light, night and day. However, the black and white deer was only wounded. The hunter chased it into the sky, and now they both comprise constellations. The people say that the hunter became the "star that is always moving," and that he still chases after the deer, trying to retrieve his arrow. Every year he gets closer. When the wounded black and white deer is finally caught, the old world will end and a new world will be created. The Sun and all the other stars will become human beings and live in the new world.

Note the last sentence: "the Sun and all the other stars will become human . . . " This is a switch from the usual spiritual belief that humans became stars. The story is typical in the sense that the heavenly bodies foretell the end of time as we know it.

Another prophecy legend originated with the White River Sioux. It is not a star story. Rather, it illustrates how myths were used to explain time; and time to the ancestral peoples was directly related to what happened in the sky. This story tells of an old woman who lives in a cave that no one knows how to find. She has been there for over a thousand years, working to complete a blanket strip made of porcupine quills for her buffalo robe. Beside her sits a big black dog whose name is Shunka Sapa. The dog's teeth are old and worn down because the old woman has used them to flatten so many quills. Close by there is a fire that has been burning for a millennium. Over the fire hangs a large clay pot in which a sweet red soup called *wojapi* is cooking. Every so often the old woman goes over to stir the pot. And when she does, the dog quickly pulls the quills out of the blanket strip. So she never makes any progress! The people say that if the old lady ever finishes the blanket strip the world will come to an end.[5]

The next story comes from a Western Rocky Mountain tribe. It seems that there was once a rabbit who had only three legs. So he made a wooden leg for himself so he could get around. Noticing that the Sun was getting awfully hot, Rabbit decided to make a trip to the Sun to see if he could find out what was going on. While it continued to get hotter and hotter, it suddenly dawned on the rabbit that the only thing the Sun doesn't burn up is cactus. So he decided to make himself a house out of cactus so he could stay cool, and to further help his cause, he would travel only at night. When Rabbit came to the east where he knew the Sun would come up, he took out his bow and arrows. When the Sun was about halfway up in the sky Rabbit shot and killed it! Standing over his kill, Rabbit declared that the white part of Sun's eye would be clouds, and the black part would be the sky. He also said that the Sun's kidneys would be a star, his liver the Moon, and his heart the darkness. Rabbit then hailed his victory, saying that the Sun would never be too hot again. And it never has. This is why rabbits have brown spots on the back of their ears and legs. They are burn spots from Rabbit's journey to the Sun. (Erdoes/Ortiz, pp.139-40)

Several things are important about this story. The first is that numerous Native American tribes believe that animals were created before humans, and that they are therefore wiser and more evolved. Many myths involve an animal being sent or going of its own accord to take care of a problem. Other points are Rabbit's discomfort at having only three legs and at being too hot. He sets out to rectify the problems and succeeds. Often, this type of story involves animals that are important to the tribe from which the tale originates. They are tribal totems.

When we bring the stars down to Earth, which we do in a number of ways, we suffer the consequences. Look, for example, how we have tried, as the Rabbit did, to harness Nature and its forces for the purposes of our "comfort." Often, we do so at great peril, upsetting Nature's precious and fragile ecological balance. Like Rabbit, we "shoot and kill." When the deed is done, we then designate "this will be this" and "that will be that," because we say so. Viewing the story from this perspective we see how Rabbit is so "human." He committed violence against the Sun. But, Rabbit carries the scars of his journey to the Sun. Notice that the scars, the burn marks, are on the backs of his legs and ears where he cannot see them on himself! We commit violence against one another, against the other kingdoms, against Mother Earth, and against our "discomforts." When we pursue, at all costs, the conquering of Nature, our actions are indelibly imprinted on us, collectively. Whether or not we see or acknowledge the burn marks of our actions, we still have them.

The Cherokee people also possess star myths that tell of a time when, in this case, *people* tried to kill the Sun because her rays were too hot. But the Sun's daughter was slain by mistake. Stricken with grief, the Sun stayed inside her house. Darkness was everywhere. The people knew they had to do something, so they traveled to the Land of the Dead and brought the Sun's daughter back in a box. The coffin was not to be opened until they reached their home. Before they came to their destination the young girl inside was pleading for air, so the people opened the box. Much to their amazement the girl flew out as a beautiful red cardinal! Since that time the Cherokee have known the cardinal as the daughter of the Sun. The Cherokee say that if the humans had only waited until the right time to let her free, there would be no permanent death as there is now. (Erdoes/Ortiz, p.253) Point made!

Two things about this story are interesting. One is that the Sun is depicted as *female* instead of the usual male. The story also contains a reprimand of sorts for the people: "if the humans had waited until the right time there would be no death." This points out that we humans don't know what is best or how to behave, and that we have brought our problems on ourselves. The problems are twofold: *darkness*, which could be said to represent ignorance, and *death*.

For some time I have felt that the starlore and the sacred ceremonies of the Ancients will return to become a greater inspiration to us all, and to serve as an integral part of human spirituality. Ultimately, this will result in our reconnection with the heavens and the Sky Gods who embody the archetypes embedded deep within human consciousness. These archetypes will in turn offer impetus for personal growth. They will release their individual power into our lives and consciousness.

There are prophetic myths that seem to point to the reawakening of the star archetype within us, for example, the prophecies of *Chilam-Balam* of the Itza-Maya. Chilam-Balam was a great prophet who appeared among the Itza-Maya around A.D. 1500. He foretold the coming of the whites, and of the problems they would bring. He said that this time of trouble would be followed by a period of glory when a new religion would bring the entire world into harmony. The prophecies also said that there will be two bearded ones who will come from the Land of the Sun in the east. One of them will awaken *Itzamma Kauil,* God of the Heavens.[6]

The idea of the "awakening" of various spirits and/or gods of Heaven is in fact a theme replayed numerous times in the last decades. It was particularly noticeable during 1986, when José Argüelles announced the international event called Harmonic Convergence, which marked the end of an important cycle of time in the Mayan calendar. It heralded the awakening of Quetzalcoatl. During the same time, many Native Elders began talking about the awakening or "return" of White Buffalo Calf Woman, a spirit of tremendous importance.

The Chilam-Balam prophecy may very well represent the activation of the star or sky archetype in collective humanity on Earth. I believe this has happened. There is evidence that what is taking place in the sky is capturing our attention more and more, that the stars and star-related teachings are playing an increasingly integral role in peoples' spiritual knowledge and practice.

Star-related mythology chronicles the oldest of the sciences: astronomy. Countless stories originating from cultures throughout the world seek to explain the celestial bodies and what goes on in the sky. Examples are seen in myths that tell of the Sun's passage across the sky and the meanings of comets and meteorite showers. Such myths provide a basis for a clearer understanding of the forces of Nature and account for the origin of Earth and the sky. They also define time, and give structure to the multilevel cosmos. It is time for our world to rediscover star myths. Through them we learn that all things are interrelated, a fundamental truth of Native American spirituality and many of the world's religions. If we learn this and adopt it as a way of thinking and as a living ideal, how different the world will be.

So far we have examined the sky and Sky Country, skywatchers, stargazers, and the unique Starwalkers, but what about the Sky Gods themselves? They are at the base of star myths worldwide. Traditionally, the gods dwelt in the sky. It is their specific task to keep the celestial order so that there will be order on Earth. The celestial divinities are the stars, the Sun and Moon, the planets, and other heavenly bodies who often manifest themselves to humans in dreams and visions. Sometimes they appear in human form. They also appear throughout the star myths as animals such as Coyote, as superhuman-like beings such as Black God, and even as objects like the star stone of the Pawnee warrior. Sometimes they come as forces of Nature, the Thunderers, Lightning, and Wind. At other times they come as monsters and/or mythical creatures like the Phoenix/Thunderbird of the Native Americans. Ancient Egyptians associated the Bird of Immortality (Thunderbird) to the time (known as the Sothic period) when the Sun and the star Sirius, known as Sothis, rise together on June 20. Other mythic creatures appear in the zodiac as the Centaur (Sagittarius) and Pegasus the Winged Horse. Today, we still respond, as our ancestors did, to the Sky Gods who set the rhythm of the day and night skies. But our response is largely unconscious.

People throughout the world have called the Sky Gods by many names. Each was a personification of and relative to a star, the Sun, the Moon, or a planet. The ancient Greeks, for example, personified the sky as Ouranous (Uranus), husband to Earth (Gaia) and father to the giant Titans. To the Sumerians the supreme Sky God was *An*, while to the early Egyptians he was *Horus*, the falcon whose eyes were the Sun and Moon, and Nut was the female Sky Goddess. In India the Emperor of Order is *Varuna*; in China he is Shang-di, the great Lord of the Heavens. The incredible Mayan skywatchers called *Itzamma* the superior god of the heavens. The Finns called him *Jumala*; to the Norse he was Odin.[7]

In some cultures the Sky Gods became human and descended to Earth. In others humans became the celestial deities. In any case, the Sky Gods ordered the universe and upheld its laws. They put the stars in the heavens, and called forth the Sun. A case in point is the ancient Egyptian goddess Maat, who symbolized natural order. In China it took "an entire heavenly bureaucracy to regulate the world." (Krupp, p.28)

Krupp says: "Stories of cosmic order are sky stories because the sky is where that order is seen. It seems to be controlled by all-seeing, all-knowing, powerful gods whose business is law and order. They modify the cosmos. They enrich it with life. They uphold its laws." (Krupp, p.29) Considering the connection our ancestors "knew" existed between Earth and sky, it is difficult to believe how long we in modern times have lived without the Sky Gods, but not without consequence.

Bill Moyers says: "[S]o we tell stories to try to come to terms with the world, to harmonize our lives with reality." (Moyers, p.4) But how well are we "coming to terms," how well are we "harmonizing?" Not very well it would seem. We live in a consumer society that knows no conscience. We face rising crime that is no longer confined to the inner cities. We face a global economic crisis, and unprecedented environmental problems that threaten our very existence. War and conflict abound. Joseph Campbell went to the root of our problems. He said we have no myths. For the most part, we are on our own in today's world. We have no Sky Gods to maintain order or help us come to terms with Nature, to live in harmony with it.

It is true that numerous examples of humans ascending into the sky are found in virtually all sacred literature, including the Bible. But that was *then*, and it happened to special people. We tend to separate ourselves from them, both in time and qualification. Star myths tell us that the sky is a transcendental place, a place of power. (Moyers, pp.32-33) I believe that we all have a need and desire to go into the sky, although it may be buried so deep inside us that we are unconscious of it. Krupp says "that is why we have wished upon the stars and yearned to fly over the rainbow. That is why we still tell stories about what we see beyond the blue horizon." (Krupp, p.33)

There is another side to be looked at too. Throughout this book my objective has been to focus on how, down through time, the Ancients viewed the sky, what relationship they had with it, and how that relationship influenced their lives. However, the sky of the Ancients and the sky we know today are *two different skies*. We have experienced a major impact to our collective psyche, taking a leap into space. We have literally gone beyond Earth and stepped onto the soil of our celestial neighbor, the Moon. We have reached for the stars in our own modern way. The Ancestors lived in a sort of Earth/sky "bubble." They saw and experienced what was in their immediate surroundings (Earth) and what was in the heavens (the skydome). Their tools were sacred rituals or sacred plants, or songs and dances. Our sky is different, though we see the same stars and the same skydome is turning overhead.

Our starwatchers and wizards are astronomers and physicists, engineers and rocket scientists. Our Starwalkers are astronauts. With bated breath, we watch the launch of manned space capsules carrying our Starwalkers into the heavens, and marvel as space shuttles allow them to stay for days and weeks on end. We talk about building space stations. Space colonization, once only a possibility, is now a probability. This has not happened over many centuries of human life, which in itself would be astounding. It has happened, rather, in a mere 40 years!

As we have watched our fellow humans go into space, we have also seen amazing live photographs of the planets in our solar system. We now know what a Martian sunset looks like. We know something about the terrain of Venus. We've seen video images of the volcanoes on Io, and learned that the other moons of Jupiter are unique worlds in their own right. We have sent space probes to fly past every planet to learn their particular nature. Technicians have held the very soil of Mars and the Moon in their hands! Through Earth-based and orbiting telescopes we have peered into the very cores of distant galaxies, discovered gas clouds that are the largest objects ever known, found mystifying quasars and suns whose composition and behavior stagger even the most competent astrophysicists. We have seen the most famous photographic image ever shot with any camera: *Earth from Space*. Earthrise is an unquestionably powerful image. It has allowed us to see the whole Earth; no boundaries, no visible problems, just a vulnerable, beautiful blue jewel suspended in the darkness of space. Earthrise has brought about a shift in human consciousness that Joseph Campbell points out. "We have today to learn to get back into accord with the animals and with water and the sea." (Moyers, p.3) And, "Reason has to do with finding the ground of being and the fundamental structuring of order of the universe." (Moyers, p.29)

Yet does it really? Haven't we really only come full circle? Our sophisticated technology has carried us physically into space and allowed us to look into its corridors, nooks, and crannies to see things we've never seen before and maybe never even imagined. Didn't the Ancients do the same thing, just in a different way? The more we learn we may come to realize something the Ancients already knew: *that we have to get back into harmony with Nature; that we have to find the fundamental order of the universe!* This was the original message the Sky Gods spoke to humanity so long ago. We were told that there would never be, could *never* be, order in our earthly world until we learned to live in the same order that exists "up there."

We can safely say, therefore, that we know a different sky, that our sky is systemic, galactic, and cosmic, literally, because we have peered to the very edge of the universe. Our sky is deeper, more distant, more complex than the relatively small, simple skydome the Ancients knew and observed. There can be little doubt that the sky has opened its doors and we have walked through them, finding doors beyond doors, and worlds beyond worlds. What we know makes greater demands upon us. Have our technological devices, marvelous as they are, shown us anything more wondrous than what the mind of the Dogon Starwalker had seen when he first told his people about *po tolo*, that invisible star that weighs so much? That starworld they knew about before we ever had equipment that could tell us they are right! Have we really discovered anything new then? And, even if we have, is what we stand to learn from it any different from the age-old value system that the Starwalkers, the first "astronauts," had already embraced? I think not.

Oh, we don't have to look at the Sun to tell what time it is, and we don't need to speculate about the physical nature of the Moon, or even the stars themselves. Computers and high-tech devices do that for us. So, what have we really gained?

Maybe the real question is what have we lost? Our sense of wonder. Our psychic connection with the sky overhead. Our understanding of the value inherent within those ancestral myths.

Skywatchers kept records, which were painstakingly accumulated and interpreted. What did it all mean? What was foretold? Shamans evolved who could "read" the sky omens. Soon came the desire, the emotional side of need, for humans to unite with the Sky Gods in order to draw their power down to Earth. Thus humans could become conscious, if but for a few precious moments, of the knowledge that we are divine. Nothing was hidden from the Sky Gods. They knew everything because they created everything. Only a special human being could approach, and the gods could not be fooled.

Discovering and working with this practice myself has led me to see that there must have been a unique kind of shaman, different from the skywatchers who interpreted sky omens and those who were the prophets and healers. There were Starwalkers, an elite sort of shaman whose journeys across the Milky Way earned them the respect and awe of ordinary mortals. They were in no way ordinary. Starwalkers communed with the Sky Gods. Both male and female, they lived in many but not all prehistoric and tribal cultures, *and they still exist today.*

Some of the star myths known in various parts of the world are about the Starwalkers, stories that tell of humans journeying into the sky. One comes to us from the early Cherokee of western North Carolina:

A long time ago, several young lads decided they would find the place where the Sun lives. So they packed a few necessities and set off on their journey toward the east. After a trip filled with exciting encounters, they came to the place where the Sun rises, the place where the sky and ground meet. Here they discovered that the sky was actually an arch of solid rock that hung above Earth, and that it swung up and down, its entrance way opening and closing. When the Sun came out it followed a path along the arch. The Sun was very bright and very hot, and it had a human form. Wanting to go into its home, the boys waited until the Sun was out. Then, one boy dashed into the open door, only to be crushed by the rock when it came down on him! The others were too scared to try to get in so they started their journey home. They were old men by the time they arrived.[8]

While this story doesn't have a "happy" ending, it does have a message. It clearly demonstrates that Starwalking cannot be accomplished without proper knowledge, training, and experience. The sky can obviously be a dangerous place. We have to know our way around. We have to know the language of the Sky Gods as the ancient Starwalkers knew it. Their modern counterparts must learn that language.

The job of Starwalkers has always been to bring the messages of the gods to the people. They have prayed over the dead, and often assisted them on their journey into the sky world. They have long conducted sacred ceremonies to honor and to communicate with distant stars. They appeased the Sun and Moon and knew of their powers. The powers of life, growth, cycles, change, and fertility are the very essence of life itself. They orchestrated the hunt by celestial portents. They were the Great Petitioners between mortals and the Heavenly Ones. They defined the moral and spiritual and literal boundaries between heaven and Earth. Most importantly they devised sacred songs and rites to protect the people from supernatural attack. Because of their training and the knowledge they inherited from those who lived before, they were keepers of the calendar that gave expression to the eternal law of cycles of life, a beginning, middle, and end. The methods by which the Starwalkers achieved their goals varied from tribe to tribe, culture to culture, but the underlying result was the same: they had *personal experience* of the sky. We can never understand something simply because we know it intellectually. We must experience it and know it to be true before we can claim it as being valid. Personal experience makes information ours and transforms mere knowledge into wisdom.

Some among the ancient peoples had a natural predisposition for shamanism. Others were appointed, or even inherited their position from their ancestral lineage. This is still true today. In any case, the position required diplomacy, for the star shaman was the ultimate arbitrator between the good and evil supernatural entities who lived in Sky Country. They had to try to reconcile differences or at least know of the intentions of the gods before their wrath fell on the people. This is what reading portents is all about.

When I began my study of the astronomy of the ancient peoples, I learned several ways celestial omens could be interpreted. One belief is that when a large circle appears around the Moon it is going to rain; if you count the number of stars visible inside the circle, you can often determine how many days will pass before the rain comes. Experimentally, I have found it to be accurate four times out of six. Also, a red Moon means rain. A comet can mean big trouble, ranging from bad weather to the decline of a ruler, a belief that was practically global. Shooting stars are good luck and occasions to make a wish come true. Old wives' tales? Maybe. But many a significant event has been heralded by a sky portent. Two come to mind immediately.

The first, with roots in paganism, occurred when Merlin the Magician "saw" a vision in the sky several years before the birth of King Arthur. When Uther Pendragon, Arthur's father, was king, an apparition appeared in the sky in the form of a star and a dragon with rays of light shining from its mouth. One of the rays shone out over the land of Gaul (France). Merlin interpreted the omen as a sign of the impending death of the reigning king. He also read that Uther would have a son who would someday lead the Britons in conquering their foes, and thus become their High King. It was owing to the portent that Uther, and later Arthur himself, came to the known as the Pendragon, the Head Dragon.[9]

The second vision is the Christian story of the dazzling Star of Bethlehem that foretold a messiah. The famous "star" has intrigued scientists and laypersons alike for two thousand years. Modern astronomers offer theories ranging from a planetary conjunction to a comet. The important thing is that it was a sign in the heavens. Although the Bible is open to individual interpretation, I think Genesis 1:14 is clear, "And God said, let there be lights in the firmament of the heaven to divide the day from the night; and let them be for signs, and for the seasons, and for days, and years." The "lights" must be the Sun, Moon, and stars and, if so, they will be "for signs." Sky portents are real and should be taken seriously. Somewhere along the way we have lost the "openness" required to take these words to heart.

The sky and its gods were not always passive or peaceful however. Through time peoples have believed that the wrath of the celestial deities has manifested as storms, lightning, thunder, clouds, wind—all moods of the Great Sky Beings. However, sometimes much more than mere moods were being mirrored by these spectacles. The Skidi Pawnee star cult had a story that the world was created during the first thunderstorm. That belief was celebrated and the ceremonial year begun when the first clap of thunder was heard in the spring, heralding a time of rebirth and growth. This is "good." There were also cultures that believed the sky and the Sky Gods were on a wild and sometimes violently destructive spree when storms came. Sky deities commanded the storm forces that often frightened humans and sometimes extracted a strict penalty for their mistakes. Storms were but another portent when viewed this way.

My experiences with Native Americans have helped me realize that they have a great deal in common with tribal cultures in other parts of the world, such as the Native Hawaiians. I am not aware of any complete body of star shaman practices still intact in Hawaii, but I do know that the earliest Hawaiians had a strong connection with the sky, and that they knew of the powers inherent in the stars, Sun, Moon, and planets. Ancient legends tell of three gods, *Kane, Ku,* and *Lono,* who came out of the night (*po*) and created three heavens, one for each to dwell in. Kane made the Sun, Moon, and stars, placing the stars in the empty space between heaven and Earth.[10]

Notice that the Hawaiian word for night, *po,* is the same word the Dogon call the invisible star that revolves around Sirius! Martha Beckwith states, "Star lore has yet to be recorded from Hawaii. Stars were named and were associated with gods and chiefs, but I know of no star incarnations or apotheoses that are related in Hawaiian story. The sun and moon are represented in myth, either as habitations of gods who descend and live on earth in human form, or as divine bodies of gods who are worshipped as aumakua by their descendants." (Beckwith, p.85) Celestial legends also tell of *Wakea,* the God of Light and the heavens, and *Papa,* the god of Earth, who were the ancestors of the earliest of the islands' inhabitants. The goddess *Hina* embodies the lunar forces. Hawaiians also found the stars useful for calendrical purposes such as the timing of planting and harvest, and they looked to the stars as omens of the success of the year's agriculture.

The few star-related legends I know indicate which stars and constellations are special to the Hawaiians and other Pacific peoples. One is the Tahitian story about *Matari'i*, the Pleiades, a rainbow-colored "fishnet" that hangs in the sky. The Pleiades was once a single bright star whose stunning brilliance so angered the god Tane that he enlisted the help of the stars Aldebaran and Sirius to help him pursue Matari'i, who hid behind a stream. Sirius proceeded to drain the stream dry. Tane then flung Aldebaran at the bright star and broke Matari'i into six small pieces. Aldebaran, called *Makali'i,* is known as the "steering star," no doubt due to its prominence as a point of navigation. The Pleiades is also associated with prosperity and the season of plenty, which lasts until these stars descend below the horizon. (Beckwith, pp.367-368) (In an interesting sidenote regarding Sirius, I was told by a Hawaiian kahuna that whales are from Sirius and that they are the "record-keepers," presumably of the secrets of the Old Ways. That was the first time that I had heard of any animal being from the stars!) Hawaiians also believe that there are times when the Sun comes to Earth as a human. This is reminiscent of the Skidi belief that humans are stars incarnate. Pacific islanders look upon the Milky Way as the sacred ocean in the sky.

I heard something else intriguing about Hawaiian mythology in a conversation in Hawaii a few years back. While we sat around "talking story" one evening, a learned person said that there was at one time a body of stellar knowledge called the "Bowl of Light." The Bowl of Light was based upon the history of a body of lore, known a long time ago by the elders of the islands, that explained the relationship between humans and the sky. I understand that part of it tells of an old man named Kai-akua, an astronomer and navigator who could read the skies and was often consulted by the first king, Kamehameha. Although I have not yet found any more information about it, it sounds similar to the body of stellar knowledge I have been talking about throughout this book.

While in Hawaii I met a *kahuna* named Makua, without doubt one of the most interesting people I have ever encountered. Kahunas are the keepers of the ancient religious secrets, and are experts whose knowledge and abilities include healing, celestial navigation, and magical practices. It was Makua who told me what to look for in my search for Hawaiian starlore. He said that there were kahunas whose expertise was astronomy. They were the *Kilo Kilo*, the readers of the skies and interpreters of sky omens. Their work was closely associated with that of the navigators. While on the Big Island I was taken to a sacred site to visit the remains of a *heiau* (an ancient Hawaiian temple) where the Kilo Kilo had once done ceremony. I was also able to visit Mauna Kea, which I knew immediately was a natural beacon vortex. When I focused psychically on the mountain I felt that this beacon is connected to the Sun, the Pleiades, and to the star Aldebaran in Taurus, but I have not been able to find any mythical references to support my feelings.

As long as we view the stars as only hot balls of gas suspended in the lifeless void of interstellar space, we simply are not open to such experiences, are we? Of course, physically, they are hot balls of gas. But they are much more, just as human beings are much more than our physical bodies! The fact is that the more open we allow ourselves to become to the indwelling spirits of the stars, planets, and other celestial bodies, the more likely we are to form and experience a personal relationship with them.

CONCLUSION

For us the universe is inanimate and separated from the conduct of human affairs. For them, it is alive and intimately attached to every activity they (tribal peoples) undertake.[1]

Anthony Aveni

As I write this—Monday, April 1, 1996—I am thinking about all the exciting astronomical events that have occurred just in the last few weeks. Fifty million "new" galaxies have been found, a number that literally doubles the amount previously assumed to exist. A planet has been discovered circling around a star above the Big Dipper, a planet astronomers say may, like Earth, have all the necessary components and conditions for life to have evolved! Two comets are currently racing through the night and predawn darkness: Hyakutake and Hale-Bopp are electrifying astronomers and the general public alike with their presence. Our knowledge of the universe grows by leaps and bounds. So fast does it grow, and so profoundly does its growth enhance and change our view of the cosmos, that we may very well be experiencing a complete revolution in our awareness and understanding of the universe, and of ourselves in the process.

My study of astronomy has changed me considerably. The journey has carried me into the domain of science in numerous ways, some of which have been frustrating and intimidating, all of which have been and continue to be enlightening. Astronomy has taken me into worlds that have both excited and confounded me. It has informed me of objects such as quasars, black holes, pulsars, whose very existence challenges and even defies the law of nature, the basics of which I thought I understood. When I committed myself to studying the universe from a purely scientific perspective, I was concerned it might eventually lead me away from the metaphysical and esoteric views I had long held dear. It didn't. In fact, I gained an even deeper respect for the universe of which I already knew I was a part.

However, in astronomy texts, I encountered various academicians and professional scientists aiming "digs" at the "kooks" and "weirdos" who believe in astrology and mythology, who know little or nothing about the mechanics of the cosmos and therefore have nothing to offer or add to true understanding. Sometimes such remarks angered me; they seemed to warrant anger. Sometimes I have felt challenged by science, and encouraged to keep going, to learn more. Sometimes I have felt like an unwelcome outsider. Then I would read something that brought me inner peace and helped me reconcile my feelings.

Anthony Aveni's work has given me tremendous knowledge of the astronomy of the ancient peoples. A scientist first and foremost, Aveni seemed as if he had been confronted by some of the same "demons" I had. He wrote:

"Astronomy was *lived* as intently as it was practiced, and much of what our predecessors viewed was devoted to purposes that, today, we would regard as religious rather than scientific. When I chip away at the bedrock of my chosen discipline, I always seem to find astrology lying at its substrate. Is it because deep down we all believe that we live in an animate world and always wish to remain in constant dialogue with it? For most of human history we believed in celestial deities, many of whom behaved like petulant, if superpowerful versions of ourselves. If we disregard the metaphysical side of our ancestor's outlook, and focus only on those aspects of their astronomy that closely resemble our own, at the same time discarding astrology and mythology on the trash heap of mysticism, then I think we may be missing an important part of humanity's outlook on the universe." (Aveni, p.164)

Ancient astronomer-priests are, so it would seem, removed and remote from their modern-day counterparts. But are they really? Their *methods* of observing the sky with such scrutiny differ from those employed by astronomers today. Yet, are the *reasons* for observing different? I think not. Through time, humans seem to be answering an innate "call," a call that beckons us to the sky, the reason that underlies our looking to the heavens. Do we somehow know that Earth is not home? Do we somehow *know* that we came from the stars, that we are star-born? If we do, we know it intuitively, not because some mathematical formula or some technological device told us so.

There are some things technology can help us to know or understand. It can help us cope, and it can make life easier. It can diagnose our illnesses, fly us across oceans, and take us to the Moon. It can even think for us using the world of cyberspace. It can show us marvelous and revealing pictures of planets and their moons, stars of all kinds, and strange and wonderful galaxies. It allows us to build space shuttles and probes by which we can explore, literally, the same alien worlds our ancestors imagined so keenly and accurately. But can it give us a direct *experience* of the universe? I say no.

We cannot change places with those elders or go back to their time, of course. After all, ultimate truth is unattainable. But there are pathways we can walk in search of greater knowledge and understanding, including meditation, ceremony, silence, and openness. We must go forward, and we have to go forward in our own individual ways. For some of us, the disciplined way of science will teach us what we need to know. For others, the metaphysical path will answer our questions and solve the mysteries of existence. In these ways we all can fill our longings to know about the stars.

As I come to the point of conclusion, it is difficult to know where to stop. There is so much to be learned, so much to know. No one can learn it all. It is challenging enough to tackle the immense body of facts regarding the ancient cultures, their religion and religious practices, and what they knew about the stars. Studying the sciences of astronomy and physics represents an equal challenge. Had I approached either subject with my intellectual ability alone, I probably would have given up or lost interest a long time ago.

Because I have allowed what I have learned to trigger my intuition, and because I have relied on what I have intuited as being equally as reliable as the facts, I have kept going. That has made the learning process itself challenging, stimulating, exciting, and rewarding. Much of the time the things I have intuited seemed off base. I wasn't always sure how or where they fit into the scheme of things; not sure how or if they were even true. No proof was forthcoming. But, there are those rare and wonderful times when there *is* confirmation. One of those times occurred recently and it seems appropriate to share that here, in the spirit of helping bring closure to this writing and, at the same time, seeing it for the true "opening" it represents. In every closure there is an opening to be found.

In April 1994, during a channeling session in Sedona, Albion gave some information that, at the time, I took as his usual prophetic insight into times to come. Albion often teaches and/or gets his point across by making predictions based upon the philosophy he espouses. This night he began by reminding those present that, although Earth changes are thought of by most as negative and dangerous times, there are very positive things that occur during these periods. It was one of these positive events he wished to tell us about.

He reminded us that Earth is not alone in the universe. He talked at length about Earth having a karmic link with the other planets in the solar system, and to the Sun and Moon, most especially the Sun who gives life to the planets, and to *all* celestial bodies in the universe. It was what he said next, however, that is relevant to the contents of this book. I have chosen to share the information with you in the Teacher's own words; his words are relevant to the times we are currently going through, to our continent, and to knowledge that will soon be available to spiritual seekers the world over.

Although we are concerned with Earth's connection and relationship with the Sun, we must go beyond that to consider its link with the stars for purposes of broadening your perspective to encompass what we wish to share at this time. Through the planet's celestial leys, star energy or force is sent into Earth's magnetic field that in turn affects all that lives. This incoming stellar energy penetrates from time to time for specific reasons. Incoming star streams are carefully managed by The Regulators who are Initiates who have reached the evolutionary stage of galactic consciousness.

Beginning on the summer solstice this year, 1994, and lasting for one solar cycle (one year), a constellation of star force will be radiating its full power to seven strategic areas of North America. This energy will "touch" a specific race of people, the red race, and seven tribes within that race. You may wonder why this race and why these seven tribes. We tell you that it is because of the imminent intensification of the current cycle of planetary change. Earth has reached a critical point in this cycle. There will soon be times when the environmental issues that confront you will become so critical that no answers as to how to deal with or solve them will be forthcoming. However, the star power will trigger in the hearts—not in the minds but in the hearts—and beings within these seven tribes a compassion for the earth that will be a stronger and deeper compassion than any that has been felt for over 200 years. Medicine men and women and Wisdomkeepers (Elders) will come forward and be willing to share their religious traditions and ceremonials with people of all races— more willing than ever before. Likewise, the people within these tribes will also be affected in many positive ways. Political, social, economical, and other issues that have plagued this race for so long will cry out for solutions. Answers will come. Medical conditions will be out in the open, resulting in opportunities to solve them coming over time. The issue of the civil rights of indigenous peoples will make great strides. The star energy will shake loose from the minds and hearts of the Wisdomkeepers. The ancient sacred knowledge they have held in safekeeping will be shared. No racial, social, cultural, religious, or political barriers will prevent these people from singing the songs and dancing the dances for eyes and ears that have never seen or heard. The seven tribes are the Oglala, the Lakota, Seneca, Hopi, Potawatamie, Chippewa (Ojibway), and the Navajo. Watch, and listen, and rejoice, and learn from these traditions as they come forward, my friends.

Albion gave this information in 1994. When I was informed about the Star Conference being sponsored in the summer of 1995 by a Sioux Elder, Standing Elk, and realized that his reasons for holding the conclave were exactly those that had spoken about, I felt a deep sense of satisfaction and anticipation. Albion was right. Granted, not all channeled information is correct, and not all things foretold by Albion or any other spirit source come to pass. And there are many reasons why this is so. This time it was true. What he said, at least in part, has come to pass, for his words foretold of star teachings being revealed that few have known about. It is time. So be it.

The study of ancient and modern astronomy often raises more questions than it answers. I suppose that is to be expected. The more we learn, the more we realize we do not know, right? I think to pursue one—ancient or modern—without the other, while by no means fruitless, is like walking into a movie that started an hour ago! How much did we miss? How incomplete is our knowledge really? Aveni tells us that "[W]e need to avoid sweeping whatever may seem foreign and irrational about the sky under the rug of ancient astronomy, and we must resist the inclination to label the exotic and unfamiliar as worthless because it hindered or retarded the development of astronomical exact science as we know it today." (Aveni, p.167) Yes. Neither should we feel the need to sacrifice our imagination and intuition in favor of the academic, intellectual "exact science" our time demands. Intellect and intuition can and must work together. When they do, we both learn about the universe and open ourselves to a direct experience and relationship with the subjects of our learning.

The period between the ancient astronomers and now seems like an unbridgable gap. Perhaps that is because the religions and religious practices of today are virtually devoid of dogma or rites than involve the stars. In Christianity for example, references to the sky are primarily in relation to the Biblical prophecies contained in the Book of Revelation. The astronomical events forecast spell a time of catastrophes, not unlike those predicted in the Hopi and other Native American prophecies, preceding a time usually referred to as "Purification." This gives the stars a rather negative connotation, not the case with the vast majority of the ancient cultures. For them the stars played a more positive role not only in the religious sense, but in daily life. I believe the time has come when this will become true for us today. I think that those individuals I term spiritual seekers will begin to remember what they already have stored in the unconscious about the stars and begin to incorporate star power and significance into their spiritual studies and practice. If this is so, there is something very important to remember.

I wrote at the beginning of this book about the role the stars and other celestial bodies played in providing a sense of *order* to people on Earth. The universe is orderly. Its activities are reliable, dependable, and predictable. I thus translate this to mean that the universe is *ethical*. (And being ethical is precisely why it lends itself to mathematical interpretation.) An ethical universe cannot be understood if it is approached *unethically*. In short, as individuals and as collective humanity, we must go to the stars with a strong, solid code of ethics. Greed, personal gain, a struggle for power, lying, cheating, all the things that separate us from the laws of nature on Earth will block us from a connection with the stars. This makes a personal evaluation of our own understanding of ethics of primary concern before the first star ceremony is done.

The stars continue, as they have since time began, to give order to our world and lives. They tell us where we have come from and where we are going. "What better place to find the clues and patterns that offer answers about the meaning of life than in the ever-dependable, supportive, and nurturing world around us?" (Aveni, p.167) What better place can we look than to the stars? The stars guide us, inspire us, intrigue us, challenge us, and sometimes frighten us. But, above all else, they give meaning to us and our lives, individually and collectively.

"Whether we use prayer to commune with the sky or the natural law of mathematics, what lies at the very foundation of our motivation to study astronomy is the will to understand and control the cosmos—with or without the gods, limitless or limited." (Aveni, p.167) I opt for *understanding* without the need to *control*; for *limitless* instead of *limited; with* rather than *without* the gods. That is my choice. What, pray tell, is yours.

APPENDICES

MEETING STAR WOMAN

In my studies of the Skidi I have learned many things; things that have baffled me, as well as things that have inspired me and activated my intuition. One of these came from a band within the Pawnee Nation, the Chawi. Bits and pieces of Skidi stellar religion filtered into the other South bands, the Chawi, the Kitkahahki, and the Pitahawirata. Von del Chamberlain tells a Chawi story about a mythical "comet women," the vivid description of which follows.

"About her throat she wore some glittering object which looked like a star. Her head was in darkness, but down feathers stood up straight from it, signifying that she was in reality a comet . . . the bird in the center represented Tirawhat (the power and the fire); the owls represented the four gods in the west. . . . In the spring he planted the two grains of corn near their grass lodge. These two grains represented the moon and a comet . . . another woman appeared before him and said 'Mother Moon promised you many things, but I cannot promise you much for I am a comet; that is why I wear down feathers on top of my head. Mother Moon is second only to Tirawhat in power. I have power only to increase your people. My corn is white and has a tassel on top . . . "[1]

This description triggered my intuition, which revealed an image of a "star woman." I invite you to "see" her in your own mind's eye as you read.

ENCOUNTER WITH A STAR WOMAN

A bronze-skinned star woman stands before me. I can see the firm muscles in her well-formed body, especially in her arms and legs. Her hair is long, black, and straight, it is silky and shines with the softness of moonlight. I see her as an American Indian, but I know it is but one of the many guises she can take. Around her neck she wears a choker made from bone, in whose center is a gold-colored symbol of a four-pointed star. Her dress is made from white buckskin, speckled all over with the same kind of tiny, black star symbols—a "robe of stars." Her feet are bare. Around her right ankle is a circlet of white corn kernels. On her head, a nest of down feathers stand up in a beautiful delicate "spray." Dark, piercing eyes peer out over her high cheekbones, her full mouth and strong nose bridge complete an ageless face. I sense that she is a "collective image" of the female Star Gods who come into the dreams and visions of Earth women. She brings to them the powers of feminine stars—the kind of power the Dogon know about, and that is inherent within their emme ya star, the star they call the "Star of Women."

Making visual, intuitive contact with Star Woman assists us in crossing into the initial stages of Starwalking. Conscious contact can be made by first quieting and relaxing yourself physically and mentally. Then "see" the great star bridge, the Milky Way, like a roadway of sparkling diamonds arcing before you, the celestial arc that links Earth and you to the heavens. See yourself standing at its terrestrial base, and then slowly step onto the bridge and begin your walk into the sky.

Slowly up the archway you walk, each step taking you closer to the realm of the Great Star Nation. As you walk skyward, know that you have left Earth's bondage . . . you have become more Star Being than human. Feel the transformation taking place . . . feel your body getting lighter . . . becoming weightless . . . becoming free.

Now, see your body glowing . . . from the inside out . . . glowing . . . radiating . . . in pure brilliance. As you come to the apex of the Sky Bridge, you see a tall, stately figure looming before you . . . awaiting you. It is Star Woman. Feel her power, and as you come closer, feel it with greater intensity.

Soon, you are close enough to feel the heat radiating from her body. Look into her face . . . see the black pools of interstellar space in them, each pupil a well of silent, whirling galaxies suspended in the watery space in her eyes. The pendant she wears around her neck begins to glow in soft, pulsating golden rays. As you move closer, she extends an arm and hand to you. Go closer to her . . . offer her your hand.

As your hands join, feel the tingling current of pure cosmic electricity flow into you body . . . activating every cell in you . . . filling and nourishing you in a way you have never before experienced. Feel the current bonding you with Star Woman in this precious moment . . . a moment that gives you a glimpse into eternity. She welcoms you . . . you are accepted . . . she has bonded with you . . . you and she are one.

Through her mind you can access the power of the stars. You can know the wisdom of the Ancients who have gone before you on this journey into her domain. Whatever question troubles you . . . whatever solutions to problems you seek . . . she, telepathically, reveals answers to you.

She renews you . . . she suckles you in her depths . . . depths known only to those who have tread this time-worn path to the stars.

It is time for you to go. Star Woman releases you . . . your light body is free . . . your mind again your own. Begin to walk away, feeling her intense heat begin to fade into a balmy, comforting coolness. When you are halfway descended down the diamond star path, turn and look up to her . . . see her slowly fade from sight.

Go on home now . . . back to Earth . . . renewed . . . strengthened . . . nourished . . . your sense of wonder beating inside your chest as your light body once more gives way to physical flesh. You are enriched . . . so very enriched. Know that she is always there . . . that she has always been there . . . for you, for me . . . for all women . . . for all times. She is our Celestial Mother . . . our Star Sister . . . our Stellar Counterpart . . . the Great Star Goddess . . . the Eternal She. She is you, you are her. She is me, I am her. We are one.

STARGAZING
NAVAHO STYLE

*When all the stars were ready to be placed in the sky First Woman
said, 'I will use these to write the laws that are to govern mankind
for all time. These laws cannot be written on the water as that is
always changing its form, nor can they be written in the sand as
the wind would soon erase them, but if they are written in the stars
they can be read and remembered forever.*[1]

Trudy Griffin-Pierce

Divination is the art of foretelling future events and discovering hidden information about a person, place, or object. Throughout history, humans have devised various methods for accomplishing this task. Some of the most familiar include the use of a crystal ball, cards such as the Tarot, palmistry, dowsing, and the use of psychic ability without the assistance of any "props." Other, less familiar methods include *aeromancy,* which is "reading" the clouds; *geomancy,* "reading" the energy and ley lines of Earth; and *pyromancy,* the art of interpreting forms in ashes.

However, among the Navajo there exists a unique type of divination known as *stargazing.* Used by medicine people, stargazing involves divining the cause(s) of illness, the source of trouble in one's life, locating lost objects, or the identity of a witch who is causing someone difficulty. It could be said that stargazers are diagnosticians when it comes to illness or determining the source of psychic attack. But they are more than that. Because they draw their power from and through personal contact with supernatural spirit forces, and perform their rituals while in a trance state, they are also shamans. (Griffin-Pierce, p.143)

Stargazing techniques vary. A basic practice involves the stargazer looking through a quartz crystal at a bright star. Questions concerning whatever problem is at hand are posed to the star. Answers are then determined by the colors refracted through the crystal. The stargazer diagnoses the problem, and prescribes the rituals and sacred sand paintings that must be done to correct it. (Griffin-Pierce, p.144)

When I learned about this unusual method of divination, I tried it, and found the results most interesting. The experiment was successful, and I did receive information. But the "receiving" was not what struck me. For many years I have trained myself to "receive" during whatever circumstances I am in at the time, from whatever "tool" I might choose to use. It was, rather, the act of holding the crystal—I chose a fairly large clear piece of quartz—up to the star (I chose Antares) that interested me most.

I noticed several things, one being the "feel" of the crystal in my hand. It fit. It felt solid and heavy, like a real "tool" right away. It was a clear star-filled night, typical for the desert of northern Arizona. When I held the crystal up to Antares, the star's light became distorted, its rays extending like a candle flame does when you look at it with your eyes squinted. The rays became elongated, and were white and red in color, with a blade of blue showing through. It was beautiful and very empowering. The experience made me feel "closer" to Antares somehow, as if in some way the crystal blocked out the world, and there was no distance between me and the star!

The entire experience was a good and positive one. I have since experimented with stargazing numerous times, and recommend it highly.

DEEP-SKY OBJECTS

The following is a list of constellations and the selected deep-sky objects found in the vicinity of each, including nebulae, open and globular star clusters, and galaxies. I suggest that you compare the zodiacal listings with your natal horoscope to see whether any of these objects are located in any of the houses, as the houses would be where these energies would be coming through.

Objects in the constellations that are not part of the zodiac can help you learn what areas of the sky they are located in, and something about the nature of the object or body involved. The energy of these objects, particularly the open and globular clusters and galaxies—because they are such high concentrations of stars—enhance and intensify the house within which they appear, as well as any planets that are posited there. For example, the supercluster of galaxies in Virgo adds tremendous energy to that sign, and certainly contributes to its being a highly concentrated area of stellar power. The list will also tell you where to look in the night sky (with a good pair of binoculars or a telescope) and see some of the most beautiful of all the sky wonders.

CONSTELLATIONS

PEGASUS: Within the Great Square of Pegasus are more than 160 nebulae, which are dark patches caused by distant stars and clouds of gas and dust. Based on my intuition, I view the Great Square is a cosmic "window" through which we can focus on a tremendous, valuable source of stellar energy to empower ourselves on all levels.

Note that during the early morning hours of May 30, the annual Pegasids meteor shower comes forth.[1] I view meteor showers as "carriers" of energy from one place to another, somewhat like "celestial networkers." The radiant point (the area from which the meteors seem to come) is highly active, and is therefore a "hot spot" of energy during the time of their appearance. Keep in mind that, although it may look as if meteors originate in a given constellation, in truth they do not. The shower's apparent radiant point, as it is seen against the backdrop of space, makes it look as if the meteors are coming from certain constellations. Showers are named for the constellation from which we see them come. (Staal, p.13)

ANDROMEDA: The Andromeda galaxy is the closest galaxy to Earth. It is located northeast of the star Mirach. When drawing upon Mirach's energy, you can easily make contact with this beautiful spiral star vortex. The star Andromedae is the radiant point of the annual Andromedids meteor shower. Astronomers believe these meteors are the fragments of the Biela comet. (Staal, p.13)

ARIES: The Arietids meteor showers activates this sky region from the 12th to the 23rd of October every year. (Staal, p.26)

PERSEUS: The Perseid meteor shower appears annually between the 10th and 12th of August. The constellation also contains a double star cluster known as ηψ-Persei, that has been known about as far back as 2585 B.C. (Staal, p.73) I feel these clusters are too far away from any of the constellation's fixed stars to exert any real influence. However, the region where they are located is a source of potent stellar energy.

ORION: Officially listed as M42/NGC* 1976, the Great Orion Nebula is the most beautiful sight I have seen through a telescope. Sometimes visible to the naked eye as a faint, fuzzy patch, the nebula is heavily populated with young, hot stars, leading me to often refer to it as a "star nursery." This entire area of the Nebula is a wonderful source of empowering energy. The radiant point of the Orionids meteors lies between the star Betelguese in Orion, and Castor in Gemini. The Orionids appear annually from the 19th and 22nd of October. (Staal, p.81)

AURIGA: The Aurigids meteor shower is visible just south of the great star Capella from the middle of August through the first part of October every year. (Staal, p.178)

CYGNUS: This constellation is the location of an interesting cloud of ionized hydrogen located near the tail of the Swan called the North American Nebula. The nebula got its name from its being shaped like the continent of the same name. Interestingly, someone once commented to me that when the nebula's shape is studied closely, it looks like what our continent will look like if and when the earth change prophecies made by Edgar Cayce and others were to come to pass!

Two meteor showers, the Cygni, have their radiant point in Cygnus during July and August. (Staal, p.215)

SAGITTARIUS: When we look toward Sagittarius we are looking toward the *center* of the Milky Way galaxy. The region is filled with stars and may, if the newest theory is correct, be the location of a black hole. The constellation is also the location of numerous nebulae and star clusters,

North American Nebula

including the beautiful Lagoon Nebula (M8), the Trifid Nebula (M20), and the Horsehead Nebula (M17). (Staal, p.186) Keep in mind that nebulae create an intense grid of stellar power.

LYRA: Lyra is the location of the famous Ring Nebula (M57). Such nebulae are very large, sometimes as much as a thousand times larger than our solar system—a very large star grid indeed! This rich region is the radiant point of the Lyrids meteor shower, which appears in the early morning hours of April 20-22. (Staal, p.247)

CRUX: Early seamen looked upon this constellation, which they called the Southern Cross, as a "good omen sent to guide them through unknown waters." (Staal, p.156) This provides a clue to the general nature of the stars when worked with as a whole constellation. I turn to these Star Spirits to ask for signs regarding making major decisions.

BOOTES: Boötes contains a globular cluster made up of 30,000 suns. The cluster is known as M3, and lies northeast of the star Arcturus. (Staal, p.156) Since globulars are composed of old stars, these are good to tune into for help to propel yourself back into time for whatever purpose desired. During March 10-12, the Boötids meteors appear just east of Arcturus. (Staal, p.84)

GEMINI: The star cluster M35/NGC 2168—which can sometimes be seen with the naked eye—is located near the star Propus, (left toe of the star Castor's twin). (Staal, p.84) The cluster makes this region of the sky a good source of energy for personal empowerment. Gemini is also the radiant point for the Geminids meteor shower, which seems to come from just above the Twins' heads. These meteors stream in annually between the 4th and the 16th of December. (Staal, p.119)

LEO: Leo is the radiant point for the Leonids, which come every year during mid-November. Astronomers believe these meteors are also the remains of a comet. (Staal, p.198)

OPHIUCHUS: Ophiuchus is the location of a number of star clusters, making the region an abundant source of stellar power. (Staal, p.198)

*NGC: These initials stand for New General Catalog. The number following the initials represents the number of the sky object in that catalog.

ASTRONOMY GLOSSARY

A basic scientific understanding of stars and the cosmos may be gleaned from the mind-boggling technological advancements of modern times. This fundamental data, which can only be gained from a study of astronomy, coupled with archaeological, anthropological, and intuitive information, can help us gain a conscious, holistic relationship with any given stellar body, and ultimately with the entire universe. Knowing the kind of star it is, how old it is, and where it is located, advances the goal of putting the universe, and our connection with it, in a clearer perspective.

How far are various stars from Earth? How big are the different stars? How do other stars compare with our Sun? To what constellation does a given star belong? The answers to these and other questions help us balance the physical, cultural, and spiritual information about stars. Astrology should be accompanied by, if not preceded by, a basic knowledge of astronomy. Together, the two form a foundation of knowledge that will have the result of increasing your education about the physical universe so that your awareness of and place within it can grow and expand.

STAR: A self-luminous spherical celestial body that emits light and heat due to its interior nuclear processes.

VARIABLE STAR: A star whose brightness varies due to changes within the core that affect its output of energy, or by its being eclipsed by another celestial body.

BINARY PAIR: Two stars that are revolving around a common center of gravity.

CONSTELLATION: A number of stars grouped by humans into designs and patterns that depict various forms. Star groups are based upon the star's appearance from Earth. The most well-known of the constellations are the twelve "signs" or "stations" of the zodiac, which is the zone along the Sun's apparent path during a year.

WHITE DWARF: A star in its final stages of evolution. White dwarfs have exhausted most, or all, of their nuclear fuel, and have collapsed to very small dense objects.

ECLIPTIC: Earth's orbital path around the Sun, and the Sun's apparent path around Earth.

GALAXY: A body composed of billions of stars in various stages of evolution, a stellar vortex if you will.

GIANT STAR: Any star two or three times larger than our Sun. There are also sub-giants and super-giants.

RED GIANT: An aged, dying star that has swollen to gigantic size and appears red in the night sky. *Antares* in Taurus and *Betelgeuse* in Orion are examples of red giants.

LIGHT YEAR: The distance light travels in a vacuum in one year. Light travels at the relativistic speed of 186,000 miles per second.

SUPERNOVA: An exploding star.

LUMINOSITY: A star's brightness and output of energy combined.

VISUAL MAGNITUDE: A star's brightness as seen from Earth.

FIRST MAGNITUDE STARS: Very bright stars as seen from Earth. *Sirius* is a first magnitude star.

CIRCUMPOLAR STARS/CONSTELLATIONS: Stars and constellations in the northernmost and southernmost parts of the skydome. These stars never set, meaning that they never disappear from northern or southern latitudes, respectively.

OPEN STAR CLUSTER: Bright stars that are relatively distant from each other and bound together by gravitational force. The Pleiades is the best known example of an open cluster.

GLOBULAR CLUSTER: Dimmer stars bound together by gravity in much greater density than open clusters. The center of a globular cluster is so thick with stars that a large telescope can resolve only a few of them into single stars.

ANNUAL METEOR SHOWERS

QUADRANTIDS - 3-4 January

LYRIDS - 21-22 April

ETA AQUARIDS - 5-6 May

DELTA AQUARIDS - 28-29 July

PERSEIDS - 12 August

ORIONIDS - 21 October

TAURIDS - 3 November

LEONIDS - 17-18 November

GEMINIDS - 13-14 November

URSIDS - 22 December

ASTRONOMY OF
THE GREAT PYRAMID

In the international bestseller, *The Orion Mystery*, Robert Bauval and Adrian Gilbert report that their research reveals little or no doubt that the shafts within the Great Pyramid at Giza were oriented to specific stars. The following excerpts (from pp.172-173) reveal the painstaking, long-awaited results of years of research that contradict long-held previous assumptions, theories, and calculations.

> I [Bauval] realized immediately that because all slopes were slightly steeper than previously assumed, the age of the Great Pyramid would prove slightly younger, and I quickly did the calculations. The south and north shafts of the King's Chamber were targeted to Al Nitak (Zeta Orionis) and Alpha Draconis respectively; the south shaft of the Queen's Chamber to Sirius. . . . The conclusion was inevitable. The Great Pyramid was built somewhere between 2475 B.C. and 2400 B.C., thus an average epoch of c. 2450 B.C.

The authors also point out that other stars and constellations that figure prominently in the pyramid shafts are Thuban in the Draco constellation—the Pole Star at the time the Great Pyramid was built—and the star Kochab in Ursa Minor. There were/are four constellations involved with the shafts, or certain individual stars within them. These include the center star, Al Nilam, one of the so-called "belt stars" in Orion, Thuban, Sirius, and Ursa Minor. So, the pyramid's shafts pointed to stars that were significant to the ancient Egyptians.

APPENDIX SEVEN

STONEHENGE AND THE ANCIENT ART OF GEOMANCY

Stonehenge has a magic that is undeniable. While there may be many explanations for the magic of this megalithic site, one method for searching is the ancient art of *geomancy*. Practiced since the earliest times, geomancy is a sort of "spiritual physics" or "landscape geometry" that relies on the real, albeit subtle, *connection* between human beings and the land. Geomancers have long known that the origin of the power that dowsers are able to sense and tap into actually lies in the vast recesses of the cosmos. Direct, personal experience with it often leads to a spiritual awakening and, ultimately, to Enlightenment.

Fundamental to the practice of geomancy is the existence of *leys*. A term coined in the early 1920s by British geomancer Alfred Watkins, leys form a terrestrial system of "trackways" that run throughout the global landscape. Being particularly interested in ancient sites like wells, mounds, churches and cathedrals, stone circles, fords, wayside crosses, castles, and various other antiquities, Watkins became enthralled by the idea that many of these were sited on straight lines which he dubbed leys. His alignment theory was proven to be true in many cases.

Having worked with and taught various aspects of geomancy for years, I find that an in-depth study of leys reveals a subject far more complex than one might first think. Though others may perceive them differently, I "see" leys and ley networks as slightly luminous "tubes" that usually run just below ground, or crisscrossing the surface of the landscape. I have found that where leys intersect, intense energy vortexes often form.

I know geomancers who suggest that leys mark actual subterranean tunnels. This is the case with the Navajo Indians, who believe that the "mysterious straight tracks left by the lost Anasazi culture around Chaco Canyon in New Mexico were 'not really roads' but 'tunnels' along which the Anasazi could travel with invisibility."[1] I view leys and the systems they form as natural "transport systems" that convey Earth's life force from one place to another, much like the circulatory system in the human body. The knowledge and practice of geomancy is more prominent in England than anywhere else, with the possible exception of China where it has long been practiced as the ancient art of Feng Shui. In the west its survival is due in great part to the work of Alfred Watkins and Alexander Thom. Thom was at one time the professor of engineering at Oxford University, and an avid geomancer and author on the subject. There are other, more contemporary, practitioners such as John Michell and Paul Devereux.

Arguably the most popular English researcher and writer on the subject of leys and sacred sites, Michell comments about ley intersections: "These lines across the country were as sacred as the temples and shrines they linked, and evidently played an essential part in the mystical megalithic science. . . . the old stone monuments have a variety of strange reputations, as the scenes of supernatural events or for power of healing and fertility."[2]

One has to wonder if Stone Age priestcrafts not only chose ley intersections as building sites for sacred monuments, but if they also intended to mark the ley systems so that future generations would know where they were so as to draw upon their inherent power. We cannot be sure, of course, but we can be sure that they knew of the existence of leys, and valued them highly. Few among us doubt that the ancestors had a much different relationship with the land than we do today. The knowledge by and through which they achieved and maintained that relationship came about as a result of instinct, intuition, and experience.

Curiously, three of the most celebrated of the British leys pass directly through Stonehenge. One, the *Stonehenge Ley*, runs through Silbury Hill at Avebury and other lesser-known points. Another, the *Old Sarum Ley*, runs north-south from the ancient hill fort by the same name. The famous *St. Michael's Ley*, by far the most well-known, connects numerous of the well-known sacred sites of Great Britain.

Beginning at the off-shore St. Michael's Mount in Cornwall, the St. Michael's Ley runs through the Glastonbury Tor in Somerset, the site of the ancient Avalon. From there, it passes through Stonehenge, on past the beautiful Salisbury Cathedral, through the Rollright Stones in Oxfordshire. Stonehenge is the most famous site on the ley, and is one of my favorite places.

However, of all the stone circles I have visited in England and Scotland, I find the Rollright Stones the most intriguing. I have done ceremonies there at various times, and found the site to possess strong healing power.

STARGATES:

COMMENTARY ON PARALLEL UNIVERSES AND LAKOTA CEREMONIALS

We all seek understanding of the universe of which we are a part. True understanding comes only when we truly experience the whole of reality. Likewise, true experience is a *whole experience* that involves and requires logic, reason, intuition, and the insight that comes from their unity. We also have to observe, but in a different way than simply looking. *We have to see.* Author and physicist Fred Alan Wolf tells us the importance of: " . . . simply observing. Observing oneself in a dream. Observing oneself in this world when awake. Observing the action of observing. If we are brave enough to venture into this world with consciousness as our ally, through our dreams and altered states of awareness, we may be able to alter the hologram by bringing more conscious 'light' to the hell worlds that also exist side-by-side with our own."[1]

"Alter the hologram." Now that is an interesting statement. It implies that the mind determines reality! It is not necessary to have science *prove* that Starwalkers could have or did—and do—travel into space and/or other dimensions. It is not necessary for science to prove that black holes exist for them to exist. How thin is the line between something existing or not existing. All too often the answer lies in whether we can prove it or not by scientific standards and requirements. This gives rise to the attitude—or worse, the belief—that something exists because we *can* prove that it does. It *is* because we say it is! It *is* because it can be validated. Are there not things in existence that we cannot prove to be? Was that not the case only a few years ago with black holes? They existed in theory only. We now know there are such phenomena. We got lucky! But what objects or celestial phenomena might exist that we have not, and perhaps cannot by the present standards of science, even begun to conceive of?

I believe stargates exist because I *intuited* their existence before I knew that there is religious, mythical, or philosophical evidence of them, some of which has been around for thousands of years! It seems that there are scientists today who, theoretically at least, believe that stargates exist, and that they play a role in what is generally called the parallel universe theory. Universes are connected, and may be entered into through "star-gates," if you will. Is the fact that I arrived at my conclusion by and through my intuition any less valid than the same conclusion/theory arrived at by an astrophysicist by and through mathematics? After all, neither I nor the astrophysicist can prove that we are correct. Neither can any intuitive or astrophysicist prove either of us is wrong! I believe that, someday, *both* of us will be proven right in terms of the *methods* used to arrive at our theory or conclusion. Will the scientist who comes to the same conclusion as the intuitive be more right? No, I think. Ancient peoples such as the Maya, Aztec, ancient Egyptians, knew the "mathematics" of the universe. Questioning how they knew what they knew seems to invalidate *what* they knew in the eyes of some.

It takes courage to allow the imagination and the intuition to entice us into believing that myths, ceremonies, or some other esoteric source of information and experience, can reveal things—real things—not known of before. Sometimes the imagination and intuition tell us about things that smack of science fiction, not science fact. Imagine, for example, what the first scientist who conceived of black holes, parallel universes, or space-warps must have thought. He or she probably found the idea hidden within a mathematical formula—the numbers said it. Would that scientist have felt himself or herself less out on a limb than the intuitive who conceived of the same "weird" thing, conceived of through another way? I remember reading somewhere that when Einstein was told about the theory of the expanding universe, which was based upon the implications of his own theory, he responded, rather emotionally, that God doesn't play dice with the universe!

I am interested in the end result, the truth, no matter how it may have been come by. There is so much we do not yet know about our intellectual and intuitive powers. But more is being revealed. A case in point is what we have learned about how close the new physics is to proving the power of the mind, and its affect upon and role in things like interdimensional or time travel, indeed in *proving* that such *can* and *does* occur! Quantum mechanics may also be close to proving that other dimensions do exist, and to proving what star shamans have long known is possible, because they have experienced its truth while in altered states. Quantum physics will surely continue to bring many things out of the realm of impossibility into one of possibility, even probability.

Starwalkers were, and are, well-acquainted with our immediate neighborhood in the galaxy, and most likely the entire universe. That they can know where the entryways into other worlds of time/space are is not outside the realm of possibility nor probability. If stargates exist, and I believe they do, their existence and locations can be intuited, and someday will be scientifically validated. Whether you choose to attempt to experience them because someone intuited that they are real or decide to wait for "proof" is entirely a personal matter. One thing is for certain. Real or not, only your mind can determine.

I have a deep respect for Lakota sacred rites. Over the years I have participated with various Lakota Elders and medicine people in Sweats and other rituals. I have felt the power generated by these rites unlike those I have felt at other times, and in other ceremonies. I have had the experience of having Grandfather Wallace Black Elk come to my home and do a house blessing ceremony and tell stories of his people for hours. I have participated in a Sweat with a Lakota "spirit talker", and done a sacred lodge in honor of the Grandfather Eagle Spirit. Ronald Goodman had it right when, regarding the Lakota spring ritual journey, he stressed the importance the Lakota placed upon enacting on Earth what was going on in the heavens. This led to right living, and right living can only take place under the watchful eye of the Sky Gods.

RΈFΈRΈNCΈ SΈCTION:
CONSTΈLLΔTIONS ΔND FIXΈD STΔRS

CONSTELLATION: CETUS

Cetus the Whale is a sprawling stellar configuration that is visible near the southern horizon during September and October. As you can see by your star map, picking out the shape of a whale takes some imagination. A dragon or sea serpent is easier. Within Cetus is the star *Difda*, 2 degrees 35" (minutes) Aries. The star's energy embodies the *memories* of the earliest periods of life on Earth. When its power is emitted to our planet it results in archetypal memories being awakened within an individual or in the masses. This often has the effect of bringing some historical event back to our attention in order to help us prevent history from repeating itself. On an individual, personal level *Difda's* energy enables us to get into conscious touch with the contents of the collective unconscious. Another Cetus star, *Baten Kaitos*, 21 degrees 57" Aries, exerts a powerful energy to awaken that which is dormant, to instigate change.

Menkar, 14 degrees 19" Taurus, is a star whose energy provides a "shield" of protection for those members of the animal kingdom who reside in Earth's oceans. At present the whales and dolphins are the needy recipients of this stellar power. The Regulators began letting *Menkar's* energy into Earth's energy field during the early 1960s. Without this star shield to protect them, many species of sea mammals would already be extinct due to the excessive slaughtering perpetrated upon them and the pollution of their habitats. *Menkar's* energy will provide protection long enough for these species to survive until humans have evolved to the point of being capable of recognizing their value to the ecosystem. On a human level *Menkar* provides mental stimulation for those working in the fields of marine biology, oceanography, medicine, and, to some degree, meteorology. Its force will result in discoveries and breakthroughs in these fields.

CONSTELLATION: PEGASUS

Algenib, 9 degrees 9" Aries, is a star whose energy is part of what I refer to as the Dark Forces. By this I mean that no life on Earth, including humans, has evolved to the point of responding to its energy positively. Such star energies are therefore experienced as negative, and can be used by the members of the Dark Forces to entice humans into lust for power, greed, and other ailments that cause resistance to the Light. Such negativity and the pain that results ultimately become the very tool by and through which one evolves. In this way the Dark Forces serve an all-important purpose to Earth and all life-bearing planets, as well as to the universe as a whole. Such stars will be referred to in the text henceforth as "dark stars." Remember that as time goes by and the Age of Aquarius finally becomes the dominant force on the planet, humans will eventually evolve so that we are able to respond to these stars' energy in a positive manner. Astrologers say that those who come under the influence of *Algenib's* power can develop a violent nature and suffer various misfortunes as a result.[1]

The star *Markeb*, 23 degrees 29" Pisces, sends its energy to Earth to stimulate and sustain the life force that empowers the mineral and plant kingdoms, an energy that the Regulators allow in at all times, making it a constantly influencing starstream. *Scheat*, 29 degrees 22" Pisces, is also a dark star whose energy causes disruption of the energy flow of whatever person or object it touches, resulting in blockages and stagnation on some level.

CONSTELLATION: ANDROMEDA

The Andromeda constellation is empowered by the Great Nebula, a large spiral galaxy that lies some 2,300,000 light years from Earth. I feel that this galaxy uses the Andromeda constellation as the channel through which to transmit its energy to our planet. This transmission serves to link Earth and the Milky Way galaxy to other galaxies in the cosmos, and in doing so provides for the possibility of intergalactic communication. It is by means of the Andromeda "link" or "network" that much of the channeled information being received by intuitives is coming through.

Alpheratz, 14 degrees 18" Aries, emits a power that helps bring about freedom, liberation, and independence. This star's energy operates purely on the mental level of a human being.

Vertex, 27 degrees 51" Aries, operates primarily on the astral or emotional level. Its energy also stimulates the brow and crown chakras in the human etheric body. The star *Mirach*, 00 degrees 24" Aries, embodies the power of love and sensitizes us to an appreciation for the positive and the beauty in all things. It is also one of the stars that promotes prosperity. *Mirach* and the star *Almach*, 14 degrees 14" Taurus, work in a similar fashion for astrologers say that *Almach's* power bestows honor to recipients, and inspires us to open to an appreciation for the arts. (George/ Parker, p.15)

CONSTELLATION: PISCES

Astrologers report that *Al Pherg*, 26 degrees 49" Aries, emanates a power that provides steadiness and strong will power, which may be used for success in any field of endeavor. (George/Parker, p.13)

CONSTELLATION: ARIES

The star *Sheratan*, 3 degrees 58" Taurus, is currently emitting a vital force that is playing a major role in the current cycle of Earth changes. Its energy triggers physical changes by setting off seismic events at various intervals and locations worldwide. When responded to by an individual or a nation, *Sheratan's* power can provoke warfare. It is greatly stimulating to the element of fire. In addition, the star *Hamel*, 7 degrees 40" Aries, is a dark star that often manifests itself as an intense surge in violent crime in society.

CONSTELLATION: PERSEUS

Perseus has numerous dark stars. One, *Capulus*, 24 degrees 12" Taurus, blocks insightfulness in humans. *Algol*, 26 degrees 10" Taurus, is known as the most evil of stars, and embodies the power of the goddess Lilith. If responded to negatively, *Algol* can adversely affect and even bring death to the body and consciousness, particularly in women. This star was triggered into action with the advent of the women's movement and the reawakening time of the Great Goddess. It brings the challenge of teaching human beings the value of the feminine in all things, including its operation within human consciousness regardless of gender.

CONSTELLATION: AQUARIUS

Sadalmelik, 3 degrees 21" Pisces, is a star of the Light that works through the Dark Force of Destruction for positive ends by tearing down forces of deception and illusion. The Regulators make use of *Sadalmelik's* power during times of planetary change and periods when the Dark Forces are attempting to entice and deceive humanity. *Sadalmelik* dispels glamour.

The star *Skat*, 8 degrees 52" Pisces, is another star of prosperity. (George/Parker, p.163) Its most important purpose is its role in sustaining Earth's cycles, including the regulation of the seasons, the cycles of civilization, and all major cycles involved in human affairs.

Sadalsuud, 23 degrees 24" Aquarius, is a star whose energy serves the Karma Lords for the purpose of enforcing the Law of Karma, or Cause and Effect, on Earth. On an individual basis it can cause problems in relationships. (George/Parker, p.153)

WINTER CONSTELLATIONS

CONSTELLATION: TAURUS

Aside from its recognition as a constellation, Taurus contains two famous open star clusters, the Pleiades and the Hyades. Of these, no star group has been more widely recognized and honored throughout history than the Pleiades. Known to astronomers as M45, the Pleiades cluster is composed primarily of hot, white stars. One of them is *Alcyone*, 00 degrees 00" Gemini, a stellar body that also exerts tremendous influence on women. Its power was exceptionally strong during the first twelve centuries A.D., when it inspired the holy priestesses throughout the world, particularly in Europe. *Alcyone's* power is being felt today as it serves to awaken the priestess archetype in women in North America, Hawaii, Australia, and Europe. Individuals who are not ready and/or capable of responding to this star's power properly are prone to use its influence for sorcery. Astrologers say that *Alcyone's* energy is "mixed" and can bring love on the positive side, and accidents and disease on the negative.

Next there is the Hyades and the star *Prima Hyadum*, 5 degrees 48" Gemini. Hyadum is a star cluster whose components are moving in the same approximate direction at the speed of 40km a second! The cluster's stars number 132. Such a cluster can trigger sudden events of conflict and war. It is important to realize however that conflicts that result in establishing harmony are necessary and ultimately serve a positive purpose.

Aldebaran, 9 degrees 47" Gemini, is a red giant elder star that is 36 times the size of our sun! Its energy stimulates human intelligence, and it is the location of one of the Halls of Records for the Earth. The star *Elnath*, 22 degrees 35" Gemini, embodies an energy that makes it a stellar source of healing, harmony, and balance. The Regulators have been letting in the energy of both *Aldebaran* and *Elnath* since the beginning of this century.

The star *Al Hecka*, 24 degrees 47" Gemini, is a dark star whose energy often triggers violence in human beings collectively. Its energy is also reaching Earth at this time.

CONSTELLATION: ORION

Orion has been of tremendous significance since the earliest times. Its energy, particularly of the "belt" stars, is currently being released to Earth by the Regulators. Known as Orion the Hunter, the constellation influences sacred rites and all religions. One of its prominent stars, *Rigel*, 16 degrees 50" Gemini, embodies the force of pure masculine power and is currently stimulating the male force within individual humans (regardless of gender). It also embodies the power of progress and intelligence when responded to positively, and will bring breakthroughs in various fields of scientific development and knowledge. If responded to negatively, *Rigel* will promote aggression and the need for dominance and control. *Bellatrix,* 20 degrees 57" Gemini, emits a force that influences military affairs and leaders, and stimulates positive diplomacy. (George/Parker, p.29) But if responded to negatively, it will become a dark star that will bring dishonor and ruin. *Bellatrix's* energy has been let in by the Regulators for over a thousand years.

Betelgeuse, 28 degrees 45" Gemini, is among the best known of the fixed stars. It is a red giant whose energy helps sustain the flow of life force in all bodies on Earth. *Betelgeuse* is one of the stars that the Regulators have used since Earth's earliest times because it stimulates the flow of evolution. The star *Alnilam,* 23 degrees 28" Gemini, is a tool by which Innerplane Teachers can telepathically connect with their students and disciples on Earth. It enhances human intuition, and can assist humans to open as "channels" for spiritual information, prophecy, and guidance that can influence humanity in positive ways.

CONSTELLATION: AURIGA

The energy of the star *Menkalinan,* 29 degrees 55" Cancer, is currently being let in by the Regulators. Its energy is exerting a tremendous current of pure stellar power to Earth that is serving to reactivate sacred sites worldwide. Many of these sites have been dormant and/or abandoned for a long time. Another powerful star, *Capella,* 21 degrees 51" Gemini, serves as a transmitter for the Melchizedek energy, as well as for the Cosmic Logos and other highly evolved members of the Spiritual Hierarchy.

CONSTELLATION: COLUMBA (THE DOVE)

The star *Phact,* 22 degrees 10" Gemini, embodies the power of peace. When its energy is being sent to our planet, as it is now, increasing steadily until the year 2000, it can bring tranquillity into any conceivable situation or imbalance that exists. *Phact* is a source of power that is often utilized by the Regulators to help "regulate" the evolutionary energy of Earth during the change of significant time cycles such as the changing of a Great Age or the millennium.

CONSTELLATION: CARINA - ARGO NAVIS

The star *Foramen,* 22 degrees 09" Libra, emits a strong starwave that pierces the veil around Earth so that powerful systemic and cosmic energy from various parts of the solar system and universe can enter our planet's auric field and vitalize consciousness. An example of this was the shift in consciousness that resulted from the photograph *Earthrise* taken by the Apollo astronauts in the late 1960s.

Canopus, 14 degrees 58" Cancer, is a well-known star whose energy has long affected human consciousness. It is highly transformative and changes evil into good. When drawn upon consciously, *Canopus'* power can have an extremely positive effect upon spiritual insight, development, and growth.

CONSTELLATION: ERADINUS

Achernar, 15 degrees 19" Pisces, is a dark star that is in direct conflict with the energy of love. When received by unevolved humans, its influence can cause people to freeze their religious beliefs into strict dogma that can lead to fanaticism. This star's force has been witnessed throughout time in the numerous conflicts where war is waged over religious differences. We see its influence today in the Middle East, Bosnia, and other countries where religious conflicts rage.

CONSTELLATION: CANIS MINOR

The star *Procyon*, 25 degrees 47" Cancer, is playing a significant role in the current meteorological planetary changes, and often triggers natural disasters that involve water, i.e., floods and droughts, extremes of the same continuum.

CONSTELLATION: CANIS MAJOR

Canis Major is the constellation through which the powerful *Sirius*, 14 degrees 05" Cancer, transmits its energy to Earth. It was known as Sothis (Isis) and the Nile Star to the ancient Egyptians, and is the star that is central to the Dogons in Africa today. *Sirius* is the location of the Great Hall of Records that chronicles human events, so it forms a celestial ley that opens up the Akashic Records for humans to remain in touch with their ancestral past.

CONSTELLATION: GEMINI

Gemini is another constellation through which several of the fixed stars transmit their power. Among them are *Tejat/Propus*, 3 degrees 26" Cancer, whose energy stimulates the human ego, promoting confidence when responded to positively, and egotism when its rays are used for self-promotion and ego-centered advantages.

Dirah, 5 degrees 18" Cancer, emits an energy that stimulates both human and animal consciousness. *Alhena*, 9 degrees 06" Cancer, provides inspiration for the arts as they manifest in various forms and expressions through humans.

The star *Wasat*, 18 degrees 31" Cancer, exerts a power that is currently being utilized by the Regulators to help sustain the physical health and well-being of Mother Earth. Wasat also assists in the formation of organizations such as Greenpeace whose task it is to promote ecological awareness and help solve the environmental problems we now face. A particularly significant capability of this star's energy is that it helps neutralize the effects of various toxic chemicals.

Propus (not to be confused with *Tedjat/Propus*), 18 degrees 57" Cancer, emits a power that denies stagnation and promotes change. The most prominent stars in Gemini—*Castor,* 20 degrees 14" Cancer, and *Pollux,* 23 degrees 13" Cancer—have pronounced effects upon spiritual matters and development of our planet. *Castor* symbolizes the Law, both the written and oral Divine Word. *Pollux's* power opens a celestial ley through which human thoughts and feelings may be transmitted into space. Astrologers are well aware of the intense powers inherent within these famous "twins." When they are not responded to positively they can bring a sudden gain, then sudden loss of fortune, disgrace, and troubles that include sickness (*Castor*), and a rash and even cruel nature (*Pollux).*

CONSTELLATION: VELA

The star *Markeb,* 28 degrees 54" Virgo, embodies an ancient power that assists the human mind in gaining an appreciation for and interpretations of patterns and designs. This has assisted humans in becoming able to create structure in both their inner and outer lives, and is responsible for the varieties of architecture that have appeared down through history. It should be remembered how architecture has reflected the ambitions, beliefs, culture, and religion of humankind since the earliest times. On the psychological level, it is also important to note the significance Jung placed on mandalas, a form of "mental architecture," and what they indicate about the innermost human nature.

SUMMER CONSTELLATIONS

CONSTELLATION: CYGNUS

Cygnus is sometimes called the Northern Cross or the Swan. Both have esoteric connotations embodied in their symbolism. The cross is the symbol of the Crucifixion, which embodies the pain and suffering we encounter in our learning to overcome the many trials involved in being human. The swan is also one of the correspondences of the sephirah Kether in the Kaballistic teachings, Kether being great Source of All Things. One of Cygnus' stars, *Albireo,* 1 degree 15" Aquarius, embodies the energy of the Christ Consciousness, which is the same as that of the World Teacher or the Bodhisattva power. This star's force is currently being transmitted to Earth and will eventually result in the formation of a new world religion, the appearance of an avatar, or some other significant planetary spiritual and/or religious event.

Another Cygnus star is *Deneb Adige,* 19 degrees 48" Aquarius, the star through which the Archangels connect with the human kingdom, and by which spirit guides form a telepathic link with humans. Stellar rays emitted by *Deneb* form a sort of celestial ley through which telepathic thoughts are channeled directly to individuals and, occasionally, to collective human consciousness. The Regulators have been letting this star's energy in since the dawn of human history.

CONSTELLATION: AQUILA

I sense that the constellation Aquila, the Eagle, has special spiritual significance to the American Indians and the North American continent, which they call Turtle Island. One of its stars, *Altair,* 1 degree 47" Aquarius, emits an energy that activates the so-called Rod of Power of the Planetary Logos and other spiritual leaders of this world, both incarnate and disincarnate. As its rays are transmitted to Earth they form a galactic ley that links the Milky Way with other galaxies throughout the Local Group (the group of which our galaxy is a part). Another Aquila star, *Deneb,* 19 degrees 48" Capricorn, focuses its rays only on North America and its people, and it has been doing so for the last thousand or more years. It embodies the wisdom of the ancestral peoples. Wisdomkeepers of all Indian tribes are telepathically linked to Deneb's energy, and the star serves as a stellar patron to medicine men and women, tribal elders, and all individuals and groups who serve as planetary stewards. I feel that it was the influence of *Deneb* that caused renewed interest in Indian culture and religion, an interest that has spread worldwide.

CONSTELLATION: SAGITTARIUS

Sagittarius contains numerous fixed stars, one of which is a triple star system, *Polis,* 3 degrees 13" Capricorn, located in the upper part of the bow of the Archer. *Polis* emits an energy that stimulates ambition and motivates people into action. Next is *Facies,* 8 degrees 18" Capricorn, which is actually M22, one of the several open star clusters in the constellation. Its rays form a celestial ley that connects to the center of the galaxy and allows for interdimensional travel and mental telepathy between humans and extraterrestrials. The people who serve as channels for extraterrestrials are doing so in part through the assistance of this star's rays, which the Regulators began letting in during the early 1940s.

The star *Pelagus* (sometimes called *Nunki*), 12 degrees 23" Capricorn, has been energizing Earth for over five thousand years! It empowers ceremonial magicians and shamans worldwide. *Ascella,* 13 degrees 38"

Capricorn, embodies the power of transformation and operates on the highest levels of human consciousness. *Manubrium*, 15 degrees 00" Capricorn, is a warrior star whose force empowers heroism and bestows strength and courage in battle. *Terebellum*, 25 degrees 51" Capricorn, is a star whose rays form a celestial ley through which the angelic kingdoms link themselves to other stars and galaxies throughout the universe. *Spiculum*, 0 degrees 39" Capricorn, is composed of two star clusters and three nebulas (M8, the Lagoon Nebula, M20, and M21). A nebula is a concentrated area of star energy, a stellar vortex if you will. This kind of power energizes the full force of a person's willpower. *Spiculum's* energy will be released by the Regulators just after the year A.D. 2000, and it will bring about a leap in human spiritual evolution. On an individual basis, *Spiculum's* influence will eventually help bring us to the point of self-realization.

CONSTELLATION: LYRA

As a constellation, Lyra's collective rays form a celestial ley that transports incoming cosmic force into our system. The star *Vega*, 15 degrees 19" Capricorn, is destined to become the next northern Pole Star. *Vega's* energy empowers the feminine force in human beings regardless of their gender, and operates within the part of the human psyche that Jung called the *anima*.

CONSTELLATION: CAPRICORN

Several fixed stars in Capricorn are currently transmitting their power to Earth. Among them is *Giedi*, 3 degrees 46" Aquarius, whose energy vitalizes the mountain ranges and specific peaks (many of which are sacred mountains) throughout the world. These include Mt. Shasta in California, Denali (Mt. McKinley) in Alaska, the San Francisco Peaks in northern Arizona that are sacred to both the Navajo and the Hopi, and Mt. Kailas, the holy mountain of Tibet. It is *Giedi's* power that is currently causing the energy of many sacred mountains, particularly the Great Smoky Mountains in the Southern Appalachians, to be reawakened to their full physical and spiritual power. The star also serves to activate dormant volcanoes, and is the power by which active volcanoes receive their power.

Dabih, 4 degrees 03" Aquarius, operates on the astral plane and on human emotions, both individually and collectively. When responded to properly, *Dabih's* energy restores emotional harmony to any given situation, relationship, group, or organization. When responded to negatively however, the power has the reverse effect, making it a dark star to the unevolved and the self-serving.

The star *Oculus*, 4 degrees 43" Aquarius, is one whose influence has been felt since ancient times. Its rays form a celestial channel for incoming cosmic power that inspires communication and occult education responsible for the transmission of ancient Hermetic wisdom to Earth. Entities such as Hermes Trismegistus, Plato, Socrates, Merlin, and—in more modern times, Einstein, David Bohm and other "thinkers"—have, both consciously and unconsciously utilized this star's power as a source of intellectual and spiritual stimulation.

Bos, 5 degrees 10" Aquarius, is a stellar source that vitalizes and sustains various cycles on Earth, specifically those that have to do with the feminine force of fertility in Nature. *Bos* provides power for the physical life cycles of the females in all kingdoms on the planet, including the cycles of estrus, menstruation, menopause, ovulation, and reproduction and the Crone or Wisdomkeeper rhythms.

The star *Armus,* 12 degrees 44" Aquarius, emits a power that stimulates the heart chakras of all the lifeforms on Earth. *Dorsum,* 13 degrees 51" Aquarius, on the other hand, is a dark star whose power has been used to energize the rituals and magic of black magicians down through the ages. The Hitlers and Mansons of the world have responded to *Dorsum's* available power, which can be accessed easily. The star *Castra,* 20 degrees 12" Aquarius, is also a dark star that emits rays that trigger hostility within unevolved humans.

Nashira, 21 degrees 47" Aquarius, emits a force that can be drawn upon to assist in our being able to overcome evil and temptation. In this way its power provides an antidote to the ever-present darkness that entices and entraps us in the glamours that are a part of living on Earth.

Deneb Algedi, 23 degrees 33" Aquarius, is one of what I call "cycle stars." Its energy perpetuates the cycles of birth and death on Earth, and in this way affects all that lives on the planet.

CONSTELLATION: CORONA BOREALIS
The star *Alphecca,* 12 degrees 18" Scorpio, sends a ray to Earth that opens a communication channel for incoming energy from the Cosmic Initiators known as the Lapikas or Karma Lords. This stellar wave is responded to only by highly evolved incarnated human souls and their counterparts within the other kingdoms.

CONSTELLATION: SERPENS - CAPUT - SERPENTIS - OPHIUCHUS
Various cultures have named this constellation, as evidenced by the four names. Serpens, however, is the most commonly used. The star *Unukalhai,* 22 degrees 05" Scorpio, provides a stimulus that helps perpetuate the life force within the plant kingdom. It enhances the medicinal and nutritional value of plants throughout the world. It is being utilized at this

time by the Regulators to benefit the forests of the world, particularly to help sustain the vitality of the rainforests and old growth forests before it is too late.

The star *Rasalhague,* 22 degrees 27" Sagittarius, is a dark star that does "Light" work by serving to bring negative karma into manifestation in individual humans. (The star *Lesath* works in a similar manner but solely through the constellation Scorpio.) Even though this may seem negative, we are reminded that evil exists within all of us, and efforts we make to become aware of it and overcome its effects provide the grist for the mill of human evolution. Stars such as *Rasalhague* and *Lesath* are therefore providing a necessary and positive service when viewed from this perspective. (Remember, the stellar forces that I have labeled as "dark" are only so to those who are incapable of or unwilling to respond to their energy in positive ways, namely those who are unwilling to take responsibility for themselves and their thoughts and actions.) Another Serpens star, *Sabik,* 17 degrees 58" Sagittarius, also emits a power that is most often experienced as a dark energy that serves to corrupt and pervert morality within society.

Yed Prior, 2 degrees 18" Sagittarius, periodically sends its energy for the purpose of generating a revolution of some kind and purpose in some segment of the human race. Such energy, though it may seem negative, is positive in the long run because revolution often serves to depose tyrants and clear the air of tyranny.

The star *Sinistra,* 29 degrees 45" Sagittarius, emits an energy that allows for human consciousness to access the individual collective unconscious specifically for the purpose of past-life recall when and as it pertains to individual karmic revelation. *Sinistra* works in conjunction with other fixed stars that have some connection with the Law of Karma and the Hall of Records.

The star *Han,* 9 degrees 14" Sagittarius, embodies the *kundalini* force, a force that is intimately connected with the elevation of human consciousness. *Han's* energy can also block the free elevation and flow of this force when and if our objectives are unclear and/or self-serving to a fault.

CONSTELLATION: SCORPIO - SCORPIOS

Scorpio is a powerful and intense constellation of stellar force that is the channel through which numerous fixed stars transmit their energy to our planet. Among these is the star *Lesath,* 24 degrees 01" Sagittarius, mentioned earlier. Another is the red giant *Antares,* 9 degrees 46" Sagittarius, which I often refer to as the Warrior Star due to its ability to empower a human being physically, emotionally, mentally, and spiritually. Its power works in much the same way as a sacred ceremony, sacred object, or sacred place empowers a person or a group. Aside from its direct influence on humans, *Antares'* rays open an important "pathway" between one dimension and another, resulting in a sort of "interdimensional connector" or "bridgeway" between parallel universes. In the near future science will discover the actual existence of this connecting link, and in doing so make one of the most profound scientific discoveries of the next millennia!

Graffias/Acrab, 3 degrees 11" Sagittarius, emits energy that causes a veil of illusion to be cast over the intellect of unevolved and unaware people, resulting in ignorance being bliss, so to speak. In this way its energy has the same type of effect that astrologers attribute to the planet Neptune.

Isidis, 2 degrees 34" Sagittarius, is a "death star" whose energy brings ending and closure to human and planetary affairs. The Regulators are beginning to let *Isidis'* energy in to propel us into the next millennium. Humanity will have to handle this energy carefully, and learning to do so will no doubt teach us many hard lessons.

The star *Aculeus,* 25 degrees 44" Sagittarius, activates the anal and solar plexus chakras in the etheric bodies of humans and animals. A sort of side result of this is the "grounding" effect these lives experience in their relationship with the planet. *Acumen,* 28 degrees 45" Sagittarius, emits rays that form the Light Ley that allows light from our Day Star to nourish the plant, animal, and human kingdoms. This star, for example, is responsible for the process of photosynthesis, and has been sending to Earth since its birth as a planet.

CONSTELLATION: LIBRA

Two fixed stars operate through Libra and both are known as "Scale": *North Scale,* 19 degrees 22" Scorpio, and *South Scale,* 15 degrees 05" Scorpio. The energies emitted by these stars work in conjunction with one another to form a strong star band that is regulated by the most highly evolved Beings who have a karmic relationship and responsibility for Earth and all that lives upon her. *South Scale* is utilized by the Karma Lords for the purpose of maintaining the balance between planetary and human law, which manifests as cosmic justice. The ultimate and end result is karmic justice. Those who work in the field of law, and those who teach and train others in the laws of the Occult are highly subject to this star's influence. *North Scale* transmits a force that influences social justice in individuals and nations globally. Its energy oftentimes works in conjunction with other fixed stars whose power affects human morality issues. *North Scale* energy is exclusively regulated by Sanat Kumara, the Solar Logos.

SPRING CONSTELLATIONS

CONSTELLATION: BOOTES

Seginus, 17 degrees 40" Libra, affects the physical nervous system of both humans and animals. It also activates five of the seven human chakras, excluding only the brow and crown.

The famous *Arcturus,* 24 degrees 14" Libra, is one of our Star Teachers —a Star Shaman if you will. It emits a pure stream of stellar force that awakens human intuition and plants a mental seed that often results in an individual entering into shamanic training. *Arcturus* also enhances learned magical skills, particularly those of prophecy, rainmaking, divination, and knowledge of plants and sky omens. The Regulators are currently letting *Arcturus'* energy into North America and Europe.

Princeps, 3 degrees 09" Scorpio, operates on the mental level and enhances intellectual power. This is a star energy that benefits all affairs that concern education and communication, and it has been used by the Regulators since the beginning of the twentieth century.

CONSTELLATION: VIRGO

The great star of Virgo, *Spica,* 23 degrees 50" Libra, emits a star wave that inspires those men and women who are engaged in or wish to become engaged in the justice system and the law, both spiritual and human—God's law and human law. *Spica's* energy has been let in by the Regulators since the dawn of civilization, and has influenced the evolution of justice systems worldwide.

The star *Vindemiatrix,* 9 degrees 56" Libra, emits a force that plays upon the human persona. When not responded to properly it can facilitate a fall from grace among the masses.[2] *Zaniah,* 4 degrees 50" Libra, embodies the power of the Law of Love, and is often utilized by the Regulators to instill love as a human value and expression. *Zaniah* works in conjunction with other stars of similar power, and is currently being let in to influence the human species.

Caphir, 10 degrees 08" Libra, bestows the skill of prophecy in humans and perpetuates and enhances instinct in animals, reptiles, and birds. *Zavijava,* 27 degrees 10" Virgo, is particularly useful to the Regulators because its energy promotes the desire within human consciousness to serve others. This star's influence has, for example, played a significant role in helping humans form organizations such as the Red Cross and other humanitarian groups. *Zavijava's* energy also inspires groups like the New Group of World Servers, the work of the Dalai Lama, and various ashrams and light centers throughout the world. This star's force, currently coming to Earth, is being gradually intensified as the current period of planetary change moves into its critical stage.

Khamballa, 6 degrees 57" Scorpio, is another star that serves as a channel for peace energy to manifest on Earth.

CONSTELLATION: CORVUS

Algorab, 13 degrees 27" Libra, transmits energy that stimulates the life force and protects the wing-eds in the animal kingdom. Its energy is also conducive to the appearance of Spirit Birds that have long been a part of mythology down through time. The Phoenix, or Thunderbird, is a prime example.

CONSTELLATION: CENTAURUS

Two fixed stars operate through Centaurus. They are *Agena,* 23 degrees 48" Scorpio, and *Bungula/Toliman,* 29 degrees 29" Scorpio, the nearest star to our solar system. *Agena* stimulates the economy of the world, and is therefore a star of prosperity. *Bungula's* rays form a systemic ley that allows for incoming telepathic communication from the Solar Logos, Sanat Kumara, to his disciples worldwide.

CONSTELLATION: LEO

Leo is the channel through which six fixed stars operate. The first is *Zosma,* 11 degrees 19" Virgo, which, working in conjunction with other stars, is responsible for and perpetuates the law of ethics within all the kingdoms on Earth. This law determines and sustains the balance of power and the rights of all lives.

Denebola, 20 degrees 42" Leo, has specifically to do with human law, courts, and judges, and to that end works in close conjunction with other stars such as *North Scale* in Libra.

Algenubi, 20 degrees 42" Leo, could rightly be called the "Destroyer Star." Its rays serve to tear down obstacles that threaten to inhibit the flow of evolution. It tears down the old in order to make way for the new. Its power purges in ways somewhat akin to that of the planet Pluto. In similar fashion *Adhafera,* 27 degrees 34" Leo, serves to break up congealed energy so that activity (of whatever kind) can begin anew.

Al Jabha, 27 degrees 54" Leo, operates on a soul level of human consciousness by activating the heart chakra. *Regulus,* 29 degrees 50" Leo, is a high energy star that stimulates the minds and hearts of Earth's political and social leaders. It is *Regulus,* for example, that is the guiding force for monarchs and presidents worldwide.

CONSTELLATION: CANCER

Praesaepe, 7 degrees 20" Leo, is the primary star for a profusion of silvery stars known as the Beehive Cluster (M44). The Beehive is an open cluster lying in the midst of Cancer. It serves an extremely important purpose for our planet—indeed for our entire neighborhood of the universe—in that it maintains the physical laws that dictate and sustain order in our world and our dimension of time/space. Without *Praesaepe's* influence there would be, for example, no law of gravity. Stars that have such monumental tasks often need numerous others to facilitate their purposes, hence *Praesaepe's* use of the Beehive stellar cluster.

Asellus Borealis (North Asellus), 7 degrees 32" Leo, and *Asellus Australis* (South Asellus), 8 degrees 43" Leo, operate through Cancer. *Asellus Borealis'* rays stimulate various philanthropic organizations worldwide and activate the nurturing nature within animals and humans. *Asellus Australis* is one of the sources of and sustainers of the Law of Polarity.

The star *Acubens,* 13 degrees 38" Leo, has the effect of activating dormant energy of all kinds. In light of Einstein having said that all is energy, it is easy to see how *Acubens'* power is a potent vitalizing force in Nature.

CONSTELLATION HYDRA

I call the star *Alphard,* 27 degrees 17" Leo, "The Wisdomkeeper Star" because it embodies the cumulative wisdom gained over the ages by collective humanity. In this way the star works closely with others that embody various levels and types of memory, including the Hall of Records stars.

CONSTELLATION: CANES VENATICI

Composed of several of the faint stars below Ursa Major, *Canes Venatici* is the location of M51, one of the galaxies known as the Spiral Nebula. It is the star *Copula,* 25 degrees 08" Virgo, whose force is channeled through spirits and highly evolved extraterrestrials in other parts of the universe. The Nebula forms a channel for new knowledge to come through the human mind, and for ancient knowledge to be reawakened into activity for use by humanity. Because of this it would be appropriate to think of Copula as the "Regulator Star."

CONSTELLATION: CRATER (THE CUP)

The ancient symbolism embodied within the Crater/Cup constellation bears mentioning. The Sacred Chalice or the Holy Grail has long been a token of the spiritual wisdom avidly sought by human beings down through time. Motivated by their ideals, individuals have embarked upon their individual and collective spiritual paths. When the spiritual journey truly begins, each person acquires the influence of the star *Labrum,* 26 degrees 41" Virgo, whose energy serves as a stimulus along the way, continually providing the courage and power to proceed ever forward toward Enlightenment.

⟨IRⲤUMPOLⲀR ⟨ON⟩TⲈLLⲀTION⟩

CONSTELLATION: CRUX

Acrux, 11 degrees 52" Scorpio, is also known as the Southern Cross. It is another star that influences the world's religions and religious leaders. It also emits energy that is utilized by magicians, shamans, and medicine people in the Southern Hemisphere.

The preceding information on the fixed stars is, with the exception of the astrological implications which were clearly stated as such, my own. Again, you must weigh what I have said carefully, seek to apply my interpretations to their natal birth chart, and then work with drawing down the various stars' power through the meditation and ceremonial techniques provided. Remember, the information represents an effort on my part to "fill in the gaps" of what has been lost of the original body of esoteric stellar knowledge, and is presented here in the spirit of making a contribution to the evolution of all that lives.

Being able to sight and identify fixed stars the final step in familiarizing yourself with the night sky. It takes time, but it is time well-spent. The value the Ancients placed in these 110 fixed stars also tells us that they knew the power inherent within each of them. This is an integral part of the stellar knowledge humanity has possessed for millennia. Knowing where in the heavens these stars are, and learning how to draw upon their power is imperative if you are to become a Starwalker. Also, still another approach to using the knowledge of fixed stars is fixed-star astrology.

As a science, astrology concerns itself with planetary energies and influences, as well as the timing of Nature's cycles and other events. When you go to an astrologer and have your horoscope erected, the astrologer explains what the chart reveals about your potentials and tendencies. The chart is therefore, in essence, a *blueprint* of your character.[3] As the astrologer Isabel Hickey says, "The blueprint we call the horoscope or the birth chart plots the energies that flow in your magnetic field."[4] Astrologers are generally known as mundane or natal astrologers. Fixed-star astrologers, on the other hand, calculate the presence and position in a natal chart, by house and sign, of fixed stars which, like the planets, have both positive and negative qualities. Which quality a given individual will experience is determined by that person's response to the star or stars positioned in their chart, his or her personal karmic condition, and the specific level of personal development and spiritual evolution. Not everyone has fixed stars in their birth chart: either that individual has not chosen to work with any such energy or has no lessons to learn that can be taught by any of the fixed stars. Should one or more fixed stars appear in a natal chart, it means that it or they represent karmic configurations that would be difficult to release until the individual has experienced all that they bring forth. (George/Parker, p.2)

This clearly suggests that fixed-star astrology concerns the power inherent in fixed stars. In a natal horoscope, the star's power is triggered by the movements of the planets. This means that the influence of a given star is not in effect all the time, but requires a planetary trigger for the power to be released. In their book, *The Fixed Stars: Health and Behavior Imbalances,* Ted George and Barbara Parker state: "The greatest affect [sic] on fixed star positions occurs with the transits of the heavy planets, Saturn, Jupiter, Uranus, Neptune and Pluto." (p.3) What George and Parker describe as a "most uncomfortable position" indicates that, if one is dealing with a difficult and negative stellar power, when a planet returns to a natal fixed-star position, the fixed stars are not progressed in a birth chart. They are fixed. It takes the progression or transit of a planet to touch them off. Whatever house and sign a star is located in at the time of one's birth is where it will remain. Because a star's movement is very slow, moving approximately eight minutes every ten years, it seldom moves enough over the course of a human life to change its natal degree.

Determining whether one or more fixed stars are present in a given birth chart is a relatively simple matter that involves consulting a fixed star ephemeris. Books that offer additional information about interpretations of fixed star energies are also available. It is important to point out, however, that interpretation, whether of a planet, star, or other celestial body or phenomenon's presence in a birth chart, is an art that is highly dependent upon an individual's ability to grasp, both intellectually and intuitively, the nature of a given body's energy. Over time, as you learn the location of the fixed stars and constellations, do ceremonies to draw upon stars' energies (see chapter 3), and meditate upon them, the stars' true natures will be revealed.

Patterns created by the planets and stars are guides that show which planetary and stellar waves are influencing us at any given time. We always have the free will to succumb to these influences or to make conscious use of and allowances for their energy in our lives. All of us are dealing with planetary energy all the time. But those who are working with fixed-star energy are dealing with a very human and very karmic relationship with the stars. Stars embody powers that in turn represent and transmit spiritu-

al truths to those who are open and ready to receive them. They have personified Cosmic Law since time began. The lives on Earth, including
humans, are vessels through which star waves flow. In this way stars and
planets are our teachers—teachers that serve as tools of self-understanding
and that aid in our individual and collective spiritual growth.

I would now like to make some additional comments regarding the
Regulators in hopes of inspiring you to pursue a deeper understanding of
these Enlightened Ones. While I have focused purely on their work of regulating incoming and outgoing stellar energies, their work with Earth and
all the kingdoms that live here is far more extensive. Working through the
Law of Karma, the Spiritual Hierarchy assures that Earth's life is maintained
until all lives have reached a point of God consciousness. In my opinion,
a particular function of the Hierarchy, which is not discussed or explained
in any detail in other teachings, concerns the regulation of various terrestrial, systemic, and cosmic energies in a synthesis of pure cosmic force that
plays upon all lives, including that of the planet herself. In part, this regulating power determines the source and degree of incoming stellar and
planetary forces. Referring to the Hierarchy as "Elder Brothers" is mislead-
ing because the group is composed of both male and female initiates. Each
has undergone the necessary experiences, and has learned the lessons life
on Earth has to offer. They have overcome the ego or personal self, and
the trappings of the material world and, in doing so, have earned the right
to serve in a highly refined capacity.

I particularly appreciate Alice Bailey's comment that "they have
worked their way from the bottom of life and of evolution well nigh to the
top."[5] While this information concerns only the most basic tasks of the
Hierarchy, you can determine the tremendous responsibility and influence
they wield to assure the unfoldment of the Divine Plan. Though never
interfering with free will, their regulation of incoming star energy super-
sedes our intellectual understanding, but surely follows a pattern that is in
keeping with the influences needed to impact the lives on Earth at any
given time. This task is not taught by many teachers, an exception being
the work contained in Alice Bailey's *Treatise On Cosmic Fire.* I think that
the time has come for it to be taught in a way that it can be understood
by the majority. Star energies unleash specific forces that come to the planet in "starwaves" which manifest as principles, inclinations, potentials, conditions, and events within the consciousness of the planet, and in the lives
within all the kingdoms. However, only human beings can deal with star
energy consciously. It requires a different *level* of consciousness to deal
with stellar energy than with the planetary, solar, and lunar energies that
are explained and worked with in astrology. Astrologers who work with
fixed stars inform an individual of the presence of one or more fixed stars

in the natal chart, and offer interpretations as to how those stars affect life, as well as the lessons the star(s) brings for personal growth. Determining what, if any, fixed stars are present in a horoscope also serves another purpose: many have made their first connection to the Star Nation because a major planet in their chart is strongly aspected by a star or stars.

However, the information I am presenting involves what might be called "esoteric astronomy." This, and fixed-star astrology are valuable tools for helping us pursue a more in-depth, conscious knowledge of ourselves and the powers that are inherent within the Star Nation. After all, the stars are influencing us whether we are conscious of it or not. This influence involves cosmic energies and cycles that are beyond human control, and are of the sort that we cannot exert any power or influence over. But we can become more conscious of this perpetual, ever-changing stellar activity and, in doing so, become more compatible with it and its effect upon our lives.

SELECTED BIBLIOGRAPHY

Allen, Richard Hinckley. *Star Names: Their Lore and Meaning.* New York: Dover Publications, Inc., 1963.

Argüelles, José. *The Mayan Factor.* Santa Fe: Bear & Company, 1987.

Ash, Russell and Ian Grant. *Comets: Earth's Most Mysterious Visitors From Space.* New York: Bounty Books/Crown Publishing Inc., 1973.

Ashe, Geoffrey. *Mythology of the British Isles.* London: Methuen London, 1990.

_____. *The Landscape of King Arthur.* London: Webb and Bower, Ltd., 1987.

Astronomy magazine. Waukesha, Wisc.: Kalmbach Publishing Co.

Aveni, Anthony F. *Native American Astronomy.* Austin: University of Texas Press, 1977.

_____. *Ancient Astronomies.* Washington, D.C.: Smithsonian Books, 1993.

_____. *Skywatchers of Ancient Mexico.* Austin: University of Texas Press, 1980.

Bailey, Alice A. *Initiation Human and Solar.* New York: Lucis Publishing Company, 1951.

_____. *Esoteric Astrology.* New York: Lucis Publishing Company, 1952.

Baines, John and Jaromir Malek. *Atlas of Ancient Egypt.* New York: Facts On File Publications, 1980.

Balthazar, Richard. *Remember Native America!: The Earthworks of Ancient America.* Santa Fe: Five Flower Press, 1992.

Bauval, Robert and Adrian Gilbert. *The Orion Mystery.* New York: Crown Publishers, Inc., 1994.

Beckwith, Martha. *Hawaiian Mythology.* Honolulu: University of Hawaii Press, 1940.

Bierhorst, John. *The Mythology of North America.* New York: Quill Edition/William Morrow, 1985.

Blavatsky, Helena Petrovna. *The Secret Doctrine,* Vols. 1 and 2. Pasadena, Calif.: Theosophical University Press, 1974.

Brennan, Martin. *The Stars and the Stones: Ancient Art and Astronomy in Ireland.* London: Thames and Hudson. 1983.

Bryant, Page. *Terravision: A Traveler's Guide To The Living Planet Earth.* New York: Ballantine Books, 1991.

_____. *The Earth Changes Survival Handbook.* Santa Fe: Sun Publishing Company, 1984.

_____. *Awakening Arthur! His Return In Our Time.* London: Thorsons/ Aquarian Imprint, 1991.

_____. *The Spiritual Reawakening of the Great Smoky Mountains.* Waynesville: Mystic Mountains Teaching and Retreat Center, 1994.

Burl, Aubrey. *The Stone Circles of the British Isles.* New Haven: Yale University Press, 1976.

Caine, Mary. *The Glastonbury Zodiac: Key To The Mysteries Of Britain.* Surrey: Kingston, 1978.

Carlson, John B. "America's Ancient Skywatchers." *National Geographic:* March, 1990.

Chamberlain, Von del. *When Stars Came Down To Earth.* Los Altos, Calif.: Ballena Press/Center for Archaeoastronomy Cooperative Publication, 1982.

_____. *Once Upon A Starry Night: Star Mythology From Around The World.* Salt Lake City: Salt Lake City Planetarium, 1984.

Chippindale, Christopher. *Stonehenge Complete.* England: Thames and Hudson, 1985.

Clow, Barbara Hand. *The Pleiadian Agenda.* Santa Fe: Bear & Co., 1995.

Comets. New York: Crown Publishers, 1973.

Cronin, Vincent. *The View From Planet Earth.* New York; William Morrow and Company, Inc., 1981.

Dames, Michael. *The Silbury Treasure: The Great Goddess Rediscovered.* London: Thames and Hudson, 1976.

Devereux, Paul. *Earth Memory: Sacred Sites—Doorways Into Earth's Mysteries.* St. Paul, Minn.: Llewellyn Publications, 1992.

Erdoes, Richard and Alfonso Ortiz. *American Indian Myths and Legends.* New York: Pantheon Books, 1984.

Ferris, Timothy. *Coming of Age of the Milky Way.* New York: William Morrow and Company, Inc., 1988.

Fidler, J. Havelock. *Ley Lines: Their Nature and Properties.* Northhampton-shire, England: Turnstone Press Ltd., 1983.

George, Ted and Barbara Parker. *The Fixed Stars: Health and Behavior Imbalances: A Delineation of Planetary Positions on Fixed Star Degrees.* Jacksonville: Arthur Publications, 1985.

Gilbert, Adrian and Maurice Cotterell. *The Mayan Prophecies.* Shaftesbury, Dorset, England: Element Books, 1995.

Goodman, Ronald. *Lakota Star Knowledge.* Rosebud, South Dakota: Sinte Gleska College Press, 1990.

Gore, Belinda. *Ecstatic Body Postures.* Santa Fe: Bear & Company, 1995.

Griffin-Pierce, Trudy. *Earth Is My Mother, Sky Is My Father: Space, Time, and Astronomy In Navajo Sandpainting.* Albuquerque: University of New Mexico Press, 1992.

Hadingham, Evan. *Early Man and the Cosmos.* Norman, Okla.: University of Oklahoma Press, 1984.

Haile, Berard. *Starlore Among the Navajo.* Santa Fe: William Gannon, 1977.

Halifax, Joan. *The Fruitful Darkness.* San Francisco: HarperSanFrancisco, 1993.

Hancock, Graham. *Fingerprints of the Gods.* New York: Crown Publishers, 1995.

Hickey, Isabel M. *Astrology: A Cosmic Science.* Watertown, Mass.: Isabel M. Hickey, 1970.

Holy Bible: King James Version. Grand Rapids: The Zondervan Corporation, 1990.

Hope, Murry. *The Psychology of Ritual.* Dorset, England: Element Books Ltd., 1988.

_____. *Practical Egyptian Magic.* New York: St. Martin's Press, 1984.

Hoyle, Fred and N.C. Wickramasinghe. *Diseases From Space.* New York: Harper & Row, 1979.

_____. *Lifecloud.* New York: Harper & Row, 1978.

Jung, C.G. *Flying Saucers: A Modern Myth of Things Seen In The Sky.* Princeton: Princeton University Press, 1978.

Klepesta, Josef and Antonin Ruki. *Constellations.* Feltham, Middlesex, England: Hamlyn Publishing Group Ltd., 1969.

Krupp, E.C. *Echoes of the Ancient Skies.* New York: Harper & Row, 1979.

_____. *In Search of Ancient Astronomies.* New York: McGraw Hill, 1978.

Lee, Pali and Koko Willis. *Tales of the Night Rainbow.* Honolulu: Night Rainbow Publishing Company, 1988.

Lewis, John S. *Rain of Iron and Ice: The Very Real Threat of Comet and Asteroid Bombardment.* Reading, Mass.: Addison-Wesley Publishing Company, 1996.

Locke, Raymond Friday. *The Book of the Navajo.* Los Angeles: Mankind Publishing Company, 1978.

Malville, J. McKim and Claudia Putnam. *Prehistoric Astronomy of the Southwest.* Boulder, Colo.: Johnson Books, 1989.

Mann, Nick B. A. *Glastonbury Tor.* Great Britain: Annenterprise, 1986.

McLaughlin, Corrine and Gordon Davison. *Spiritual Politics: Changing The World From Inside Out.* New York: Ballantine Books, 1994.

Michell, John. *The Traveler's Key to Sacred England.* New York: Alfred A. Knopf, 1988.

Monroe, Jean Guard and Ray A. Williamson. *They Dance in the Sky: Myths and Legends of the Stars.* Blacksburg, VA: The McDonald and Woodward Publishing Company, 1988.

Mooney, James. *Myths Of The Cherokee and Sacred Formulas Of The Cherokee.* Nashville, Tenn.: Charles and Randy Elder, 1982.

Morse, Eric. *The Living Stars.* New York: Amethyst Books, 1988.

Mountford, Charles. *The Dreamtime Book.* Hong Kong: Prentice Hall, Inc. (first American edition), 1973.

Moyers, Bill and Joseph Campbell. *The Power of Myth.* New York: Doubleday, 1988.

Neely, Henry M. *A Primer For Star-Gazers.* New York: Gramercy Publishing Company, 1970.

Oxford American Dictionary. New York: Oxford University Press, 1980.

Pearson, Carol S. *Awakening the Heroes Within.* San Francisco: HarperSanFrancisco, 1991.

Pennick, Nigel. *The Ancient Science of Geomancy.* London: Thames and Hudson, 1979.

Peterson, Natasha. *Sacred Sites: A Traveler's Guide to North America's Powerful, Mystical Landmarks.* Chicago: Contemporary Books, 1988.

Peterson, Scott. *Native American Prophecies.* New York: Paragon House, 1990.

Pinch, Geraldine. *Magic In Ancient Egypt.* Austin: University of Texas Press, 1994.

Povenmire, Harold R. *Fireballs, Meteors and Meteorites.* Indian Harbor Beach, Ok.: JSB Enterprises, Inc., 1980.

Raymo, Chet. *The Soul of the Night: An Astronomical Pilgrimage.* Englewood Cliffs, N.J.: Prentice Hall, 1985.

———. *365 Starry Nights.* Englewood Cliffs, N.J.: Prentice Hall, 1982.

Roberts, Elizabeth and Elias Amidon. *Earth Prayers Around The World: 365 Prayers, Poems, and Invocations For Honoring The Earth.* San Francisco: HarperSanFrancisco, 1991.

Robertson, Robin. *Beginner's Guide To Jungian Psychology.* York Beach: Nicolas Hays, Inc., 1992.

Rush, Annie Kent. *Moon, Moon.* New York: St. Martin's Press, 1971.

Spencer, John R. and Jacqueline Mitton. *The Great Comet Crash: The Collision of Comet Shoemaker-Levy 9 and Jupiter.* New York: Cambridge University Press, 1995.

Spilsbury, Ariel and Michael Bryner. *The Mayan Oracle: Return Path To The Stars.* Santa Fe: Bear & Company, 1992.

Squier, E.G. and E.H. Davis. *Ancient Monuments of the Mississippi Valley.* Glen Arm, Md.: The Sourcebook Project, No. 1847.

Staal, Julius D.W. *Patterns In The Sky.* Blacksburg, Va.: The McDonald and Woodward Publishing Company, 1988.

Stein, Kenneth. "The Star-Gods of Neoplatonism." *Gnosis* #38, Winter 1996.

Sun Bear and Wabun Wind. *The Medicine Wheel: Earth Astrology.* New York: Prentice Hall Press, 1980.

Temple, Robert K.G. *The Sirius Mystery.* New York: Penguin Books, 1976.

Waters, Frank. *The Book of the Hopi.* New York: Penguin Books, 1963.

Watkins, Alfred. *The Old Straight Tracks.* London: Abacus Sphere Books Ltd., 1974.

Weltfish, Gene. *The Lost Universe: Pawnee Life and Culture.* Lincoln, Nebr.: University of Nebraska Press, 1965.

Williamson, Ray A. *Living the Sky: The Cosmos of the American Indian.* Boston: Houghton Mifflin Company, 1984.

Wright, Barton. *Hopi Kachinas: The Complete Guide to Collecting Kachina Dolls.* Flagstaff, Ariz.: Northland Press, 1973.

Wolf, Fred Alan. *Parallel Universes: The Search For Other Worlds.* New York: Simon and Schuster, 1988.

NOTES

PREFACE

1. Stein, Kenneth. *The Star Gods of Neoplatonism. Gnosis* #38 Winter 1996, p.31.
2. Swimme, Brian, in *The Pleiadian Agenda,* p.xiii
3. Bauval, Robert and Gilbert, Adrian. *The Orion Mystery.* (jacket).
4. Jung, Carl G. *Flying Saucers: A Modern Myth of Things Seen In the Skies.* p.22.
5. Robertson, Robin. *The Beginner's Guide to Jungian Psychology.* p.6.

CHAPTER ONE

1. Krupp, E.C. *Beyond the Blue Horizon.* p.43.
2. Hadingham, Evan. *Early Man and the Cosmos.* pp.128-129.
3. Williamson, Ray A. *Living The Sky: The Cosmos of the American Indian.* pp.43-44.

CHAPTER TWO

1. Staal, Julius. *New Patterns in the Sky: Myths and Legends of the Stars.* p.xiii.
2. While the Sun is a star, it is my purpose here to deal with suns other than our Day Star.

CHAPTER THREE

1. Krupp. E.C. *Beyond the Blue Horizon.* p.29.
2. Morse, Dr. Eric. *The Living Stars.* The Archangel Stars were discussed throughout this book., but only on page 83 are they mentioned as a whole concept.
3. Ferris, Timothy. *Coming of Age of the Milky Way.* p.20.

CHAPTER FOUR

1. Chamberlain, Von del. *When Stars Came Down To Earth.* p.142.
2. Eicher, David J. *Here Comes Hale-Bopp. Astronomy,* Feb. 1996, p.69.
3. Spencer, John R. and Mitton, Jacqueline. *The Great Comet Crash.* p.vii.
4. Hoyle, Fred and Wickramasinghe, Chandra. *Lifecloud.* (jacket).
5. Hoyle, Fred and Wickramasinghe, Chandra. *Diseases from Space.* (jacket).
6 Cronin, Vincent. *The Viewpoint from Planet Earth.* pp.58-59.
7. Lewis, John S.. *Rain of Iron and Ice.* p.11.
8. Bauval, Robert and Gilbert, Adrian. *The Orion Mystery.* p.201.

9. *The Meteor Crater Story* (pamphlet). p.34.
10. Lewis, John S. *Rain of Iron and Ice.* p.11.

CHAPTER FIVE

1. Aveni, Anthony. *Ancient Astronomers.* p.17.
2. Raymo, Chet. *The Soul of the Night.* p.ix.
3. Chamberlain, Von del. *When Stars Came Down To Earth.* pp.247-248.
4. Williamson, Ray. *Living The Sky.* p.166.
5. Pearson, Carol S. *Awakening the Heroes Within.* p.6.
6. Griffin-Pierce, Trudy. *Earth Is My Mother, Sky Is My Father.* p.142.

CHAPTER SIX

1. Aveni, Anthony. *Ancient Astronomers.* p.164.
2. Raymo, Chet. *The Soul of the Night.* p.205.

CHAPTER SEVEN

1. Krupp, E.C. *Echoes of the Ancient Skies.* p.22.
2. Information about Osiris was gathered throughout the text of *The Atlas of Ancient Egypt* by John Baines and Jaromir Malek.
3. Bauval, Robert and Gilbert, Adrian. *The Orion Mystery.* p.89.
4. Detailed information about this theory may be obtained from reading *The Sirius Mystery* by Robert K.G. Temple. See Bibliography for publisher information.
5. Bauval, Robert and Hancock, Graham. *The Message of the Sphinx.* p.225.
6. Allen, Richard Hinckley. *Star Names: Their Lore and Meaning.* p.307.
7. Thompkins, Peter. *Secrets of the Great Pyramid.* p.147.
8. de Lubicz, Schwaller R.A. *The Sacred Science.* p.283.

CHAPTER EIGHT

1. Krupp, E.C. . *Echoes of the Ancient Skies.* p.229.
2. Michell, John. *The Traveler's Key To Sacred England.* p.105.
3. Cooke, Ian. *Journey To The Stones.* p.23.
4. Hadingham, Evan. *Early Man and the Cosmos.* p.51.
5. Brennan, Martin. *The Stars and the Stones.* p.10.
6. Dames, Michael. *The Silbury Treasure.* pp.14-17.
7. Aveni, Anthony. *Native American Astronomy.* p.149.
8. Peterson, Natasha. *Sacred Sites.* p.100.

CHAPTER NINE

1. del Chamberlain, Von. *When Stars Came Down To Earth.* p.26.
2. Ibid, p.1 of Preface.
3. Ibid, p.21.
4. Ibid, p.43.
5. Weltfish, Gene. *The Lost Universe: Pawnee Life and Culture.* pp. 80-83.
6. del Chamberlain, Von. *When Stars Came Down To Earth.* p.63.
7. Weltfish, Gene. *Lost Universe*, pp. 79-80.
8. del Chamberlain, Von. *When Stars Came Down To Earth.* pp.43,60.
9. Krupp, E.C. *Echoes of the Ancient Skies.* pp.211-213.
10. Gilbert, Adrian and Cotterell, Maurice M. *The Mayan Prophecies.* pp.157-158.

CHAPTER TEN

1. Aveni, Anthony. *Ancient Astronomers.* p.131.
2. Waters, Frank. *The Book of the Hopi.* p.13.
3. References to the kachinas are spread throughout a large portion of *The Book of the Hopi* by Frank Waters; pp.137-247. I have also learned a great deal about these deities from reading *Hopi Kachinas: The Complete Guide to Collecting Kachina Dolls* by Barton Wright. Please see the bibliography for publisher details of both these publications. I have also been taught by Hopi friends about certain of the star-related kachinas mentioned in the text. I have some personal concern that the information gained from any text on the Hopi might not be accurate in light of the fact that there have been many changes made in Hopi ceremonials, although most are subtle and not generally known to or figured out by outsiders, and because most texts are dated.
4. Ash, Russell and Grant, Ian. *Comets: Earth's Most Mysterious Visitors From Space.* p.16.
5. Locke, Raymond Friday. *The Book of the Navajo.* pp.13-15.
6. Williamson, Ray A. *Living The Sky: The Cosmos of the American Indian.* pp.162-164.
7. Griffin-Pierce, Trudy. *Earth Is My Mother, Sky Is My Father.* p. 32.

CHAPTER ELEVEN

1. Wolf, Fred Alan. *Parallel Universes: The Search For Other Worlds.* p.20.
2. Goodman, Ronald. *Lakota Star Knowledge: Studies In Lakota Stellar Theology.* p.27. Please note that references to the "four directions" implies our relationship with the other kingdoms of life on Earth. The reference to the "good red road" concerns the Sioux term for the spiritual path.

CHAPTER TWELVE

1. Gilbert, Adrian and Cotterell, Maurice M. *The Mayan Prophecies.* p.2.
2. Spilsbury, Ariel and Bryner, Michael. *The Mayan Oracle: Return Path to the Stars.* p.14.
3. Krupp, E.C. *Beyond the Blue Horizon.* p. 203.
4. Gilbert, Adrian and Cotterell, Maurice M. *The Mayan Prophecies.* p.33.
5. Aveni, Anthony. *Skywatchers of Ancient Mexico.* p.6.
6. Argüelles, José. *The Mayan Factor.* p.19.
7. Aveni, Anthony F. *Skywatchers of Ancient Mexico.* p.294.

CHAPTER THIRTEEN

1. Temple, Robert K.G. *The Sirius Mystery.* pp.19-20.
2. Klepesta, Josef and Ruki, Antonin. *Constellations.* p.116.
3. Krupp, E.C. *In Search of Ancient Astronomies.* p.269.
4. Chamberlain, Von del. *When Stars Came Down To Earth.* p.144.

CHAPTER FOURTEEN

1. Snyder, Gary in Roberts, Elizabeth and Amidon, Elias. *Earth Prayers From Around the World.* p.237.
2. This was my book on sacred sites in five countries; India, U.S., England, Egypt, and Tibet. It also contained information on the psychology of ceremony and how to make ceremony a part of one's spiritual path as well as daily life. The book was published by Ballantine Books, New York, New York. It is now out of print.
3. Mann, Nick. *Glastonbury Tor.* p.22.
4. Krupp, E.C. *Beyond The Blue Horizon.* pp.289-293.
5. Gore, Belinda. *Ecstatic Body Postures.* p.173.
6. Balthazar, Richard. *Remember Native America!* p.82.
7. Lockyer, Sir Joseph Norman. *Bulletin of the American Astronomical Society.* (12(4):885)
8. Squier, E.G. and Davis, E. H. *Ancient Monuments of the Mississippi.*
9. Ashe, Geoffrey. *The Landscape of King Arthur.* pp.16-17.
10. Caine, Mary. *The Glastonbury Tor: Key to the Mysteries of Britain.* p.22.
11. Michell, John. *The Traveller's Key to Sacred England.* pp.93-94.
12. Dames, Michael. *The Silbury Treasure: The Great Goddess Rediscovered.* p.43.
13. Mountford, Charles. *The Dreamtime Book.* The references to Ayer's Rock are a compilation of information found throughout this book.
14. Hadingham, Evan. *Early Man and the Cosmos.* pp.153-155.

CHAPTER FIFTEEN

1. Monroe, Jean Guard and Williamson, Ray A. *They Dance in the Sky.* p.ix.

2. Moyers, Bill. *The Power of Myth.* p.4.
3. Halifax, Joan. *The Fruitful Darkness.* p.103.
4. Stein, Kenneth. GNOSIS #38. *The Star-Gods of Neoplatonism.* p.31.
5. Erdoes, Richard and Ortiz, Alfonso. *American Indian Myths and Legends.* p.485.
6. Peterson, Scott. *Native American Prophecies.* pp.18-19.
7. Krupp, E.C. *Beyond the Blue Horizon.* pp.23-24.
8. Mooney, James. *Sacred Myths and Formulas of the Cherokee.* p.256.
9. Ashe, Geoffrey. *Mythology of the British Isles.* p.180.
10. Beckwith, Martha. *Hawaiian Mythology.* p.43.

CONCLUSION

1. Aveni., Anthony. *Ancient Astronomies.* p.165.

APPENDIX ONE

1. Chamberlain, Von del. *When Stars Came Down To Earth.* p.247.

APPENDIX TWO

1. Griffin-Pierce, Trudy. *Earth Is My Mother, Sky Is My Father.* p.142.

APPENDIX THREE

1. Staal, Julius D.W. *Patterns In The Sky.* pp.31-32.

APPENDIX SEVEN

1. Devereaux, Paul. *Earth Memory: Sacred Sites-Doorways into Earth's Mysteries.* p.163.
2. Michell, John. *A Traveler's Key to Sacred England.* p.10.

APPENDIX EIGHT

1. Wolf, Fred Alan. *Parallel Universes: The Search for Other Worlds.* p.312.

APPENDIX NINE

1. George, Ted and Parker, Barbara. *Fixed Stars: Health and Behavior Imbalances.* p.10.
2. More information about the Great Smoky Mountains may be obtained by reading my book, *The Spiritual Reawakening of the Great Smoky Mountains.*
3. Ibid. p.78
4. Hickey, Isabela. *Astrology: A Cosmic Science.* p.5
5. Bailey, Alice A. *Initiation: Human and Solar.* p.25

ABOUT THE AUTHOR

Page Bryant currently lives in Waynesville, North Carolina, in the heart of the Great Smoky Mountains, following eleven years in Sedona, Arizona. She has been married for eighteen years to visionary artist Scott Guynup, and is the mother of two grown children. Together, Page and Scott operate the Mystic Mountains Teaching and Retreat Center in Waynesville.

Page has been a professional psychic and intuitive counselor for twenty-five years. The first psychic to host her own radio talk show in the United States, her radio shows aired in several major markets from 1973 through 1990. While on KMPC Radio in Los Angeles, she was a daily featured guest on the popular Gary Owens Show. She also had her own television series in 1976 in Florida.

Page was the first apprentice of Sun Bear, the well-known Chippewa medicine man and founder of the Bear Tribe Medicine Society. She has been a teacher at Sun Bear's Medicine Wheel Gatherings for the past fourteen years. In 1989, shortly before his death, Sun Bear and Page led a sacred pilgrimage to England and Scotland.

As a successful lecturer and workshop/seminar facilitator, Page, along with her husband, has led students on spiritual journeys to Egypt, England, Scotland, and Hawaii. Page's broad range of metaphysical and scientific knowledge has made her one of the most popular and interesting teachers in the field of alternative thought today. Her studies include astronomy, physics, astrology, esoteric Buddhism, Tibetan Buddhism, kabbalah, theosophy, numerology, Jungian psychology, Native American spirituality, Bach Flower remedies, sacred ecology, geomancy, Earth Changes, and ancient religions and cultures.

Page Bryant is the author of numerous books, including *The Earth Changes Survival Handbook*; *The Magic of Minerals*; *Earth Changes Now!*; *The Aquarian Guide to Native American Mythology*; *Terravision: A Traveler's Guide to the Living Planet Earth*; and *The Spiritual Reawakening of the Great Smoky Mountains*. She is currently the feature editor for *Wildfire*, a national magazine that addresses ecological/environmental issues, Native American spirituality, ceremony, community living, and related issues. You can write to Page at the following address:

Page Bryant
707 Brunswick Drive
Waynesville, NC 28786